Understanding youth in late modernity

Understanding youth in late modernity

Alan France

Open University Press

Open University Press
McGraw-Hill Education
McGraw-Hill House
Shoppenhangers Road
Maidenhead
Berkshire
England
SL6 2QL

email: enquiries@openup.co.uk
world wide web: www.openup.co.uk

and Two Penn Plaza, New York, NY 10121–2289, USA

First published 2007

A catalogue record of this book is available from the British Library

ISBN 13: 978 0 335 215 348 (pb) 978 0335 215 355 (hb)
ISBN 10: 0335 215 343 (pb) 0335 215 351 (hb)

Library of Congress Cataloguing-in-Publication Data
CIP data applied for

Typeset by YHT Ltd, London
Printed in Poland by OZGraf S.A.
www.polskabook.pl

The McGraw·Hill Companies

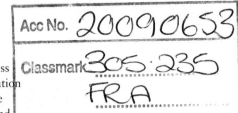

For mum

Contents

Acknowledgements x
Introduction 1
Outline of the book 3

1 The making of modern youth 6
Introduction 6
Pre-modernity: The age of place, tradition and custom 6
Early modernity and the youth question 8
The growth of the interventionist state 12
Welfare capitalism and politics of inclusion, 1945–80 14
The arrival of the 'teenager' 16
Youth in crisis: The impact of unemployment 17
Youth, crime and disorder 19
The 'girl question' in post-war Britain 21
Conclusion 23

2 Science and the age of reason: The 'discovery of adolescence' 24
Introduction 24
Modernity, science and the age of reason 24
G. Stanley Hall and the 'discovery of adolescence' 25
Adolescence as a 'normal' part of the life course 27
Criminology and the influence of 'science' 27
Positive criminology and its impact 29
The Chicago School and early sociology 32
Functionalism: Youth as a social institution 34
Anomie, subculture and delinquency 36
The influence of American social science 38
Conclusion 40

3 Social science and the politicisation of the youth question 41
Introduction 41
Youth as 'a generation for itself' 41
Class, culture and the youth question 43
Youth unemployment in the 1980s 45
Why working-class kids got working-class jobs! 46

Developments in criminology from the 1970s 47
Feminism and the study of girls 52
Conclusion 57

4 Youth transitions in the age of uncertainty 59
Introduction 59
Changing patterns of school-to-work transitions 59
New times and New Labour 62
Youth inequality and transitions into adulthood 70
Conclusion 76

5 Youth, education and the politics of inclusion 78
Introduction 78
Education and the post-welfare society 78
New Labour and inclusive education 80
Tackling social exclusion 83
The problem of (with?) social exclusion 84
Education and the social reproduction of inequality 87
Conclusion 96

6 Threatening youth and risky futures 97
Introduction 97
Youth justice policy in late modernity 97
Youth policy and policing of space 100
The politics of youth crime 103
'Popular punitiveness' in youth policy 104
Youth crime and the media 105
Social science and the youth crime question 106
Conclusion 113

7 The marketisation and commodification of youth 115
Introduction 115
Consumption in late modernity 115
Youth, new media technology and consumption 118
Youth consumption identities 123
Conclusion 131

8 Youth culture and the growth of the 'risk-taking generation' 133
Introduction 133
New Age travellers and eco-warriors 133
Rave culture and the arrival of ecstasy 134
The rise of clubbing 135
Fears for (of?) the 'E' generation 135

Risk-taking in late modernity 137
Youth culture and social research 141
Conclusion 149

9 The changing nature of youth in late modernity? 151
Introduction 151
'Political discourses' and the youth question 151
Responses to the youth question 153
Youth research and the youth question 154
The social science and policy nexus 160
The youth question and a 'new' public social science? 164

Notes *166*
References *168*
Index *191*

Acknowledgements

This book could never have been completed without the help and support of others. It has been conceived and developed over a long period of time, and special thanks must go to Nick Stevenson, Phil Mizen, Derrick Armstrong, Jean Hine and colleagues at the Centre for the Study of Childhood and Youth at the University of Sheffield for their constructive engagement with me on many of the ideas discussed in this book. I would also like to thank Harry Hendrick, Allison James, David Philips, Adrian James, Shane Blackman, Barbara Cole, Jackie Marsh and Rob MacDonald for their comments on early chapter drafts. While the final content is mine, their contribution was invaluable. I am also grateful to Annunziata Fiora for her diligent proof reading and my granddaughter, Ruth Green, for her invaluable help in organising my references. Finally, a very special thank-you to Jan, my life-long partner, who not only gives me inspiration and helps me through the tough times but also remains my best friend.

Introduction

Youth has always been under the microscope and of central concern to adults and the state. A range of fears and anxieties has consistently shaped the 'youth question' and influenced 'what is to be done about young people'. This is not just a modernist fascination. It has a long and complex history covering a number of centuries (Griffths 1996). Neither does the youth question have a single simple universal definition (Cohen 1997): it can change, dependent upon wider contextualised developments taking place in society, although, as we shall see in the discussions that follow, historical continuities in how it is shaped do exist (Pearson 1983). What is not always understood are the processes and influences that construct and restructure the youth question over time.

This book is concerned with investigating these issues in detail through an analysis of developments in Britain. While the book starts its journey in pre-modernity and then travels into the establishment of modernity in the twentieth century, its central focus will be on the developments taking place in the last twenty years, in what has been called 'late' or 'high' modernity (Giddens 1991). To achieve a full understanding of the processes underpinning the construction of the youth question, the discussion that follows will concentrate on what I believe to be two of the major influences: that of the role of government and the way that politics and policy have constructed and responded to the youth question; and that of youth research and theories of youth from within a number of core disciplines of the social sciences.

Politics has always had a major influence in shaping and reflecting core values and assumptions about the social landscape around us. Yet it also has the power to influence and shape our understandings. Through examining the political interests, the beliefs, the ideologies and the core assumptions about youth in political discourse and public policy, we can start to understand how the youth question has been understood, constructed and responded to at different historical moments. Politics and policy-making are continually concerned with driving particular political projects, usually in relation to political ideologies and utopias, and instigating social change. But it also has to manage the tensions that arise from the external forces that create new environments and challenges. Policy-making, then, needs to be responsive to these new social contexts. How youth is perceived and conceptualised in these processes can then have major consequences in shaping the youth question, and how agencies respond to the 'conditions of youth' at different historical moments. The impact of this can be significant in that it can shape the types of opportunities that are available and the way young people experience 'being young'.

But this process cannot be seen as purely political. We also need to consider the ideas and thinking generated within social science research and theorising. Over the past century, youth and the youth question has, in a number of varied ways, been of major interest to the social sciences. Disciplines such as sociology, criminology, psychology, educational studies and, more recently, cultural and media studies, have all had something to say about the activities of the young. Yet youth research is not a simple reflection of 'how it is'. Historically, youth was conceptualised and 'created' by disciplines such as developmental psychology, positivist criminology, and sociology, which were themselves greatly influenced by ideologies and values of the day:

> Youth research does not simply reflect aspects of young people's lives, nor does it *mis*represent their experiences, as though the latter were sitting around like the truth waiting to be discovered. Youth research is more complex than this, given the ideological role it plays in constructing the very categories of 'youth' and 'adolescence', and in presenting stories about the origins of specific forms of youthful deviance or resistance.
>
> (Griffin 1993: 2)

Social science has created many varied understandings, and in the chapters that follow we explore these different perspectives, and the historical and contemporary role that social science has played in constructing youth and the youth question. In this process we will examine how different disciplines have theorised the youth phase in the life course, allowing us to get underneath the complex influences and assumptions that different epistemological approaches make towards the analysis of youth.

Yet this book is about more than this, in that it is also concerned with exploring the historical and contemporary relationship *between* politics, public policy-making and the social sciences. How politics and social science have communicated (or not) over the youth question is of central importance to the discussion that follows. Social science aims to be reflexive, undertaking critical analysis of different social phenomena and providing alternative understandings and explanations. But it should also have a critical role to play in influencing the type of society and world we live in (Wright Mills 1959). As we shall see in the discussion that follows, a number of social scientists have, over the previous century, engaged in this endeavour and have offered a broad range of explanations and understandings not only of the youth question but also of youth itself to those working within the political process of government. But history shows that how politics and public policy understand and relate to social science is full of tensions and uncertainties (Bulmer 1987). How far ideas from the social sciences have influenced the political understanding of the youth question remains a complex question itself. The take-up of social science into the political arena is not a simple scientific process (Sanderson 2004). It is highly subjective and arises through the interplay between political ideologies, values and perceptions of what counts as valid knowledge. As we shall see, different ideas at different time periods have gained greater influence than others, while some ideas have been marginalised and given less credence.

Over the previous century, youth research has been a growth area in social science, and new and illuminating understandings of youth itself have emerged. How much influence this has had on political discourses is a central theme in this book. In assessing this, it is critical to understand what role and influence different disciplines within social science have had in both defining the youth question and the construction of policy solutions. The book will also explore whether there are other forms of knowledge that could have been drawn into that process. Of course, it is important to recognise that this relationship between politics and social science is not a one-sided responsibility. Questions need also to be asked about how social science, at particular historical moments, has been willing and able to make a contribution to these debates or not.

Outline of the book

The first three chapters locate our discussion within a historical context. Chapter 1 starts with an analysis of the political construction of the youth question in pre-modernity, highlighting the importance of notions such as dependence, semi-independence and independence. The discussion continues to follow these processes through the arrival of modernity, where the nation state and industrial capitalism start to institutionalise and universalise youth as a stage of the life course. It explores changes taking place in modern society in the twentieth century and examines the implications these had on the youth question. The discussion concludes in the late 1970s, when the 'crisis' of modernity is showing signs of erupting, having major implications for the young.

In Chapter 2 we turn our attention to the role social science has had in contributing to our early understanding of the youth question. Modernity is the period of Enlightenment, when science and rationality are seen as important for understanding modern social life. It is in the late nineteenth and early parts of the twentieth century that we see the 'discovery of adolescence' in psychology and the arrival of a 'new science' of criminology. Both conceptualise youth as a 'normal stage' of development. As other disciplines grow and become mainstream in universities, new ideas also start to emerge. Youth comes to be seen as 'an institution' and notions of 'subculture' are seen as a distinctive aspect of the youth phase.

In Chapter 3 we move on to the post-war period of the twentieth century. By the 1960s social science is fascinated by the 'new' teenager and the 'counterculture'. Influences and changes within sociology and criminolgy create a more radical analysis of social change that focuses on the importance of class and culture. In the late 1970s and early 1980s feminism also re-emerges as a major force, challenging the 'malestream' focus of social science, providing alternative understandings of youth and the youth question. These powerful movements set the scene for the future emergence of a 'new orthodoxy' in youth research that dominates in late modernity.

The next five chapters turn to contemporary debates on the youth question, sharpening the lens on the developments that have taken place in more recent times. Chapter 4 focuses on youth transitions, drawing out and reflecting upon the political anxieties and responses to national and global changes and especially to the breakdown of the 'school to work' transition. This highlights not only how policy constructs the problem but also how it develops new forms of interventions in post welfare society. The discussion concludes by exploring how social science has responded to claims of a growing individualisation amongst the young, showing how such distinctions fail to recognise the powerful structural continuities that still shape youth transitions.

Chapter 5 outlines how in late modernity government has understood and responded to the youth question in education. New Labour has put education at the top of its political agenda, and this chapter discusses how they have progressed these ambitions in a post-welfare society. It also explores the tensions between social science and policy. In this a critical body of knowledge has been marginalised and questions of inequality and power have been given limited recognition in the policy making process.

Chapter 6 turns our attention to debates over youth crime. In late modernity crime has been declining, although anxieties over the behaviour of the young remains and has broadened to include concerns over 'anti-social behaviour'. This chapter explores how government is contributing to these anxieties, how they are responding and what impact this is having on the youth question. Social science has contributed to debates by being fixed on 'causes' these giving limited interest in the criminalising processes that many of these changes have brought about.

Chapter 7 examines the growing influence of youth consumption. In late modernity consumption especially in areas such as the internet, mobile phones, computer games and music technology (i.e. MP3 players, IPods) has expaned at a phenomenal rate. It has been claimed that youth is the 'net' generation yet evidence suggests inequalities remain. How government has understood this and how they have responded has had major consequences on young people's access. The chapter also examines the impact these consuming practices have on young people's identities. Poststructuralist approaches are shown to have weaknesses when it comes to explaining the wider influences that are at play within the 'market place.'

In Chapter 8 we maintain a focus on 'culture' by examining the changing nature of youth culture in late modernity. In the first part of the chapter recent political anxieties about youth culture are discussed highlighting the growing concerns over the 'risk taking generation' and youth cultural activities. This is followed by discussions on the relevance of cultural theories to explain these evolving phenomena showing how poststructuralist approaches give limited attention to forces that have a shaping quality. In Chapter 9 we reflect upon historical and contemporary developments surrounding the youth question, and explore what they tell us about the relationship between social science and political discourse. New approaches to this relationship have evolved in late modernity, and this chapter will discuss the extent to which these have affected our understandings of youth and the youth question. The discussion will conclude with a review of possible ways forward for social researchers, exploring how they might start to have a greater impact in influencing contemporary understandings of youth and the youth question.

1 The making of modern youth

Introduction

This chapter maps historically the political understandings and actions towards youth and the youth question. It follows them from pre- and early modernity to the establishment of welfare capitalism after the Second World War and to the crisis in modernity in the 1970s. It concentrates on how the youth question has been understood and constructed over this time, showing the contradictions, tensions and areas of continuity. The chapter also highlights how policy has responded to the youth question at different historical moments in different social contexts, leading to the construction of 'modern youth' as an age-related stage in the life course.

Pre-modernity: The age of place, tradition and custom

It has been suggested that prior to the seventeenth century youth or adolescence did not exist (Ariés 1960). But this position has been challenged on methodological grounds. The claims made by Ariés evolved from the analysis of paintings of the fifteenth and sixteenth centuries which showed children were nothing more than 'little adults'. But the pictures were of the wealthy and bourgeoisie of the time and had little to say about the diverse experiences of those of different class backgrounds or genders (Griffiths 1996). Youth as a linguistic category did not exist, but boundaries between different age groups in pre-modern society did (Griffiths 1996). These focused more on the distinctions between dependence (childhood), semi-dependence (youth) and independence (adulthood). This form of grading was the precursor to modern youth. Evidence also showed the existence of a distinctive 'youth culture' amongst the semi-dependent groups (Griffiths 1996) and that certain festivals and activities were targeted specifically towards them, showing a recognition of separateness from childhood and adult activities (Gillis 1974). But the notion of a transitional phase that was age-graded was not universally recognised (Davis 1990). Boundaries were more likely to be blurred and locally defined around family, work and community. For example, employment in feudal society tended to revolve around the family home. Men, women and children all had parts to play in the production process of small-scale industries and agriculture (Hall 1982).

But a range of 'rites of passage' that moved children from 'dependent childhood' to 'independent adulthood' did exist. Different occupations provided varied transitional processes that 'reaffirmed economic and social distance between youth and adulthood' (Griffiths 1996: 27). For example, those going into service were more likely to start work before puberty, while those starting apprenticeships would not be taken on until they were 17.[1] Employment such as this tended to be close to the family home and both types were mechanisms for moving children out into independent living, although the status, pay and position did not reflect that of adults. In many cases it was 'lodging employment'. They worked under a master and would be both fed and lodged as a part of their payment, although they would still contribute to home life. This was for boys a mechanism for learning skills of tenancy farming and building up social connections that might further their careers (Springhall 1986).

Distinctive differences in this process existed between genders. Young women were expected to become involved in housewifery and domestic service (Springhall 1986; Mitterauer 1992), while young men entered occupations and apprenticeships that reinforced masculine roles (Griffiths 1996). Marriage was also seen as the main transitional step for young women, while for men it was employment and a trade. Young women were also denied access to public office, work on commonwealth business and office in the church, and men dominated all areas of administrative and public life. A sexual division of labour was also already well established by the mid-sixteenth century (Griffiths 1996).

Differences in transitional routes also existed between the aristocracy and the working classes. Apprenticeships could include a period of schooling, but it was normally the preserve of the middle classes and the aristocracy (Mitterauer 1992). Schooling was seen as a critical aspect of the growing-up process, starting in many cases with private tuition, public school and university. Young women would also take these routes, but once again we see their education dominated by gender distinctions and beliefs that girls should be receiving schooling solely in preparation ready for marriage (Dyhouse 1981).

The youth question itself was shaped by a range of anxieties that existed at the level of the locality (Davis 1990). Adults and the middle classes in particular had anxieties about the behaviour of the young in three major areas. First, there were concerns over the collective group identity of youth and their delay in moving into adulthood, especially on levels of local order. Part of the problem was thought to be young single men in apprenticeships. This group was seen to be involved in a range of problem behaviours such as rioting, political protest, crime and drunkenness (Griffiths 1996). Second, people generally married in their mid- to late twenties. Anxieties existed over the length of time young people were living away from home before they got married. Third, and finally, there was a major concern about 'masterless youth' or young people who resisted or rejected service and apprenticeship. The church and the aristocracy were gravely concerned that young people not placed in service or in apprenticeships would become delinquent and get involved in civil or political disorder (Griffiths 1996).

Regulation and governance of youth was far more fragmented in pre-modern society. The nation state was not yet formed, and therefore regulation and governance was on a more localised and regional basis. Youth could be highly monitored, regulated and controlled by some of these localised mechanisms. Working in service, or as an apprentice, brought with it high levels of discipline and authority. The magistrates and the church were also critical enforcers of moral codes of conduct at the local level. For example, in the late seventeenth century we see new legislation emerge influenced by local magistrates that restricted apprentices visiting public houses and brothels, from attending tennis courts, bowling alleys and cock feast days, and from playing cards, dice and billiards (Smith 1973). Being in employment also usually made young people members of local guilds or fraternity groups. These 'youth groups' had their own rules of behaviour and sanctions that legislated youthful behaviour, acting as another method of regulation (Springhall 1986). But local communities also had their own mechanisms for maintaining local control and order. For example, the custom of charivari was a ritual that acted to shame those who did not conform to community values. This was a noisy public demonstration, a form of public naming and shaming ceremony, that was used against individuals who went against social norms, values and community expectations (Davis 1990). This practice could be used against anyone in the area who deviated from social norms, although it was traditionally used by young people, acting as a form of self-policing (Davis 1990).

Early modernity and the youth question

In the eighteenth century modernity became the dominant form of social, economic and political order in western Europe. It radically changed not only the mode of production but also the political and economic systems and social organisation of life. Giddens (1991) suggests that modernity brings four critical developments. First, modernity can be associated with the introduction of industrialism and social relationships that emerge from the use of power and machinery in the production process. Second, modernity sees the establishment of capitalism as a system of commodity production that uses markets as the mechanism to distribute labour and commodities. While industrialism and capitalism are closely related, they need to be recognised as separate components. Third, modernity is linked with the creation of the modern nation state and the rise of organisation as a critical aspect of ordering social life. Finally, with the emergence of industrialism, capitalism and the nation state, we see the growth of institutions of surveillance. This involves both the visible supervision and organisation of certain populations, and the collection of information to monitor and coordinate social life.

The impact of modernity was far-reaching and substantial, leaving no area of life untouched. It not only reshaped time and space but also 'disembed [ded] social relationships' (Giddens 1991: 17) and radically changed local, national and global relationships. Its establishment took well over a century, but by the mid-nineteenth century we start to see the fundamental components embedded into the way the Western world was organised (Hobsbawm 1968). Its influence on the meaning of youth and the youth question was significant. What we see is the early establishment of the making of the modern phase called youth.

Modernity brought about major changes. One of the most important was the migration of populations from rural to urban environments. This was not unique to modernism (Hobsbawm 1968), but what was unusual was the pace and the numbers of people involved. In 1750 there were only two cities with populations of over 50,000 inhabitants; by 1801 there were eight and by 1851 there were 29, including nine with over 100,000 (Hobsbawm 1968). Eighty per cent of this new urban population was in fact aged between 15 and 25 and, while the age range was not new, the permanency of the move was. One of the major impacts of this relocation was the growing awareness of youth as a distinct age category and the emergence of an urban youth culture organised around the urban neighbourhood gang (Gillis 1974).

Industrialism also changed the nature and organisation of both employment and family life. With the growth of new forms of industrial and factory-based production whole families became involved in employment. Traditional methods of collective family working were, in the early stages of industrialism, transferred to the factory environment (Alexander 1982). Production was a collaborative process and could involve the whole family. In the early phases of industrialism there was little resistance to children and young people working in factories. As technology advanced, divisions of labour between men and women and between adult and child became more pronounced (Hall 1982). Certain tasks became the responsibility of children and young people – a precursor to the development of the youth apprenticeship infrastructure and to the low pay structure that is endemic to youth employment (Fyfe 1989). Modernity also had a major impact on the sexual division of labour:

> Amongst its many transformations the nineteenth century entailed significant changes in the positioning of women and men in social reproduction and economic production. These changes were bound up with a long run shift from a family economy to a family wage

> economy in which the need for cash income increasingly shaped family and household composition and organisation.
>
> (Irwin 2003: 569)

The 'family wage' economy brought with it a reconfiguration of gender relationships. The distinctions between roles and occupations became sharper. Men were to be the breadwinners and providers, women the home-makers. Women were also excluded from the labour market by trade unions in part because they were seen as undermining wage rates and collective bargaining (McClelland 2000). This is not to say that women did not need to work, as the family wage remained unstable (Tilly and Scott 1989). Women's employment became more focused into specific areas of employment and restructured into areas of low paid, part-time and temporary labour. The sexual division of labour was born and the context for what was to follow was set. But industrialism was not only an economic restructuring; it was also underpinned by a growing ideology of the importance of family life (Irwin 2003). Masculine status was given to men whose wives did not work. This was seen as visible proof that the family was not poor and that the man was independent (Hobsbawm 1987), while leisured women were a sign of affluence (Burstyn 1980). Home-making, childcare and family work became associated with 'naturalness' and nature, reinforcing the growing divide between the sexes (Burstyn 1980).

It is within this context that the role of girls in modern society is constructed. Social reform was dominated by this ideology, and it had a major impact on how girls' lives were to be shaped around the service or domestic sphere. For example, in the 1911 Census 34.8 per cent of all girls aged between 14 and 18 and registered as employed were involved in some form of domestic service (Dyhouse 1981). Such employment strongly encouraged the training of girls in skills that would make them either good mothers or future carers in domestic service (Dyhouse 1981). Throughout the establishment of modernism girls are seen as having a major contribution to make towards the reproduction of the species. Young women are confined to being future mothers, responsible for the socialisation of future generations. As a result, the state has a growing interest in intervening in the lives of young women to maintain the status quo. By the Victorian era we see education for girls expanding (Dyhouse 1981), and although their educational opportunities were greatly affected by class position (Walford 1993) messages of their role in society remained the same.

The emergence of modernity also increased other anxieties about the young (Pearson 1983). Urbanisation and industrialism are seen to undermine traditional mechanisms of regulation and control. Community and family sanctions are thought to have less impact on maintaining order as young people moved into the cities. Regulating behaviour became the province of the city, not local communities (Hobsbawm 1987). Similarly, as the system of service or apprenticeship broke down and was transformed, masters lost their influence and power. Regulation of youth was therefore limited to the cash-nexus system (Davis 1990). There were also growing anxieties and fears that the destabilising of society by the forces of modernity was increasing juvenile delinquency (Pearson 1983). Throughout the early stages of modernism, youth crime was perceived to be on the increase (Pearson 1983). The cause of this was located in the growing independence of youth in manufacturing towns and cities, and moral decline although this may have been a 'moral panic' over national concerns about the state of modern society and about reinforcing the status quo (Pearson 1983). Youth was being used as a 'social barometer' of social morality and order:

> the growing number of middle-class journalists and social commentators ... expressed concern not simply about the need to control criminality, but about the need to tackle a 'premature precocity', symbolized by promiscuity, irreligion, pauperism and knowledge of the 'adult world and its pleasures'. In short the problem was viewed as having as much a moral as a criminal character.
>
> (Muncie 2004: 56)

As a result of this, youth is constructed as the 'other' (Brown 2005) and the state, and its emerging agencies, take more responsibility for regulating and controlling them. New laws are passed, thus creating more criminal offences (and therefore increasing levels of crime), and greater emphasis is given to punishment. A dualistic approach between 'reform' and 'punishment' is born. What we start to see is the emergence of juvenile delinquency being 'legislated into existence' (Muncie 2004).

But as modernity became established, there was a growing movement of liberal thinkers who advocated the importance of restricting children's and young people's involvement with the harsh realities of the day. Concerns were raised about the threat to the innocence of childhood and to the physical and moral upbringing of the poor. Their efforts were focused to a large extent on the use of child labour in factories but went beyond this to argue for legislation to tackle the effects of poverty on childhood development (Fraser 1973). The result of their actions and influence was the creation, over a long period of time, of a body of legislation that structured the youth phase around specific age categories in employment. For example, Althorp's Factory Act 1833 restricted children aged 9–13 to working no more than 8 hours a day, while young persons, defined as aged 14–17, were restricted to a 12-hour day (Fraser 1973). As a result, legislation reduced children's involvement in factories and created a youth labour market that was clearly defined as transitional.

In the early stages of modernity, social reformers were also greatly concerned about the 'health of the nation' in pursuit of national efficiency and security. Sexual disease amongst young men was seen as a major social problem, and to tackle it required intervention in the lives of girls (Doolittle 2004). Throughout modernity, moral reformers, political commentators and the media continued to focus attention on the sexual behaviour of girls. This tended to be interpreted as a sign of moral decline amongst the poor. Girls who were defined as 'sexually promiscuous' were also usually defined as 'troublesome' (A. Hudson 1989). This may be framed around notions of protection, yet it has other consequences:

> In their zeal to protect working class girls from prostitution, late nineteenth-century reformers created new objects of control. Simultaneously they also established an explanatory code that portrays girls as passive and in need of protection, but also as potentially socially dangerous if they do not conform to codes of sexual respectability and domesticity.
>
> (A. Hudson 1989: 199)

These themes of motherhood, domestic responsibilities, marriage and sexual respectability remained central to how the 'girl question' is constructed in the early stages of modernity.

These anxieties over youth led to increased forms of intervention by the nation state. We see the emergence of the legislative framework and institutions that start to intervene more intensively in the lives of the young people. Much of this is with young people from poor or working-class backgrounds and with young women defined as 'in moral danger'. Social reformers were involved in this process, trying to bring about protection, but the emphasis was on regulation and control of the 'dangerous classes' and 'promiscuous girls'. The state then started, through this process, to universalise the youth phase as transitional and age-bounded. Youth became separated from both childhood and adulthood and existed in the new infrastructure constructed by the state. By the middle of the nineteenth century, youth, as a part of the life course, was well and truly established.

The growth of the interventionist state

Over the next hundred years modernity becomes embedded as the order of the modern world. From the Victorian age, through the First World War, and into the inter-war years we see the fullness of the modernising project taking hold. The nation state and its bureaucratic infrastructure, liberal democracy, and capitalist forms of production all become established. This does not necessarily lead to more stability, as there are two world wars, the decline of the British Empire, the Great Depression and continued class conflict over the sharing of the benefits of industrialism. Modernity may become more embedded but tensions remain, and it is these unresolved problems that influence the youth question.

Building on the influence of the child saviour movement and early Factory Acts, there was a growing concern about the failure of the state to capitalise on youth as a 'national asset'. The strong reformist movement of the Victorian age and beyond argued that the state of youth was not only a moral issue but also one of security and economic success (Davis 1990). Tensions existed over attempts to create a powerful nation state that was an economic power base that could be competitive. Issues of social order remained, but there was a growing anxiety that the state needed to recognise the positive contribution youth could make to society and that youth was a national asset that should not be squandered (Davis 1990). Concerns also emerged over the health and condition of youth. Evidence in 1901 from the Boer War recruitment office showed that two out of three recruits were unfit to serve in the army (Davis 1990). As a result of these concerns, levels of intervention continued to increase.

One area of anxiety was defined as the 'boy labour problem' (Hendrick 1990). Social reformers in the early twentieth century were concerned about the eclectic mechanisms and structures that shaped the transition from school to work. Concerns focused on what were called 'blind alley jobs'[2] and 'occupational mobility' (Springhall 1986). All this led to the growth of indiscipline and inappropriate independence (Hendrick 1990). In such situations it was thought that it led to 'unruly' leisure and young people having too much time on their hands. These debates continued into the Great Depression. Youth employment became a major concern of the state and issues of poor schooling and educational opportunities topped the political agenda, providing seeds for the reforms that followed after the Second World War (Davis 1990).

From the 1880s until the Second World War social reform was also aimed at improving the moral condition and attitudes of the young. Reformists such as Mary Carpenter led the way in arguing for a more interventionist role for the state in family life. She believed that youth crime was associated with conditions of working-class life, and the failure of parents to discipline their children and instil the correct morals gave justification for greater state intervention. For the first time the state took on *in loco parentis* as a core responsibility when needed. New legislation also introduced reformatories and industrial schools, where children aged between 7 and 15 could be sentenced to between 2 and 5 years. These were grafted on to a mainstream system of justice that had punishment at its heart. The emerging legislative framework that followed from 1900 until the Second World War was then constructed around a discourse of reform, treatment, control and punishment, with welfare and treatment taking a greater role (Davis 1990). Within this model the problems of youth were redefined. The causes underpinning their lack of integration were seen as a problem with family socialisation, poor parental behaviour and working-class culture. Removing the young from such influences was seen as essential if the youth problem was to be addressed (Clarke 1973).

Into the early twentieth century there was also continued anxiety about girls. Some of this focused on questions about their education, their relationship to industry and factory work and their criminal and sexual activity (Board of Education 1923). There was also concern about the impact of the feminist movement on girls' attitudes (Dyhouse 1981). Between 1886 and 1920 there was also an expansion of 'girl societies and clubs', concerned with educating girls in feminine roles and responsibilities (Dyhouse 1981). At the heart of their approach was a desire to protect young women while also helping to improve the quality of mothering and housewifery (Dyhouse 1981).

These growing anxieties about the condition of youth in the first half of the twentieth century are not coincidental or unrelated to broader global processes taking place at this time. The need to improve the youth of the nation was also linked to other problems. Britain was under threat both externally and internally. The newly established industrial order was built upon class exploitation. Economic downturn and unemployment after the First World War created resistance and conflict, expressed through protests led by the emerging Labour movement (Hobsbawm 1968). But also the British Empire was under pressure. It was a time of economic challenge and a period with a growing global conflict and wars. While tackling the 'problems of youth' was seen as morally justifiable to help address these problems, the 'youth problem' also became a mechanism for drawing attention away from the problems of the state. For example, the emergence of the term 'hooligan' is no historical accident. It is

> 'associated with imperial decline, material incapacity, the erosion of social discipline and moral authority, the eclipse of family life, and what was feared to be the death rattle of "Old England"'.
>
> (Pearson 1983: 107)

Welfare capitalism and politics of inclusion, 1945–80

War had a major impact on how the state was to respond to the youth question. Pre-war concerns about the condition of youth were once again raised as a focus of concern. Schooling had been greatly disrupted, with large sections of the youth population moved out of cities and schools, especially in London, which had suffered major destruction (Davis 1990). Children and young people were seen as undernourished and suffering from poor health. Concerns were also expressed over the need to provide a world 'fit for heroes' for the returning young soldiers. In this sense Beveridge and the Labour government-in-waiting designed a reconstruction programme built upon the needs of the young. Youth became an important metaphor and rationale for social change and for the reconstruction of a 'new' Britain that prioritised welfare reform.

With the overwhelming election victory of the new Labour government in 1945, Britain's reconstruction was built upon a vision of major welfare reforms such as full education, commitment to full employment and Keynesian economics, and the tackling of squalor and disease through principles of social justice for all. As a result the state increased its levels of intervention and its commitment to social inclusion and to improving the lives of all its citizens (Davies 1986; Mizen 2004).

In the late 1940s and early 1950s youth therefore became a major site for policy intervention, leading to the first major steps towards its redefinition and universalisation as a category across policy (Mizen 2004). The youth question was strongly focused on tackling problems and barriers that young people faced. Educational opportunities for all were to be improved by changing the school leaving age to 16, by removing the eleven-plus examination, and by increasing further and higher education opportunities for the working class. The reformist movement was also influential within youth justice, seeing welfare as the solution to young people being a social problem because of their circumstances. There came a strong recognition that delinquency was the result of 'social inadequacy' and a failure to 'fit in' (Davies 1986), rather than of 'depraved individuals'. Under the 1969 Children and Young People's Act, more reform and treatment became central to the youth justice system, seeing the welfare needs of young offenders as something that could be addressed by anti-poverty programmes. Punishment remained but was seen as less important:

> The juvenile justice system came to be perceived as a mechanism within a much wider framework of social welfare treatment. Increasingly, errant youth came to be understood as deprived rather than depraved, in need of rescue and rehabilitation rather than simple punishment.
>
> (Osgerby 1998: 145)

The creation of the Youth Service was also an important development (Osgerby 1998). Concerns over leisure-time use continued after the Second World War but became a central part of youth policy through the creation of a state-funded Youth Service. Formal youth movements, such as the Scouts, the Boys' Brigade and other voluntary organisations, had always been evident

(Springhall 1986) but after the war the state saw the Youth Service having a key role in educating and socialising the young (Davies 1986). But by the 1950s there was a growing concern that the Youth Service only reached 'respectable youth' (Jephcott 1954), and the Albermarle Commission (Ministry of Education 1960) advocated that the Youth Service should turn its attention to the 'unattached' through the use of detached work (Davies 1986).

While there was substantial evidence that the policies post-war created increased inclusion for large sections of the population, there was a growing concern that certain sections of the youth population remained marginalised. Juvenile delinquency increased, and the Youth Service failed to attract not only the unattached but also large sections of young people and especially girls (Davies 1986). There were also concerns that although youth unemployment was low, youth employment was expanding in the semi-skilled and unskilled sectors of the economy. This led to anxieties that in the long term would have an impact on their inclusion (Carter 1966). Educational reform, especially in the university sector, was also seen to be benefiting the middle classes rather than young people from the working classes (Committee on Higher Education 1963). The policy response to these issues was to treat them as technical problems that adjustment in policy could tackle (Davies 1986).

The arrival of the 'teenager'

But the youth question was not just perceived as the same 'old problems'. There was also a growing anxiety about the arrival of a new breed of young person: the teenagers who had their own distinct lifestyle and culture, born out of the affluence of the post-war boom (Abrams 1959: 5). The teenager arrived with an expanding consumption market and new styles and leisure activities (Osgerby 1998). Throughout the 1960s and 1970s there was increasing anxiety about the impact of consumption, style and leisure on the morals and behaviour of the young. There were concerns that teenagers were becoming more 'disrespectful', that they 'lacked manners', rejected tradition and convention (Davis 1990), and were causing a range of social problems (Cohen 1980). Influences such as the cinema, pop music and the fashion industries were seen as 'corrupting' youth and 'leading them astray'. Youth culture was seen as a growing problem, impacting on a growing sense of unease and feelings of social disorder, which were arising as a result of changes in modernism. But this was about more than just the growing spending power of the young. We also see the public arrival of the new subcultural groups that reinforce ideas that youth was changing or bringing about change. In the 1950s youth culture 'exploded'. We see the arrival of the 'beatniks', the 'Rockers', the 'Teds' and the 'hippies', bringing with them greater media and academic attention (Osgerby 1998).

But not only was social change seen as creating new forms of relationships for teenagers; the activities of the young were seen as a new 'counterculture', or 'generational movement', perceived as a potential threat to the existing social order. With the growth of affluence and the 'withering away of class divisions' it was claimed that youth was a force for social change through the newly formed middle-class cultural movements (Musgrove 1964). The middle-class counterculture movements saw themselves as more individualised and more diffuse in their structure. Members did not always see themselves as emerging from tensions in the social and economic order but from their own idealism. The counterculture did not represent a revolution from 'below' as such, but an attack from 'within the system' (Musgrove 1964: 19). The new emerging youth culture was challenging the existing order, being influenced by bohemian ideas of the 'avant-garde'. By the 1960s the counterculture had expanded into all walks of life, linked more to the growth of the middle classes entering into higher education (Osgerby 1998). It was from this intellectual base that the counterculture movement grew. Rock music and pop festivals, peace campaigns and movements, anti-establishment demonstrations and university 'sit-ins' were all seen as symbolic of the power and influence of this emerging movement. Youth in the 1960s and early 1970s was then being seen as the new vanguard generation of social change (Musgrove 1964).

But the counterculture was predominantly a middle-class movement. Involvement in political activities and 'dropping out' could only be afforded by material resources and freedoms found within the dominant class (Brake 1985). Middle-class militancy was also more about art and the expression of individualism than about confronting existing structures of inequality. Similarly, the political objectives of the counterculture were less to do with revolution and social change and more to do with following established paths of their parents (Abrams and Little 1965). Much of the protest was therefore more related to conformity and maintaining the existing social order (Osgerby 1998).

Youth in crisis: The impact of unemployment

The growing fear and anxieties of youth in the 1970s were compounded by changes in the economic sphere of social life. The youth question quickly refocused on the problems of youth unemployment. As a result we start to see a shift from the 'policies of inclusion' to 'policies of control' as a mechanism of managing the economic crisis and regaining the authority of the state (Osgerby 1998). Throughout the 1970s and into the 1980s we see massive global economic restructuring (Allen and Massey 1989). This transformed the youth labour market, bringing with it the highest levels of youth unemployment known in the post-war years (Mizen 2004) and a radical restructuring (Ashton *et al.* 1990). Youth employment prospects declined in the 1970s and youth employment failed to recover during periods of economic boom, showing that changes to the youth labour market had long-term impacts on opportunities (Ashton *et al.* 1990). As adult employment increased, no corresponding change could be identified in the youth labour market (Roberts 1995). Such a downturn was unprecedented in history, indicating this was a fundamental restructuring of youth labour (Mizen 2004).

We also start to see a growth in number of young people aged 16 and over staying on at school. For example, in 1974 one in three young people stayed on at school after the official leaving age had been reached. This number increased to one in two in the early 1980s, and seven out of ten a decade later (Furlong and Cartmel 1997). Most young people and their parents tended to reject other options available and saw extended schooling as a better alternative to unemployment or training. This suggested that new post-16 courses acted more as 'warehouses' for the young until 'real' jobs came along (Roberts 1995). But the growth area for opportunities for school leavers was the expansion of youth training. By the late 1970s the Youth Opportunities Programme (YOP) was launched as a mechanism for training the young in skills they needed for work. This was symbolically the final political acceptance that the commitment to full employment was dead and that a new era was about to begin (Mizen 1995). By the end of the 1970s only 162,000 school leavers had entered YOP, but by the middle of the 1980s nearly half of all school leavers had experienced a training course run by the Manpower Services Commission (MSC). This expansion of youth training in response to youth unemployment is normally defined as the birth of the 'training state' (Mizen 1995).

Throughout the 1980s the problem of youth unemployment continued to be a central concern to policy-makers. As the inclusive policies of Labour were rejected, the New Right emerged with a political agenda linked to the politics of less government and greater use of market forces (Savage and Robins 1990). As a result major restructuring took place in the role of the state in social life and the use of public services. Youth training was disliked and went against their ethos, but throughout the 1980s it grew in size and stature, although there was a shift in how it saw the problem. Young people were blamed for their own unemployment because they lacked the necessary skills or competences (Mizen 2004). Unemployment amongst the young was seen as a result of overindulgence by the state in protecting the young worker, the influence and power of trade unionism, and the dependency culture created by the benefit systems (Mizen 2004). On top of this, young people were seen to have individual failings brought about by the lack of skills or abilities (Davies 1986). Youth training was transformed, creating the work ethic and disciplines of employment for the young unemployed.

The 'blaming of the young' for the problem of unemployment impacted on other policy areas. In the 1980s vocationalism in the school curriculum was expanded. For example, in 1983 the government set up the Technical and Vocational Education Initiative (TVEI) in schools. Vocationalism was also introduced into further education, channelled through the MSC, and developed as National Vocational Qualifications (NVQs). What we see, therefore, is a concentrated stream of programmes aiming to discipline the young to the new economic environment and job market.

Major changes in the welfare benefit system and the deregulation of the youth labour market also took place. This dual-pronged approach aimed to open up youth employment to market forces and to increase their take-up of lower-paid jobs. Eleven changes occurred between 1980 and 1993 that reduced state benefits to the young (Roberts 1995). These included the repeal of employment protection legislation, 21-year-olds losing living-at-home contributions, 16–17-year-olds losing contributions to board allowance, and students losing benefits in vacations. By the late 1980s the Thatcher government was also building in 'workfare programmes' where welfare benefits were linked to job searching and availability (Mizen 2004). Getting benefits became more closely aligned to finding a job. The youth wage was also deregulated and opened up to market forces, while rates of pay set on youth training programmes were reduced. The cumulative effect of these measures saw the value of youth pay decrease substantially (Mizen 2004), leading to increasing levels of poverty amongst the young (Novak 1998). By the end of the 1980s the youth unemployment problem was being highly regulated and controlled by central government. Youth training increased and youth were put under the microscope in their attempts to find jobs.

Youth, crime and disorder

In the early 1980s the crisis of modernity was also symbolised by growing claims of problems over youth crime and social disorder. Throughout the 1960s and into the 1970s youth crimes had been on the increase and, as the recession took hold, major anxieties and concerns were raised about the youth crime problem (Newburn 2002). Government became more draconian and interventionist in dealing with young people who were seen to be a problem. Changes to youth justice policy advocated under the 1969 Children's Act had been shaped by a welfarist approach, but this legislation was never fully enacted. For example, the age of criminal responsibility was not changed from 11 to 14, and attendance and detention centres were never phased out. In fact, by 1982 the main principles of the Act were rejected and replaced by legislation that saw punishment become the centre plank of government policy towards juveniles (Newburn 2002).

By the middle of the 1980s the state and magistrates had new powers to send young people to 'short, sharp, shock' centres and youth detention centres. This is a sign of 'authoritarian populism', where government and the state put law and order at the centre of its strategy for managing society (Hall *et al.* 1978). Young people were at the forefront of such policies, leading not only to greater levels of imprisonment, but also to more intensive policing (Hall *et al.* 1978). But while conservative rhetoric on youth justice was 'being tough on crime', practice within the system was aimed to limit the use of custody for young people and to reduce the numbers of young people coming into contact with the youth justice system (Newburn 2002). Even though government gave greater sentencing powers to magistrates, the number of young people within the system was greatly reduced (Newburn 2002).

By the early 1980s the 'inclusive state' had also failed certain groups of young people. Major disturbances broke out in urban areas of large cities. In 1981 communities in Bristol, Brixton, Southall, and Toxteth in Liverpool had gangs of youths 'rioting'. Communities were destroyed, with shops, facilities and cars being burnt out or badly damaged. Other 'riots' also broke out in smaller towns, cities and communities. Areas such as Wolverhampton, Huddersfield, Derby and Nottingham saw similar patterns of violence and disorder, with youth being seen as the major culprits. In 1985 similar events took place again in other large urban centres. Young people were once again seen as the major troublemakers.

These disturbances were explained by the media and government as an outbreak of 'alien disease' or 'evil individuals' trying to encourage disorder for their own revolutionary ends (Solomos 1988). Such behaviour was seen as 'un-British', and government ministers blamed it on the breakdown of morality, lack of family discipline and bad parents (Solomos 1993). But such explanations also had a strong focus on race. The Scarman (1981) report, for example, while claiming that the Brixton riots were not 'race riots', still recognised that there was a connection between the anger of young black people in the context of deprivation, and police and youth relations. Others had stronger views linking the problem to the black community. Enoch Powell, for example, claimed that such events vindicated his arguments that black cultures were not compatible with Britishness, and that a programme of repatriating black people was needed (Bowling and Phillips 2002). Such a view attempted to pathologise black culture and individual characteristics of young black people and their communities (Gilroy 1987). Little was made of how such communities had suffered long periods of disadvantage, poverty, unemployment and racism, or of repressive policing (Gilroy 1987). Neither did it recognise that 'rioting' may well be an integral part of British life in that the history of modernity is a history of disorder and conflict.

The 'girl question' in post-war Britain

Throughout the post-war period and into the 'crisis' of modernity, there was a growing concern about the impact of social change on the lives of girls. Anxieties emerged that claimed post-war reform was bringing about major changes that challenged the 'natural' roles and responsibilities of young women (Davies 1986). Large increases took place in female employment. Figures indicate that by 1968 over 38 per cent of girls aged 15–17 were entering clerical industries (Osgerby 1998: 52, Table 5.1). This overtook domestic service and brought girls out of the private and into public spheres of economic life. Girls were seen to be entering work and becoming an important part of the workforce, although the sexual division of labour remained a strong factor in structuring the types of work and income levels (Osgerby 1998). Much of this employment was still structured around women having the core responsibilities in the home (Abbott *et al.* 2005). Concerns were also raised about young women's involvement with popular culture and consumption. Fashion, cosmetics, clothes, magazines, pop records and other forms of leisure targeted young women, who were found not only to be a viable market source but also, as a result of new forms of employment, to have incomes to spend. By the 1960s and 1970s there was a massive growth in leisure goods and services available to young women (Abbott *et al.* 2005). But anxieties also arose in the 1960s over the counterculture movements. Feminism was seen as a 'liberating' force that aimed to free women from their domestic 'duties and responsibilities', creating new forms of sexual freedom. The discovery and marketing of the contraceptive pill was seen to give young women more control over their bodies and lives and increasing equality and freedom. In this sense girls were at the forefront of social change.

The changing opportunities for girls and the increased demands from the feminist movement brought about changes in both legislation and attitudes that had major impacts on the lives of young women. For example, by the middle of the 1970s, abortion was legalised and the Equal Opportunities Act had been put on to the statute book, ensuring, in principle, equal pay and opportunities in employment. Attitudes also started to change. Women were seen as having the right to have careers outside the home, and sexual relationships were brought out into the public domain (Abbott *et al.* 2005). Divorce expanded and more women were cohabiting rather than getting married.

Different governments between 1950 and the late 1970s responded to the 'girl question' in different ways, although much policy still reinforced traditional messages and maintained inequality. For example, the eleven-plus required girls to get a higher score than boys to secure a place at grammar schools (Tomlinson 2005a), and employment segmentation and wage differentials remained (Abbott *et al.* 2005). Policy continued to focus its anxieties on the sexual behaviour of girls and especially working-class and 'troublesome' girls. For example, in youth justice policy there was a growing worry about the sexual promiscuity of girls and, as a result, the new Children and Young Persons Act (1969) introduced, under the welfare banner, new powers of intervention that would allow magistrates and social workers to respond to girls seen as being in 'moral' danger. In research that followed, clear evidence emerged that showed that social workers' interpretation of 'moral danger' related to anxieties over what they perceived as inappropriate sexual behaviour. Any girl defined as having a 'troubled' or 'troublesome' life tended to be put into care (Thorpe *et al.* 1980).

In the early 1980s, with the election of the conservative party, a 'new' ideology emerged that rejected the post-war consensus of inclusion, being also underpinned by a strong moral position. Once again this saw the individual and the family as central to social life, rejecting state intervention as a means of improving inclusion. The 'natural' family was seen as the only way of bringing up children. Any other combination was perceived as 'unnatural' and dangerous (Thompson 2004). Growing evidence of 'social problems' was seen as a result of the decline of the 'natural' family and the lack of good family values. Social policy became a major force that 'normalised' heterosexuality and punished difference (Carabine 1996). A key 'problem' was seen as the number of young single mothers. For example, girls were accused of getting pregnant as a means of jumping the queue for public housing. As a result welfare benefits were to be targeted at 'respectable' young women (Carabine 1996). How the political right employed their moral politics was instrumental in order to mobilise popular fears and gain support for other more radical programmes, yet it was a powerful force that both regulated and controlled young women's behaviour (Carabine 1996).

In this period girls' sexuality was also being regulated by social policy. For example, the 1986 Education Act took sex education out of the control of local authorities and placed it in the hands of school governors. Government also introduced Section 28 of the Local Government Act that put restrictions on how homosexuality could be presented in the classroom and what advice teachers could give. As a result of these reforms, practices of teachers, school nurses and voluntary organisations became subject to 'an atmosphere of intimidation' (Epstein and Johnson 1998: 14). Similar outcomes arose as a result of the Gillick competence ruling that proposed that doctors could not give under-16s contraceptive advice. The outcome of the case, while complicated, created anxieties amongst health professionals about how to deal with these questions (Thompson 2004). As policy developed, social policy became more confused and contradictory. On the one hand it emphasised a 'moral authoritarianism' insistence on defining anything outside of the 'norm' as wrong, but on the other it advocated a public health pragmatism where it was recognised that something needed to be done (Thompson 1994).

Conclusion

This chapter has focused on the political construction of the youth question and its impact on our understanding of 'modern youth'. As major social and economic changes have taken place, youth has been seen as both 'dangerous' and a 'threat' to the stability and maintenance of the status quo, but also as 'vulnerable' and in need of protection, especially from the ravages of modernity. This interplay between 'dangerousness' and 'innocence' has then shaped how the state, at different moments in time, has responded to the youth question. The emergence and growth of institutions such as education, juvenile justice, the youth service, and social services, all with core responsibilities for managing the problems of youth, alongside legislation that universalises the youth phase, constructs youth as a 'normal' part of the life course. This duality of anxiety, and the state's response to it, explains the contradictory nature of how, in the modern era, the young make the formal transition into adulthood.

Yet the understanding of the youth question has also varied by gender, class and, more recently, ethnicity. This has created different responses and actions, which have had different impacts on how certain groups have been constructed and understood within the political construction of the youth question. For example, being a girl has been about being marginalised from major educational and employment opportunities, understood in relation to gender stereotypes and expectations of their future role as mothers, as well as being seen and problemitised because of their sexuality. The youth question, therefore, has to be recognised as having different meanings to different social groups, bringing about different types of responses. In this sense youth is not only shaped by preconceived understandings of 'differences', but also reinforces them through social practice in both policy-making and professional practice.

2 Science and the age of reason: The 'discovery of adolescence'

Introduction

In this chapter we turn our attention to developments in social science. Modernity is also associated with the Enlightenment period, and is seen as the age of science and reason in which our modern-day understanding of 'adolescence' is discovered. Developments in American and European psychology, criminology and sociology are influential in not only explaining youth but also identifying the causes that underpin the behaviour of troublesome and problematic young people. In the discussion that follows we will explore how, in the early developmental stages of social science, a number of influential theorists approached the youth question. We will also discuss how these ideas impacted on the expansion of social scientific youth research in Britain in the first sixty years of the twentieth century and the influence they had on the political management of youth and modern-day understandings of their problems.

Modernity, science and the age of reason

Modernity was not just a reconfiguration of how society was organised, it was also the age of Enlightenment that challenged the pre-modern and traditional ways of understanding the social world. It was a period of political upheaval which saw the introduction of radical ideas (Nesbet 1967), along with the construction of and belief in the political subject (Delanty 1999). Individual rights and freedoms were seen as paramount to how the world should be ordered. The Enlightenment period also introduced the notion of the rational subject, or what became known as 'instrumental rationality' (Adorno and Horkheimer 1979), a belief that human beings are above nature and able to master their environment. Science was seen as central within this process. It provided knowledge for understanding and controlling nature. For example, it was in the seventeenth century, alongside the emergence of modernity, that saw the arrival of theory testing and the use of empirical evidence to find out how the world is and how it might be understood (Williams and May 1996).

With the emergence of modernity we also see the expansion of the reflexive subject (Giddens 1991). This becomes a defining feature of all human action,[1] and although it is present in pre-modernity it becomes a major everyday feature of social life in modernity. Reflexivity is also introduced into systems of social reproduction and all parts of human action. Tradition has less influence on how the world is understood and can only be a force if knowledge and information justifies it. Reflexivity, therefore, becomes the mechanism that drives action:

> 'The reflexivity of modern social life consists in the fact that social practices are constantly examined and reformed in the light of incoming information about those very practices, thus constitutively altering their character'
>
> (Giddens 1991: 38).

Modernity relies upon knowledge as a critical function of order. It is associated with the growth of institutions and organisations that collect and assess information as a mechanism of changing the way 'things are done'. An example of this is the collection and analysis of official statistics. In this context social science becomes a central feature of the reflexivity process with the birth and expansion of sociology, criminology and psychology. But it is also the 'new age' of reflexivity where individuals use the increased knowledge in assessing their everyday lives and activities. This reflexivity of knowledge has a central role in how individuals interpret their own lives and how they make choices about their own biographies and how governments govern (Giddens 1991).

G. Stanley Hall and the 'discovery of adolescence'

The study of youth has its roots in Victorian Britain (Davis 1990). It is here that we see the 'establishment of a distinctively modern approach towards the young as an object of study' (Davis 1990: 59). Conceptualisation of the meaning of youth becomes the focus of the newly emerging discipline of psychology. The modernist orthodoxy of what youth means today is initially formalised and justified as a universal stage of development by the discipline of psychology (Springhall 1986; Davis 1990; Griffin 1993). With the growing anxieties of the Victorian middle classes, and the growth of professionals who need to explain and understand the 'youth problem', comes a search for explanations. It is here that psychology has its influence:

> The late nineteenth and early twentieth centuries were a time when developmental and educational psychology took on an ever more professionalized, scientific and empirically based guise, and began significantly to shape policy towards the young, thus contributing to

> the objectification of the very pattern of division of the pre-adult years that these disciplines claimed to have discovered.
>
> (Davis 1990: 59)

At the heart of this approach is the work of G. Stanley Hall (1903). He is credited with having 'discovered' adolescence and been the founding father of all psychological theories of youth. While much of Hall's theoretical underpinnings would be rejected today, his influence on the understandings of the 'youth problem' in Victorian England was enormous.[2] Hall's theory was greatly influenced by his own Victorian values and beliefs. His approach was a blend of middle-class values, Christian theology and Enlightenment philosophy. In many cases Hall's starting position was shaped by the dominant ideology of the day and especially the anxieties surrounding the 'youth problem'. He saw himself as providing an explanation of why youth were problematic and constructing solutions that would help maintain the social order and status quo.

Hall was also greatly influenced by the post-Darwin movement of biological and evolutionist philosophy, believing that genes and genetics were critical factors in shaping the life course and for making a 'natural order' (Davis 1990). An earlier version of this approach provided justification for slavery, imperialism and colonial expansion (Griffin 1993). Hall took this idea and reworked it into his theory of adolescence. Infancy, childhood and adolescence were more like prehistoric cultures and at a primitive stage of human development, with adulthood being the most advanced stage.

Hall saw adolescence as a 'second birth' and the infancy of man's higher nature. It was here that the 'natural' transition to adulthood began and that through discovery and energy adults would emerge. But this was the time of puberty where physical and emotional changes took place, and as a result it was natural for youth to go through a period of 'storm and stress' in making this transition into adulthood. Youth was seen as 'a prisoner of its own nature' (Hendrick 1990: 103) and therefore not always in control of its actions. Yet Hall believed that those who managed to make this transition successfully would reach a higher level of being (the fully rounded adult), while for those who failed the future held delinquency, degeneracy and perversion. In Hall's work we see for the first time the scientific evidence of 'storm and stress' and a belief in the universalism of the problematic nature of youth transitions (Davis 1990). Hall strongly recommended that the state, and its agencies, should tighten the regulation and control of youth. Young people needed the space and opportunity to achieve their potential while learning to suppress and manage their biological changes through self-control. Young men had to be steered towards more 'normal' adult heterosexual relationships and monogamous marriage. Boys were seen as naturally superior and capable of a higher destiny, while girls were seen as lower down in the evolutionary order. Girls were plagued with having to manage menstruation. This was a critical component in their development and, until they had passed through it, they remained greatly at risk of having future problems. This position led Hall to argue for girls to be excluded from education that might encourage serious learning (Dyhouse 1981).

Adolescence as a 'normal' part of the life course

While Hall's ideological position would not be given much credence today, his assumptions and claims about the naturalness of the psychological and emotional transition to adulthood as a universalism are well embedded within both psychological and 'common-sense' discourse on youth (France 2000). Similarly, we see the common acceptance of youth as a period of 'storm and stress' entering the everyday vocabulary and debates on the nature of youthful problem behaviour. Hall is inspirational to the child psychology movement, influencing a range of significant developments in psychology and psychiatry (Hendrick 1990). He is the founding father of the child study movement and the American Psychological Association. His approach was able to connect not only with those working in the medical profession but also with 'common-sense' everyday understandings of the problem that existed in the discourse of the middle classes. The approach created its own language that also appealed outside of the discipline into everyday understandings of 'the problem' (Hendrick 1990). This has longer-term impacts on the understandings of youth, in that it locates a particular starting point for theorising 'adolescence' as a particular set of behaviours within the life course that in turn shapes 'common-sense' and everyday theories of the youth question (Cohen 1997). Hall also had a significant influence on the child reform movement (Hendrick 1990), offering the newly emerging professions a 'scientific' explanation of the 'troubled child'. For example, those concerned with the boy labour problem – social commentators and political and social reformers, such as youth workers and educationalists – were influenced by his ideas (Hendrick 1990). This interplay between theory, science and 'common sense' then gave justification for different types of interventions.

Criminology on the influence of 'science'

Hall's psychology of adolescence and the role of science in understanding the youth question also had a major influence within criminology. Its history can be located back to the very beginning of the Enlightenment and the Classical traditions (Garland 2002). Irrationalism, superstition and prejudices were rejected for a more modern theorising dominated by science methodologies and technologies (Garland 2002). Science, and especially the emerging new medical disciplines of psychology and psychiatry, offered an alternative empirical approach that would explain and understand individuals' relationships with modern society.

The movement of these ideas into practice is generally credited to Lombroso (1876) and his work on the 'science of the criminal'. He believed that the criminal was a 'naturally occurring entity, a fact of nature rather than a social and legal product' (Garland 2002: 25). He set about studying the body types and shapes of criminals in prisons to try and identify the differences between the criminal and the non-criminal. He concluded that serious offenders were born and not made, that criminal activity was biologically driven, and crime was generated by biological pathology. Such claims were challenging to the judicial orthodoxy of the time. Previous theories of crime were located in the Classical ideas of rational choice. Individuals have 'free will' and make choices based upon consequences. Lombroso's approach suggested that behaviour was more to do with biology and, therefore, determined. He suggested that, as a result, rather than punishing the criminal as a deterrent, treatment was more likely to be effective (Muncie 2004).

Lombroso and Ferrero were also interested in the 'problem girl' and especially in female delinquency. Again, like Hall, they started from the position that women were lower down the evolutionary scale and this was reflected in their particular nature. So, for example, because girls were passive, and more domestic, these were signs that they had not evolved as far as men. To explain both the offending and non-offending of girls they made two claims. Firstly, women were less inclined to be criminals because they were the 'weaker sex', less evolved than men and not subject to the powerful natural forces of the male. Men had the biological strength and the developed abilities to be criminals, unlike women. In other words, women lacked the evolutionary development and biological power to be criminals. Secondly, when women did commit crimes, it was because they were 'unnatural', taking the criminal elements of men and combining them with the worst of women. It was also suggested that female criminals were being more like men in their actions than women (Smart 1977).

But Lombroso and Ferrero were intrigued by the fact that a large proportion of the women they investigated were in prison for sexual crimes. It was here that biology was seen as critical. Lombroso and Ferrero believed that prostitution was a stage in evolution and, as a result, involvement in it was linked to the lack of personal development within individuals. Women were therefore slaves to their biology, which then pushed them to certain sorts of crimes (sexual). It never occurred to them that the number of women, defined as prostitutes, in prison was because of the moral outrage and political attention of the Italian bourgeoisie. They were deeply concerned with the moral probity of women, and prostitution was identified as a particularly vicious activity. The women's prisons which Lombroso visited were therefore most likely populated with women accused of prostitution, hence Lombroso's focus on the sexual nature of women's delinquency.

Positive criminology and its impact

Outdated as many of Lombroso's ideas are today, his influence on criminology, like Hall's in psychology, was enormous, leaving an important legacy. After his thesis was published, a major new international movement arose that saw a flurry of publications, texts, and conferences, all aimed at developing his initial ideas (Garland 2002). This had a major impact on American and European thought and was a major influence in the expansion of the positivist movement.[3] The positivist approach to social research is committed to the application of methods used in the natural sciences to study social behaviours. It is interested in identifying 'cause and effect' and developing robust scientific methods of measurement. Social life is seen as being tangible and quantifiable, creating objective knowledge about the behaviour of human beings.

While psychology and positivism took hold and became major influences in the late nineteenth century, psychology, as a social science discipline, did fragment and become far more diverse. The tradition set by Lombroso was continued by writers such as Hooton (1939), Sheldon (1949) and Glueck and Glueck (1950). Their approach attempted to measure physiology through scientific means and make claims concerning the relationship between body size and shape and criminal behaviour. In this model it is not causes that are revealed but correlations.

A more influential tradition has been that of genetics and the idea of the 'pathological family' (Hollin 2002). Such an approach relies very much on attempts to isolate genetic causes that are either located in individuals (i.e. the criminal gene) or are inherited from family (genetic dysfunctioning passed on from generations). It was argued that certain traits, such as low intelligence, impulsivity and aggressiveness, can be transmitted through genes.[4] Similar approaches have focused on the impact of biological factors such as hormone imbalances, excess testosterone, lack of vitamins, and abnormal levels of adrenaline and blood sugar, to name a few. While the research is intensive, it has not yet been able to prove a direct link to offending behaviour (Muncie 2004).

The third development of psychology was to recognise 'multiple causes' and the importance of environment to criminal behaviour. One of the most significant early contributors to this debate was Cyril Burt (1925). He argued that juvenile delinquency could not be attributed solely to one (biological) cause. There was no such thing as a 'born criminal', rather criminal behaviour was the outcome of the interaction between the individual's psychological make-up and their social environment. By using positivist methods of measurement he identified 170 different influences which seemed to correlate with delinquency. These included individual family and societal characteristics such as body shape and size, impulsiveness and low intelligence, poor family relationships, inappropriate parental discipline, and unconducive and poor neighbourhoods. While this approach focused on the importance of multiple factors, psychology was seen still to make a significant contribution:

> Burt sought to organise these factors in order of importance and the result was a psycho-dynamic explanation. If delinquency reflected people's inability to follow rules and act responsibly, then this inability had to be referred to people's emotional and moral development. Genetic factors were certainly relevant to this, but the key to a healthy moral growth was the family.
>
> (Frith 1984: 27)

Burt's contribution can then be seen as the intellectual rationale for the 'common-sense' understanding of juvenile delinquency in that some people have psychological problems which are then compounded by 'bad families', 'broken homes' and 'poverty'. This approach underpins what is called 'developmental criminology', where multiple risk factors are seen to impact on child and youth development, pushing them towards a life of crime and rule-breaking (see Farrington 2002).

Positivist criminology also had an impact on the continued study of girls and delinquency. The research by Cowie *et al.* (1968) on delinquent girls in a detention centre is a good example of this tradition. They claim that official statistics support the idea that girls commit less crime than boys. Girls do not normally become delinquent, but when they do it is doubly problematic. To explain this they use a similar methodology to that of Lombroso and Ferrero, arguing that correlation science can help identify cause and effect. They believe that for girls to become delinquent a far greater concentration of problem biological and social factors is needed than for boys. In other words, girls need a bigger push into becoming delinquent. A central place is also given to the role of genetics in that they believe that girls' biological programming presupposes some girls towards delinquency. They locate the 'problem' within hormonal or chromosomal imbalances, which they argue explains why girls are involved in more sexual offences than boys. Part of the problem, they suggest, is that girls who become delinquent are more physically mature and attract greater sexual attention, which then leads them towards forms of moral degeneration.

Other examples of studies in this tradition have continued to influence the study of girl delinquency (Smart 1977). While the methods have become more sophisticated, the assumptions on gender differences that underpin them remain strong. The ideas and assumptions of Lombroso and Ferrero may not have maintained academic credibility into the present day, but they have historically remained underpinning theories of gender differences and explanations of delinquency (Smart 1977). This position articulates a range of patriarchal concerns and stereotypical images that have pervaded the study of girls and have been generally absorbed into dominant ideologies of gender. These ideas remain strong, partly because they find support within external institutions and agencies of the state: 'An additional reason for the continuing "relevance" of these particular works is the compatibility of their ideological stance with the prevailing interests of professional pathologists and agents of social control' (Smart 1977: 27).

Positivist criminology had a significant influence on how the youth question in the early stages of modernity was understood and how it was to be dealt with by the newly formed state. Social commentators, critical thinkers and reformers were greatly influenced by ideas emerging from early developments in criminology (Garland 1994). Questions remained over how social order and the status quo were to be maintained in the early stages of modernity. Writers such as Beccaria and Bentham drew upon the 'new scientific' to propose new forms of social policy in managing criminal activities (Garland 1994). Data collected by scientists that started showing trends and patterns of offending also impacted on wider political discourses about what was to be done about the 'youth problem'. The methods of investigation used by positivist criminologists also helped 'amateur social scientists' investigate local social problems (Garland 1994) and, especially, the problems of juvenile delinquency (Pearson 1994). By using data collected locally they were able to make connections between social problems and their own beliefs about the 'moral' causes of crime. Henry Mayhew, for example, was a British journalist concerned with the 'social question of the poor'. His approach to investigating this question was very much shaped by the empiricism of early positivist criminology (Brake 1985).

The work of Lombroso and colleagues also had a major impact not only on social science, but also on the political process. His ideas received international acclaim and influenced the setting up of a new scientific criminology that was 'concerned to develop a "positive", factual knowledge of offenders, based upon observations, measurement, and inductive reasoning' (Garland 1994: 39). It focused attention on the individual criminal and the characteristics that marked them off from 'non-criminals' and on identifying 'causes of crime'. His theory and approach had practical applications in the political world and brought about radical changes to how the state was to respond to the offender. For example, his approach influenced changes in the British criminal justice system. This had always relied on the belief that 'free will' was a critical feature of criminal choice. But Lombroso was influential in challenging this view, seeing offending as more deterministic and linked to biological predisposition to criminality. As a result, sentencing and intervention in Britain were changed to reflect this view, seeing the condition of the individual and the possibility of them being reformed as factors critical to how the state would deal with them: 'Criminal justice was to cease being a punitive, reactive system and was to become instead a scientifically informed apparatus for the prevention, treatment, and elimination of criminality' (Garland 1994: 40). This is the start of the formal political processes of categorisation and surveillance of offenders, leading to systems being put in place to assess the risk of them being reformed or becoming future serious offenders.

British criminology had its roots in a medical form of science and the work of Lombroso was superseded by social scientists such as Goring and Freud who drew upon medical approaches to understand the causes of crime (Garland 1994). Yet even though British positivist theorising and research in this area expanded dramatically during the late nineteenth century, British politics remained reasonably resistant and untouched by its influence (Garland 1994). In fact crime policy in the late nineteenth century and early twentieth century in Britain was more interested, not in searching for causes of delinquency, but in the analysis of the administrative structures created under modernity and the impact different policies had on crime levels. By the early 1930s administrative criminology, a form of positivist science used in understanding institutions, had a larger influence in British policy-making than other forms of social research (Tierney 1996). Although positivist criminology had limited impact at the level of national policy, it did start to have an influence on the professions responsible for managing young offenders themselves (Garland 1994). British criminology as a social science discipline became fully established in the late 1930s, catering for the needs of new professions that have a core responsibility for managing the offender and, in particular, the young delinquent. Criminological teaching, influenced by the early scientific approaches discussed here, was used to help professions such as social work, probation and youth work identify and control the criminal problem (Garland 1994). Positivist criminology, like that propagated by Lombroso and Hall, gained support amongst reformers and professionals working with 'troubled and troublesome' youth, thereby giving justification to their work on the surveillance and control of problem and criminal populations (Brown 2005).

The Chicago School and early sociology

As the social sciences developed, so did the approaches to the youth question. In America we see the influence of sociology through the work of social scientists working in the Chicago School. It has a disparate and varied history[5] and a different approach to exploring the youth question, seeing ecological factors as important. As a school of thought, it was politically motivated and wanted to investigate the impact of rapid urbanisation in the city of Chicago. As a city, it was undergoing a massive expansion in its infrastructure, its economic growth, and its population, but especially its immigrant population. Researchers in the Chicago School were fascinated by this development and wanted to understand what impact it was having on residential life, on issues of social cohesion and on crime levels. For them Chicago was like a laboratory and gave them the perfect opportunity to study city life as a 'whole culture' that was undergoing social change. A range of disciplines influenced the approach taken by the Chicago School, although the anthropological study of human life and its consequences was at its heart (Downes and Rock 2003). Robert Park is recognised as one of its founding fathers. He was a scientist by profession and was interested in what has been called 'the social ecology of the city'. For him city life was like that of the plant kingdom (Downes and Rock 2003).

As the city 'evolved' it was claimed that a number of concentric zones could be identified where social life was differentiated or had its own 'natural areas'. At the centre was the business zone, with a small residential population and high property values. Next to this was the 'zone of transition'. This was where the poor lived, where the worst housing was, and where new immigrant families settled when they first arrived. It was this area that interested the researchers of the Chicago School. It was never their expressed ambition to study crime and delinquency (Downes and Rock 2003), but part of the draw to researching such an area was what was seen as the pathological behaviour of large sections of the population. It was thought that such behaviour could not simply be explained by the individual characteristics of people living there, but that there was something distinctive about the social organisation of the neighbourhoods and local area.

The Chicago School became focused on the 'youth problem' in this area. Much of their work concentrated on those groups of young people who were seen as creating problems for their communities. There were four main reasons for this (Brown). Firstly, the methods of investigation that the Chicago School used inevitably drew them towards those cultures that were seemingly more interesting. So, for example, the hobo, street gangs, prostitution and especially juvenile delinquency became the focus of their studies. Secondly, there was the question of access. It was, of course, much easier to study the powerless, and the visible, and especially the juvenile gangs, than the powerful in their offices and casinos. Thirdly, the progressive liberal movement in America provided much of the funding that underpinned the Chicago School. These were equivalent to the child saving movements in Britain (Tierney 1996) and they greatly influenced the problem-focused work of the research, wanting to discover the best type of policies that could improve people's lives. Finally, their central thesis related to the way that, within the zone of transitions, 'social organisation' and 'cultural living' were transferred across generations. They believed that at the root of this was the socialisation process of the young, therefore they became transfixed on this generational experience. As a result of these influences the Chicago School was dominated by studies on youth delinquency (Brown 2005).

Out of this work a number of theses emerged. Shaw (1929), for example, argued that crime was a result of 'social disorganisation' in that neighbourhoods that had little regulation, or had a breakdown of social ties, led to greater levels of delinquency. He later expanded on this theorising of juvenile delinquency by suggesting that many of the problems in disorganised neighbourhoods arose because of the 'cultural transmission' of criminal values as a 'way of life' (Shaw and MacKay, 1942). Young people learned criminality by association with criminal gangs and individuals and, therefore, just being around crime created a culture of criminality. It is then passed on from generation to generation. Sutherland (1939) was more interested in what he called 'differential association'. Crime was not seen as being caused by personality but by whom you associate with. It is the nature and quality of the interaction between a young person and the criminal gang or individuals that is important. Learning is therefore about motivations, techniques and moral justifications. These arguments have found much favour in theorising that followed, although the work of the Chicago School has been much criticised. For example, the theory of social disorganisation is accused of being a tautology (Tierney 1996). Social disorganisation is a sign of delinquency and delinquency is a sign of social disorganisation. Contradictions between the two positions of 'structure' and 'culture' also exist. On the one hand the Chicago School argues that social disorganisation is the cause, on the other it is a 'cultural transmission' of delinquency (Taylor *et al.* 1973). What is it to be?

Functionalism: Youth as a social institution

Other theorists in American sociology were also trying to explain the youth question. Talcott Parsons (1942), influenced by the work of Durkheim, was concerned with the function of the youth phase in the transition to adulthood. Functionalist theory, and structural functionalism in particular, was very influential in the mid-1950s. It starts from the point that society is like a biological body structure. Each institution is like a body part and has a critical role to play in keeping society functioning. In this context youth (and especially the age grading system associated with being young) is understood as an institution in a system with distinct roles and purpose. Age – and, in particular 'age differentiation' in the life course – is seen as critical. Age grading maintains social continuity (Parsons 1942, 1964; Eisenstadt 1956). It acts to distribute roles and enhance socialisation, while also helping to make connections to other structural components of the system, for example, kinship, educational and occupational structures. It is here that individuals find self-identification and recognition of their place in society: 'For the social system it [age differentiation] serves as a category according to which various roles are allocated to various people; for the individual, the awareness of his own age becomes integrative elements, through its influence on his self-identification' (Eisenstadt 1956: 28).

Functionalist arguments suggest that in all societies children have to be socialised into adult roles. They have to be taught the values and morals of the society they live in. Age definitions ensure that individuals know their place in the world. At different stages young people learn appropriate behaviour and values for their full participation in adult society. Eisenstadt (1956) saw these processes as universal to all societies, although he recognised that, in modern society, problems were emerging that were creating difficulties for young people. In pre-modern and primitive societies the family undertook these roles, but in modern and industrial society there is a 'structural gap' where families fail to fulfil this function. Modern society therefore needs to create special institutions to make sure this process takes place. As modern society grew more complex, tensions emerged in how young people move from one age grade to another, with their socialisation and, therefore, their transitions into adulthood. This was creating identity crises for the young and problems of adjustment (Eisenstadt 1956).

One solution for young people was to turn to their peer groups for help (Parsons 1964; Eisenstadt 1956). In 1950s America it was thought that youth was becoming a more separated group with its own 'culture'. Adolescents were thought to be spending most of their time together in schools, and therefore a distinctive culture with its own values and norms was developing (Parsons 1964; Coleman 1961). This culture emphasised irresponsibility, the importance of sport as an avenue for achievement, negative feelings towards the adult world, and physical attractiveness as a source of peer-group status (Davis 1990). While this was seen as potentially problematic, Parsons and others saw this development as a 'new institution' that could aid the transitional process for the young (Parsons 1964).

The relationship between functionalist theorising and biologism and positivism is complex. It does not totally reject arguments that locate behaviour and problems in either psychological or physiological difficulties. While this approach focuses on the structural processes of transition, psychology is still seen as important. Parsons's position has much in common with psychologists' modelling and assumptions of human nature and the biologically given properties that seem so evident in youth (Cohen 1997). He also draws upon positivist social science methods to support his arguments. His model of social systems as biological organisms that are evolutionary and adaptive takes much from the works of Social Darwinism. Parsons also draws upon

Freudian theory in explaining mother–child relations of socialisation, suggesting that personality is a critical factor for the internalising of values and beliefs (Cuff and Payne 1979). Underpinning much functionalist theorising, then, is a set of psychological assumptions about the very nature of youth itself. But Parsons does have some fundamental differences from psychologists. He is interested in the functioning of the social system and its impact on social life. Parsons's questions around social order may be similar to those of psychologists, but his starting point is different (the influence of the social context), although his approach is still underpinned by a series of givens or assumptions about the very nature of youth in modern society.

Anomie, subculture and delinquency

Functionalism also had a major impact on criminology. Robert Merton, for example, a long-time admirer of Durkheim, introduced the idea of 'strain theory' and the importance of anomie as a cause of juvenile delinquency. Unlike the theories of the Chicago School, Merton argued that the location and causes of juvenile delinquency were in American society itself. Crime did not emerge out of geography or deviant values in small neighbourhoods but through the problems of mainstream American values themselves. The American dream emphasised the importance of material and monetary gain as something everyone should strive for; in an open democratic society like America, the dream could be achieved by those who were willing to work hard. Merton suggested that, in reality, America was not open and that sections of the population found their aspirations blocked. As a result 'a strain' emerges that leads some to find other ways of achieving their ambitions.

This notion of strain theory is continued in the work of Cohen (1955) and Cloward and Ohlin (1961). It is also here that we see the emergence of 'subcultural theory' within criminology. Cohen (1955) rejected the notion of anomie, arguing it failed to address non-utilitarian actions of delinquent youth (Muncie 2004). He suggested that delinquency was a form of 'status frustration' and adaptation by the working class to their experience of being discriminated against. The solution for young people was to create subcultures that rejected dominant middle-class values and allowed the young to develop alternative social systems where adjustment to their environment could be made. Cloward and Ohlin (1961) developed this further by suggesting that deviance was clearly a collective activity and that subcultures were mechanisms used by young people to gain high status in their own working-class communities (rather than as responses to middle-class discrimination). At the heart of these different subcultural theories of juvenile delinquency is a belief that it is a response to how young people experience issues of exclusion in American society. As Brown (2005: 31) suggests:

> The notion of subculture, despite significant differences between studies, was used to denote the coping mechanisms adopted by lower-class young males in a social system which denied them legitimate access to the material and status rewards enjoyed by the affluent.

Most of these studies can also be described as a form of sociological positivism (Muncie 2004) and are concerned with explaining juvenile delinquency as some form of pathology or, at the very least, a dysfunction of social systems. Strain theory is a good example in that it takes as its starting point, similar to the Chicago School, the belief that there are 'criminal' and 'non-criminal' groups. Sociological positivism may reject biological differentiation but it still accepts and assumes that there remain criminals and non-criminals as a social fact. It takes statistical representations of crime as unproblematic and suggests that delinquency amongst the young is a white working-class male problem. It assumes that middle-class boys and working-class girls do not get involved in delinquent activities. Crime is a working-class phenomenon that is evidenced by scientific forms of measurement. Not only did it build upon positivist notions of how to measure and understand crime, but also it continued to reinforce the notion that the problem was one of white, working-class boys. There is no recognition of differences, either between different classes and genders, or even within different groupings. For example, strain theory has been much criticised for its failure to explain why it was only certain young people who transgressed into criminal activity (Tierney 1996). Why did only a small proportion of young working-class males become delinquent or join subcultural groups? Surely if the problems lie in 'status frustration' then large groups of working-class youth would have reacted in the way suggested. Gender is also a marginalised subject. By drawing upon statistical representations of the youth problem, girls are seen as less of an interest, therefore most of the early studies of subcultural studies ignore the question of girl delinquency (Smart 1977). Much of the theorising by subcultural theorists also takes an 'oversocialised' and deterministic view of the delinquent. Young people are seen as passive and responding to the forces around them almost unquestioningly. There is no recognition that young people are social actors in these processes or that their behaviour can be defined differently in different contexts. 'Sociological positivism continues to view the individual as a body that is acted upon, and whose behaviour is determined by external forces. Little or no role is given to the process of choice, voluntarism or self-volition' (Muncie 2004: 99). Young people's voices and perspectives are therefore marginal to these forms of analysis, leaving us with a perspective of 'causes' that are defined by the researcher's interpretation and moral judgements.

The influence of American social science

In the early twentieth century, American sociology and, in particular, structural functionalism and subcultural theory had limited impact on the study of the youth question in Britain. While it had a major influence on British sociology, it did not seem able to explain the 'problems' British youth were 'expressing'. It is important to remember many of these theorists developed their arguments in America between the 1930s and 1950s, during a particular phase of capitalist development and in relation to a specific set of questions that related to youth social integration in affluent 'Middle America' (Downes and Rock 2003). For American sociologists issues of class were always seen as less important, and they tended to assume that a meritocracy was the best way to order social life and that it existed in all Western societies. Parsons (1964), for example, focused on trying to explain what was happening in American high schools and especially on the activities of middle-class, white males. Youth and 'youth culture' was seen as homogenous and reflected the middle-class lifestyle of Middle America. The problems were about the institutions of society – the family and the age-grading system needing to adapt to new changes. Such a theory had difficulty in being transferred into an explanatory model of youth transitions in the United Kingdom, as it was unable to address differences that existed within the diversity of British youth groups (Frith 1984). It was recognised, for example, that in Britain class, in particular, had always had an important role to play in structuring a young person's transitions (Allen 1968).

The 'problems of youth' in Britain in the 1960s were in fact seen as being closely aligned with the industrial context of the division of labour evident within society at any given moment: 'youth is problematic for adults within given social contexts that . . . exist within industrialised societies' (Allen 1968: 326). Youth, therefore, was a problem that was socially constructed, having a close relationship to industrial capitalism and class relationships. Structural functionalism did not recognise such complexities and differences, and British studies tended to reject it as a model for understanding the complexities of youth transitions and culture (Brake 1985). As we shall see in the next chapter, while structural functionalism has limited influence, a more distinctive British version of subcultural studies does emerge, one that is influenced by Marxist thought and that has a closer relationship to class inequality than those devised in America (Brake 1985).

American criminological research also had a mixed impact on criminological youth studies in Britain (Brake 1985). Early American theorising had little impact on early community-based studies, but by the 1950s and early 1960s British sociology and criminology were concentrating more on the 'youth problem' (Tierney 1996), and both positivist criminology and subcultural theories seemed to offer a route into explaining social life (Brown 2005). American sociology, in particular, started to have a growing appeal within the British context, offering a 'vocabulary of motive' that was able to offer possible explanations of why the post-war inclusion project of the then Labour government was struggling, and why juvenile delinquency seemed, in a period of affluence, to be on the increase (Downes 1966). The work of American sociologists started to influence the British area studies of community life, suggesting that juvenile delinquency was related to local subcultures and geographical boundaries (Pearson 1994). Yet the American approach to these questions did not turn into large-scale empirical research programmes or help develop new British-based theories, resulting from a view that such approaches were not transferable to the British context. Youth in Britain and their communities were seen as distinctively different to those in America. Not only was class an important historical factor but also Britain did not have a gang culture or such a diverse immigrant population, therefore transferability of learning across cultural boundaries was seen as inherently problematic (Brake 1985).

Politically, transferring functionalist theorising into policy-making was also problematic, being a contradiction in terms (Downes and Rock 2003). Functionalism suggested that when problems emerged they would 'naturally' lead to adaptive mechanisms arising that would restore the equilibrium (Gouldner 1971). Policy then was seen as irrelevant and might even interfere with the natural reordering of society (Downes and Rock 2003). At most, policy should be non-interventionist, letting the 'natural' order be restored. Such a position in the 1960s and early 1970s was in conflict with the post-war consensus and politics of British welfare capitalism. In a political sense it therefore had little impact on the national policy-making process in the UK.

The ideas of the Chicago School had most political impact on the locality in America. Shaw and McKay, for example, set up the Chicago Area Project, which is still in existence. It aimed to draw upon the results from research to make changes in the different communities in Chicago. The sociologists were seen as having a critical role in making their findings have an impact (Downes and Rock 2003). A range of subcultural theorists also had an influence on American national policy. For example, Cloward and Ohlin took their ideas on anomie, delinquency and opportunity and helped construct the Mobilization of Youth Project. This became a major influence on the American 'War on Poverty' campaign that dominated American domestic policy in the early 1960s (Downes and Rock 2003). The British government did not adopt this approach in its policy, although a smaller version was created called the Community Development Programme. It differed from previous government interventions in that it aimed to intervene at a community level. Similar to the American War on Poverty programme, it floundered due to the lack of adequate resources and lack of national action on tackling those structures that created feelings of anomie (Downes and Rock 2003). A more influential theory that has impacted on British policy, and has been longer-lasting, is the idea of 'social disorganisation'. Historically, this approach has influenced the development of a wide range of British initiatives that have aimed to increase social cohesion and tackle anti-social behaviour of the young within communities; for example, the 'broken windows thesis' (Wilson and Kelling 1982), 'zero tolerance' (Walklate and Evans 1999), and, more recently, theories of social capital (Putman 2000). All aim to regenerate community norms, values and networks as mechanisms to tackle the 'social disorganisation' of local neighbourhoods.

Conclusion

As we saw in Chapter 1, the British state in modernity constructed the youth question in a particular way. Not just this, but the universalising of services and interventions for young people helped construct a modern meaning of youth. In this chapter we have seen how the developments in psychology, criminology and sociology, especially from America, drew upon 'positivist' science to construct a particular model of youth. It is a model that reinforces the view that youth is a state of transition between childhood and adulthood, and that it tends to be a troublesome and problematic period of the life course. It is claimed that this is a stage of development that is greatly influenced by a young person's genetic make-up, and biological and physiological evolution. It is also a model that is highly gendered, seeing boys as the more developed species and also potentially the more problematic. Girls are usually ignored, or at the very least marginalised, although still defined by their biological development and, in particular, their sexuality. Methodologically the 'youth problem' is 'discovered' by 'scientific methods of investigation'. Young people are constructed as passive agents in this process, being 'driven' by either internal forces (biology) or external forces (social systems).

As we have seen, these ideas did not emerge in a political vacuum. Social science was itself shaped by the political values and moral positioning of key contributors to these debates at these times. We cannot separate out the man from the ideas. This form of social science was very influential in shaping and justifying political understandings in these early stages of modernity of the youth question. While social science had a limited impact on the policy-making process of the time, it did have an influence at the level of professional practice. It was here that social science training impacted on the 'new class' of professionals in social work, probation and youth work and, in particular, understandings of child development and the problem(s) of youth.

3 Social science and the politicisation of the youth question

Introduction

In this chapter we concentrate our analysis on the relationship between social science and politics from the end of the Second World War to the 1980s. This is a period of rapid and radical change, where modernity is underpinned by welfare capitalism until the emergence of the economic crisis in the 1970s. This is followed by the emergence of Thatcherism: the politics of the New Right. Other major social and cultural changes are also taking place that traditional social science theories struggle to explain. We see the emergence of the teenager, the rise of youth unemployment and crime, the restructuring of the youth labour market and the rise of feminism. The youth question comes more to the forefront of the political agenda, and explanations by social scientists become influenced by specific political projects and interests, although, as we shall see, their influence on the youth question remains limited.

Youth as 'a generation for itself'

As welfare capitalism became embedded as a key strategy of government in modernity, it was thought that policies of inclusion were reducing the significance of class in shaping life chances (Lee and Newby 1986). Politicians claimed that the British population had 'never had it so good' as welfare capitalism not only expanded welfare rights and services, but also created a more affluent society. Changing occupations and a growing economy were seen as leading to major social changes in society. Class differences were seen as less important, with social attitudes and values converging into what was called the 'embourgeoisement' of the class system (Lee and Newby 1986). Anxieties over the youth question in the 1950s focused less on the problems of unemployment and the transition from school to labour market and more on consumption and, especially, on the emergence of the 'new teenager' and their response to social change.

While structural functionalism had little impact on British explanations of these changes, the same could be said for class theories (Frith 1984). As a result, new theories and ideas emerged that located explanations not in the functionalist idea of age categorisation nor in Marxist theories of class differences, but in a 'generational theory' (Pilcher 1994). One such contribution to this discussion was identified in the work of Karl Mannheim (1952). He was interested in how specific historical circumstances shaped generational values and beliefs and how they contributed to social reproduction in a period of social change. Youth, as a generation, is seen to help loosen the connection between chronological age and class in the youth phase. It becomes associated with ideas about social, political and cultural renewal (Davis 1990) rather than class conflict. Youth is unique because it 'firmly locates generation within a social-historical context' (Pilcher 1994: 483). The notion of generation is seen as a social category not dissimilar to that of social class, but class is linked to the economic and power structures of society, while generation is linked to the interaction of an individual's biography and social location. The exposure, at specific historical moments, to certain experiences and/or crises is claimed to have a more lasting ideological effect than class similarities. People born into certain historical moments and circumstances can, therefore, be seen to develop a shared set of outlooks, values and beliefs that stay with them for life. Individuals all pass through different stages of life or go through what Mannheim (1952: 290) calls 'the biological rhythm of life', and it is the interplay between this and the historical circumstances and situations that creates a certain feeling of collective location and identity.

Generational theory comes to be seen as more significant in social differentiation than concepts such as social class (Pilcher 1994). But its influence on explaining social change and the youth question is limited, having fundamental methodological weaknesses (Pilcher 1994). For example, we are still left unclear about when one generation ends and when another begins. It is also assumed in much of this work that there is the inevitability of a 'generational gap'. Young people will hold different values and perspectives than those of generations that have gone before, yet the evidence supporting such a claim is weak. In fact young people are very conservative and hold similar views and perspectives to their parents (Springhall 1986). There also remains a core problem with the attempt by generational theory to disassociate itself from a class analysis:

> the study of generations brings to light consequential differentiations within generations as well as between them. Far from exempting us from the study of social structure, an attempt to grapple with the problem of the historical formation of identity forces us in just that direction.
>
> (Abrams 1982: 262)

Class, culture and the youth question

As we reach the later part of the 1960s, there is a growing body of evidence from empirical studies that suggests embourgeoisement is a myth (Goldthorpe *et al.* 1968). As a result a more radical analysis re-emerges within social science. Structural Marxism, led by Louis Althusser (1969), for example, becomes more fashionable and the discipline of cultural studies starts to have a major impact on academic thinking. Youth research is not immune to these changes, seeing the teenager's cultural activities as signifiers of problems and tensions in the class structure in a period of social change (Griffin 1993).

At the leading edge of this analysis is the Birmingham Centre for Contemporary Culture Studies (CCCS). For the CCCS, the analysis of the youth question is a political project that aims to understand how class reproduction is undertaken in a period of rapid social change. Sociology and the study of youth become highly politicised and radicalised (Griffin 1993). At the heart of their analysis is the notion of 'culture'. This was the way that 'groups handled the "raw" materials of their social and material experience and, especially, their class experience' (Clarke *et al.* 1975: 10). The role of class is paramount to this process. The principal structuring of divisions arises from capitalist society, but differences emerge and become complicated by generational differences associated with particular subcultural forms.

The CCCS then becomes interested in how youth used subculture as a response to their economic and social conditions. Much of their early work focused on the politics of resistance evident within subcultures (see Hall and Jefferson 1975). Drawing upon the tradition of neo-Marxist Gramscian hegemony theory, the CCCS argued that youth subcultures become class sites of 'winning space' or resisting the dominant bourgeoisie ideology. Groups do not have political solutions to their structural positions as their solutions are always 'magical' or 'imaginary' (Hall and Jefferson 1975). Other influences on their ideas came from the work of Lévi-Strauss and his usage of the concept of 'bricolage'. Clarke (1975), for example, writing in his paper on 'Teddy boys' suggested that subcultures reordered and recontextualised objects with fresh meanings. The example he used was the way that 'Teddy boys' took the 'Edwardian' dress and recontextualised it with the present.

But class was not the only focus of the CCCS. Hebdige (1979) wanted to shift from a class-based analysis to a more complex understanding of social difference (McGuigan 1992). His main writing focused on the emergence of punk and the Rastafarian subcultures. Hebdige was writing at the height of the punk movement and argued that punk was a 'semilogical guerrilla warfare of subversive practices' (Hebdige 1979: 105). This was aimed at the dominant culture and it took its resistance to extremes by creating anarchistic cultural forms that involved 'cutting up' and 'mixing' previous styles of youth culture.

So, for example, punks are associated with the use of safety pins, plastic clothes, leather bondage and the use of horror and 'dark' movements to state their perspectives alongside anti-establishment and violent protest. Punk becomes a menace and threat to the social order. But, as Hebdige shows, it is ironic that the very establishment appropriates the very anti-establishment style of the punks it aims to challenge. Punk becomes codified, commodified and commercialised in that while the young create 'new' styles the cultural industries appropriate them for the mass market (Hebdige 1979). The example Hebdige gives is of the plastic bag and punk clothing, which aim to be 'anti-commercialism'. By the summer of 1977 punk clothing could be bought through mail order, and fashion houses where busy re-creating new fashions for the mass market. Plastic bags and safety pins became all the rage and could be bought on the high street in mainstream shops.

The CCCS started to broaden the notion of 'resistance' to include a racial dimension. Writing in the late 1970s, CCCS identify that it is a significant point in racial history. Second-generation young blacks are encountering greater levels of racism, with political tensions increasing over immigration and community spaces. This is seen as the start of a structured 'resistance' or 'colony' culture that creates 'oppositional' lifestyle to mainstream white society (Hall *et al.* 1978). These developments take place in distinct neighbourhoods and young blacks express their own newly formed identities and develop 'oppositional' and 'resistant' values to white society. 'Race' becomes a site of 'resistance' for second-generation young blacks who are experiencing extreme disadvantage and racism in the urban centres of Britain. This form of 'resistance' is expressed through the emergence of Rastafarianism and the 'rude boy' (Hebdige 1979). Jamaican culture and religion are drawn upon to construct a unique British style of Rastafarianism that includes dreadlocks, khaki camouflage, reggae and a language of its own. It becomes a style connected with alienation and the economic position of young blacks in the UK. This alternative cultural form of 'resistance' is also appropriated by white working-class youth. British subcultures are 'reinterpreted as a succession of differential responses to the black immigrant presence' (Hebdige 1979: 29). For example, the skinheads appropriate black music (i.e. 'ska' and reggae) and punk bands such as the Specials, Madness and the Beat draw upon black culture, reggae, and the 'rude boys' in constructing different cultural forms.

The CCCS has been much criticised and I do not intend to go over these debates.[1] But it did have a major impact on youth studies. Its legacy remains, and even today it is a central focal point for theorising of youth culture. It has also reached international significance in framing research in other countries.[2] The CCCS study of youth provided a less pathologised understanding of young people's social actions (McGuigan 1992). Even though it maintained many of the 'common-sense' assumptions surrounding the meaning of the youth phase (i.e. as a state of transition) it did take a different approach to the individual. Notions of 'storm and stress' were replaced with ideas of 'storm and dress', which tended to emphasise the creativity of youth (Cohen and Ainley 2000). Youth as 'a problem' was still its focus, generalising from the spectacular subcultural activities of the few to the many (Brown 1987). But unlike previous theories, this was not associated with 'individual failings' but more with the problems of social and economic structures.

The CCCS also introduced the importance of consumption to our understanding of youth activity. It broadened the notion of 'culture' to draw in other conceptualisations from cultural and literature studies. The focus on consumption was the first of its kind. Previously youth had been conceptualised within a narrow framework of either production or community. Their use of culture gives an indication that the young are 'active social agents' in the construction of their own lives. This being said, the CCCS could still be criticised for a rather deterministic view of the young and could be accused of over-reading the different activities of the subcultural groups they investigated (McGuigan 1992).

A major part of its impact has been the reaction it created. A number of studies emerged that challenged the 'malestream' focus of the work (Griffin 2000), its lack of attention to 'ordinary' youth (Brown 1987) and issues of 'difference' and, in particular, sexuality (Mac an Ghaill 1994) and race (Gilroy 1987). This critical positioning led to the emergence of a more radical form of cultural research represented within youth studies as the 'new orthodoxy' (Griffin 1993).

The writings of the CCCS were clearly developed for an academic audience, even though it claimed to be a 'political project', but its expansion as an approach to researching the youth question emerged at a time when the New Right were in government. As a political party it was anti-intellectual in its approach to social science research, and especially research that seemed left-wing and radical. Social science funding was also cut and it became increasingly difficult to get funding for more qualitative research (Griffin 2000). Those researchers who 'questioned the construction of particular groups of young people as the source of specific "social problems", were themselves represented as "troubling"' (Griffin 2001: 151). In this context the 'voice' of more radical approaches was marginalised within discussions about the 'problems of young people'.

Youth unemployment in the 1980s

As we saw in Chapter 1, the late 1970s and early 1980s were a time when political questions were being asked about young people and unemployment. Much mainstream social science research on unemployment at this time tended to focus on questions of 'causes'. National statistics were not a source of reliability, with what constituted unemployment being redefined over 16 times between 1979 and 1986 (Griffin 1993). Large-scale surveys were conducted to explore the reasons why young people were unemployed, but most of these contributed to 'victim-blaming', seeing the problem as a consequence of individual failings (Griffin 1993), and giving limited attention to structural problems and their consequences.

But not all work around the 'crisis' was 'victim-blaming'. A number of more marginal studies took a more critical perspective, suggesting that the problems and 'causes' needed to be located in a broader context. For example, it was suggested that in this period of 'crisis' there was a breakdown of the social contract between young people and society, and that traditional routes into adulthood were being fractured and broken as a result of major global and local changes. Class relationships remained important and the range of opportunities open to the young were becoming more limited, therefore impacting upon their future pathways and trajectories (Coffield *et al.* 1986). Young working-class people were offered limited choices, ranging from 'shit jobs' and 'groovy schemes' to 'unemployment', which in effect was no real choice. A range of other studies, such as Wallace (1987) and Hutson and Jenkins (1989), made similar conclusions. Yet while such studies were received within the social sciences as insightful, making a major contribution to our understanding of the process at work, they had little impact on political understandings of the problem, being seen by the New Right as 'unscientific' and politically motivated (Griffin 1993). Given their ideological positioning towards the individual in society, such a perspective was unsurprising.

Why working-class kids got working-class jobs!

Youth researchers within education were also asking why was it that working-class young people got fewer qualifications than middle-class young people, why they were underrepresented in universities, and why the majority of them ended up in 'dead end' jobs (Willis 1977). Within education research, explanations for these differences tended to focus on schooling as a form of 'educational differentiation', where schooling acts as a function of either reproducing existing social inequalities (Bowles and Gintis 1976) or 'cooling out' aspirations of working-class youth, ensuring they are distributed into working-class jobs (Roberts 1975). But both approaches tend to be functionalist in their theorising, giving limited attention to the micro-processes of schooling and the interplay between systems, teachers and pupils, and to pupils' perceptions and actions themselves (Brown 1987). As a result, educational studies turned their attention to exploring 'cultural differentiation', where explanations suggested that 'it is not the school's but the pupil's selection process which held the key' (Brown 1987: 19). Once again this type of approach lays the blame for 'failure' at the door of the young and their families, not recognising the schooling process and the impact of the interconnection between structure and agency (Brown 1987).

Others had more radical perspectives, showing how the educational processes worked to disadvantage working-class pupils (Hargreaves 1972). Schools that tended to put pupils into low streams helped create an 'anti-school culture'. Working-class pupils evaluated their performance and future prospects against the 'middle-class measuring rod' of success, recognising their future place in society. Aspirations are seen as resulting from school performance, which allocates them to the lower streams. Willis (1977), on the other hand, saw the 'counter-school culture' not as a consequence of educational failure but a 'cause'. Working-class pupils did not assess themselves in terms of their position in the school, but in terms of the consequences of what it means to be successful as a future working-class adult. Yet such an argument had problems, as it did not explain the differences within working-class culture or why large numbers of young people rejected school but tried to 'get on' (Brown 1987). Others have also suggested that 'counter-school culture' constructed the problem as 'bipolar', in that pupil culture was defined, for example, as either conformity and non-conformity, or anti-school and pro-school (Woods 1983).

Moving into the late 1980s, this use of cultural reproduction explored the operation of youth training programmes, showing how working-class trainees got working-class jobs.[3] For example, writing about a BTEC training course in Fashion Design, Bates (1992) showed how the process of 'cooling out' young people's expectations prepared them for the real world of retail mass production. This had a strong gender dimension, in that this was not only a class issue but also one that reinforced the sexual division of labour (Cockburn 1987). Such work was significant in showing how the process of social reproduction could work outside the school, although it tended to ignore the cultural processes within community life and institutional settings that also helped 'structure' transitions in certain ways (Jenkins 1983). As a result youth theorising of transitions had to go beyond the simple negotiation processes of work and recognise the importance of history and culture in this process (Jenkins 1983).

Developments in criminology from the 1970s

By the early 1970s British criminology was also undergoing a radical change. As we saw in Chapter 2, the discipline had been historically influenced by positivist and medicalised approaches drawing upon psychology and forensic psychiatry (Garland 2002). But by the 1970s it was in 'crisis', struggling to find solutions and explanations to the youth crime 'problem'. Positivist criminology became even more atheoritical and unable to move explanation further (Griffin 1993). One important development was the emergence of 'new deviancy theory' (Tierney 1996). British criminology made a significant break from orthodoxy, severing the links with its 'political paymasters' and creating a space for a more radical approach to the questions of deviance (Tierney 1996). Its roots can be found in the National Deviance Conferences of the early 1970s, leading to different strands of more radical theorising being developed over the next 30 years. One particular development was that of 'labelling theory'.

Moral panics and labelling theory

Labelling theory offered new ways of understanding why young people become deviant (Becker 1963). In a UK context it had limited influence on social science research (Tierney 1996). The most important work influenced by this tradition was that of Stanley Cohen (1980). His classic text on *Folk Devils and Moral Panics* attempted to utilise the American theory to illustrate the role of social interactionism in the creation of moral panics: 'Societies appear to be subject, every now and then, to periods of moral panic. A condition, episode, person or group of persons, emerges to become defined as a threat to societal values and interests' (Cohen 1980: 9). He focused on how the activities of a group of young working-class males, over an August bank holiday in Brighton, became defined. For him, deviancy and the moral panic are a result of the reactions of certain sections of the population to specific events. This is ultimately linked to adults who are able to label the young who are powerless in this process. Moral panics are not simply a misrepresentation of 'fact' or an invention, but a complex set of processes within the social relationships of adults in different institutions. Not only do they manage to demonise the young, but they also manage to activate closer societal controls and regulations. In this sense moral panics tend to connect with growing anxieties of parents and adults, usually reinforcing notions that youth of the day are out of control and need punishing, controlling or rehabilitating. In this context, a moral panic is also a panic about standards of conduct and fears about the decline of morality amongst all young people. Cohen's work is seminal in this area of 'deviance amplification'.

Hall and his colleagues (1978) combined both labelling and Marxist theory in an attempt to construct a more political understanding of moral panics, seeing them as helping the state manage its internal crisis. It was suggested that a closer relationship existed between the institutions of power and influence and the media, arguing that at a time of crisis the state needed to mobilise its forces to regain its legitimacy and influence. It was at this time that welfare capitalism was in crisis, and young people were a good scapegoat to justify the expansion of the 'authoritarian state'. Using the case study of the 'mugger', Hall *et al.* (1978), showed how, even though the term did not have any legal status, it enjoyed popular usage in the discourses of the media and Parliament. It tapped into, and played to, a set of moral anxieties that already existed amongst the public about the growth of crime and the decline of morality in mainstream society. This had direct implications for how society was then to be policed and the type of laws and regulations created. Hall *et al.* (1978) recognised that it not only increased forms of policing but also targeted specific populations, showing how it became racialised. Evidence from crime statistics did not reflect either the extent of mugging or that it was purely a 'black issue'. It was seen as no coincidence that immigration was a large political issue and the crisis of the 'black mugger' contributed to this debate (Hall *et al.* 1978).

While Hall and his colleagues brought a more political analysis to the discussions on moral panics, Pearson (1983) located the debate in its historical context. By examining historical documents and newspaper articles he was able to identify the labelling of youth as a phenomenon of every generation, showing that, at different time points, anxieties about youth remained consistent. His point is not so much the idea that history merely repeats itself but that nothing really changes. Rather, he is concerned to demonstrate that the history of hooligans is also a history of 'formidable stability which repetitiously identifies some aspect of "social change" as the cause of the loosening of tradition, but which is itself paradoxically immune to change' (Pearson 1983: 208). The nature of complaints and societal responses provides a consensual and normative language for understanding social change in modernity. In doing so, attention is detracted from the past, which points to juvenile crime and delinquency as a *continual* feature of British life, and which, for him, reflects persistent, middle-class anxieties about the impact of social change on the young working class. It is these specific concerns that make *Hooligan*, at least for Pearson, a 'history of respectable fears'.

Radical criminology and 'New Left Realism'

As labelling theory was taking hold in the UK, so was critical criminology. This took root within the expanding 'new' university sector led by a new group of Marxist criminologists influenced by the sociology of deviance. This was not just a difference of opinion or a new perspective, but a 'paradigm war' in which old Classical administrative criminology and positivism were rejected (Tierney 1996). This new approach to the study of crime became a political project that highlighted the notion that a society based on socialist (and non-capitalist) order could be crime-free (Taylor *et al.* 1973). It attacked traditional approaches to criminology, suggesting that critical criminology intended to create a situation where what is opposed is inverted: 'If crime was previously pathological, it was now "normal". If criminologists had previously sided with official versions of reality, they now sided with the deviant's. If previous research was aimed at correction, it was now aimed at "appreciation"' (Tierney 1996: 128–9).

Critical or radical criminology, as it became known, had at its heart a focus on class analysis. Deviance was seen as a class issue, one where the powerful bourgeoisie made the rules of law and had the forces and power to enforce them. Criminal activity was a political class acting against the ruling elite and its laws (Taylor *et al.* 1973). Once established as a method of analysis, it fragmented as a discipline, seeing a wide range of different perspectives emerge, although the central thesis remained strong (Tierney 1996).

By the 1980s New Left Realism had emerged from this approach. It argued that critical criminology failed to take crime seriously, not recognising the harm it could and did do to the poor. It was also utopian in its ideals, failing to engage with the real practical problems of addressing crime, tending to romanticise it and ignoring the impact it had on everyday life (Tierney 1996). As a result, a more radical agenda was launched that aimed to gain a broader understanding of the relationship of crime in disadvantaged neighbourhoods, highlighting the important non-criminal events that make life distressing and harmful. One of the major developments was the introduction of victimisation studies as a way of understanding the impact crime had on the lives of the working class. In terms of the youth question, the work of Anderson *et al.* (1994) was significant in that it undertook, for the first time, a major survey of young people and their encounters with crime. They showed that the young working class experience crime in a range of complex ways, not only as perpetrators but also, importantly, as witnesses and victims (Anderson *et al.* 1994). Crime for the young working class is a major part of their everyday lives.

The impact of new deviancy theory

These new approaches to the study of youth crime varied in their impact. At the level of ideas, they challenged the orthodoxy within criminology and created a new academic focus on crime and deviance as a social process, or as a form of political action. New deviancy theory expanded its interest in the deviant beyond the criminal into new areas of study. But apart from the work of Cohen (1980) and Hall *et al.* (1978), youth deviancy did not feature in labelling theory research agenda. Issues of mental health, poolroom hustlers, nudists, the blind and many others became the focus of American labelling theorists. They became interested in what were called 'nuts, sluts, and perverts' (Liazos 1972). Similarly, critical criminology focused on class conflict and its impact on working-class life, giving limited attention, until the 1990s, on young people's everyday experience of crime. Ethnography and area studies became the central method of research. Detailed examination of how different groups negotiated and managed deviancy became the norm. As a result, the study of the 'youth problem' and the 'juvenile delinquent' became marginalised within much of the new deviancy theory analysis (Brown 2005). An opportunity was therefore missed to develop a forceful critique of the demonising and criminalising of the young within criminology.[4]

This being said, they did make an impact in a small number of ethnographic youth studies. These studies emerged around youth-related issues and focused on the interrelationship between structure and agency, seeing a more holistic and inclusive theorising develop. For example, Parker (1974) and Robins and Cohen (1978) both attempted to capture, through the voices of boys, the interplay between their experiences of living in poor and disadvantaged communities, and their involvement in criminal activities. They were able to provide insights into how structural conditions impacted on values and beliefs, and shaped life chances. Even though this was the case, new deviancy theory did continue the tradition within criminology (and sociology) of focusing attention on white working-class males (Brown 2005). Little attention was given to young women or other diverse ethnic groups, or to the more mundane criminal or deviant activity.

At a national political level, new deviancy theory seemed to have little relevance and impact, especially in government policy. While it challenged the mainstream orthodoxy of administrative and positivist criminology, it did not engage with and contribute to national policy-making. Administrative criminology, while under attack from within criminology, still held a significant place in policy-making (Tierney 1996). The Home Office still retained a positivist approach to its research agenda, seeing the search for 'causes' and the impact of policy on crime levels as its central agenda. This type of criminological research maintained its power base within government and continued to have a significant influence not only on the types of methods, but also on the questions to be asked around youth crime (Tierney 1996). Even when the New Right government of the 1980s reduced funding, criminological research within the Home Office remained for this type of work.

This being said, new deviance theory and, in particular, labelling theory did have an impact at a more 'grassroots' level. In the 1980s the New Right was advocating the new 'authoritarian popularism' as a mechanism for dealing with the 'youth crime problem' (Newburn 2002). Yet at a local level, and within the Civil Service itself, there was a commitment to a professional practice that argued that 'the kids are left alone'. Writers such as Rutherford (1986) argued that most young people involved in crime grow out of it by the time they are 18, and that state intervention is a central part of the problem. As a result policies of diversion, decriminalisation and decarceration take hold. Young people entering the youth justice system are taken out as quickly as possible to avoid them being stigmatised and labelled as 'criminal' (Newburn 2002). Such a strategy has a major impact on removing young people from the youth justice system (Muncie 2004) and has led to claims that the decline in youth crime in the 1990s is a direct result of this type of intervention (Newburn 2002). While this approach was abandoned in the early 1990s, new deviancy theory seemed, even in an environment difficult for social scientists, and for a short period of time, to shift blame away from the young to the system itself.

One final impact that we should not ignore is the influence new deviancy theory had on the educational curriculum of criminology and sociology. Not only do we see the emergence of the sociology of deviance (Downes and Rock 2003) within sociology departments in the UK, and the expansion of teaching in criminology that incorporated the new approach, but also social work, probation training and youth work encounter labelling theory as an explanation to youth crime. Its impact is hard to measure, yet it is reasonable to say that it encouraged a broader understanding of the processes at work, and could well have helped make fertile ground for the introduction of the 1980s diversion strategies discussed above. But labelling theory also becomes a major part of O- and A-level courses within schools (Tierney 1996). Cohen's (1980) debates on folk devils and moral panics, alongside the arguments of new deviancy theory, also become a central part of the school sociology curriculum. Sociology in schools therefore is greatly influenced by the radical agendas of the left. As a set of ideas, new deviance theory becomes embedded in critical thinking over the youth crime question.

Feminism and the study of girls

As we have seen in our previous discussion, most concern and theorising around the youth question between the 1930s and late 1960s focused on the behaviour and activities of boys. But during the 1960s feminism became a major contributor to political ideology and social theory. Not only did it challenge the political, economic, social and cultural ordering of British society, but also social science was radicalised and asked serious questions about understandings of gender differences. The impact of feminism cannot be underestimated. It rejected the dominant theories of gender differences that had located differences in biological factors, seeing gender as a social construct that is shaped and influenced by social, political and cultural factors (Oakley 1972; Sharpe 1976). Feminist writers also wanted to tackle the 'invisibility' and the 'silence' surrounding gender questions ensuring that the 'male as norm' was challenged (Griffin 1993). Such ideas were strongly influential in youth studies. Claims of gender 'blindness' and a failure to understand how girls' lives were shaped led to a range of studies that took gender as a central focal point of analysis. Young women were encouraged to speak about what it was like to be a girl (McRobbie 1980; Griffin 1985; Lees 1986). This is a radical departure within youth studies as male-dominated studies had historically not only marginalised gender from its analysis but also marginalised the voices of the young.[5]

The most significant and influential early work on girls has to be credited to the feminist cultural studies writer, Angela McRobbie. Based at the CCCS in the late 1970s and early 1980s, she produced some of the most challenging work in opposition to the 'malestream' perspective of youth culture. For her, girls' marginalisation was as much a result of male academics not giving girls serious attention as of their 'real' invisibility. McRobbie maintained the CCCS approach to class analysis (McGuigan 1992), although she gave more emphasis to how production relationships helped construct a sexual division of labour that separated girls from the public into the private spheres of life and socially reproduced femininity.

McRobbie undertook a study of girls in Birmingham intended to mirror Willis's *Learning to Labour* study. In her research, girls understood their own class position and gender subordination,[6] having a more fatalistic attitude to their futures. Marriage and all its baggage, such as housework, children and poverty, were seen as an inevitable part of their future life. As a mechanism of coping with this, girls had two strategies: firstly, they valued the important role of their 'best friends'; and secondly, in these friendships, girls fantasised about romance and love. This created a form of escapism for the girls and gave them hope for the future. This culture of friendship and romance was practised in the private world of the 'bedroom culture'. Much of this was centred around girls' magazines, pop stars and pin-ups, all of which helped them cope, and even to laugh in the process, in the face of pressures of family and home. Indeed, not only did it allow them to cope, but the 'bedroom' was also a central site for their resistance and non-conformity. Through the elevation (or celebration) of the central aspects of feminine ideology, 'female' commodities, such as beauty and fashion, became a display of femininity, which was then used as a form of resistance by the girls. This provided an opportunity, not in overt and often spectacular ways that subcultures permitted boys, for girls to construct a 'feminine form of intransigence' (McRobbie 1978: 103). But this could also work towards increasing social control of girls and increasing their conformity:

> Marriage, family life, fashion and beauty all contribute massively to this feminine anti-school culture and, in doing so, nicely illustrate the contradictions inherent in so-called oppositional activities. Are girls in the end not simply doing what is required of them – and, if this is the case, then could it not be convincingly argued that it is

> their own culture which in itself is the most effective agent of social control, pushing the girls into compliance with that role which a whole range of institutions in capitalist society also, but less effectively, directs them towards?
>
> (McRobbie 1978: 104)

How older girls conform to traditional roles and positions also emerged in research on the transitions from school to work (Griffin 1985). Girls did not just think about their lives as manual workers but were forced to manage competing economic and social pressures located in the family. The lives of girls were structured by the need to manage the transition into both the labour market and the marriage market, treading the tight rope of availability (Griffin 1985).

Feminist writers in criminology also had much to say about conformity, asking why girls commit less crime and what makes girls conform to 'normal' patterns of behaviour. Feminist analysis focused on the process of social control (Heidensohn 1985). Women both contribute to these processes while also being on the receiving end of them. They have the main responsibility for child-rearing, standards of domestic order, and care of men. These processes are ideological, in that if women step outside these roles, they are blamed for any social problems that emerge. They can also act as regulators in women's own behaviour. The processes that ensure women conform are both formal and informal and can include gossip, anxieties about reputation, fear and stigma, alongside the structural constraints that shape the choices women have. Women therefore have a high stake in conforming to these social norms and roles, while also finding it difficult to step outside them. It is these processes that explain the limited involvement in rule-breaking and criminal activity. While social control theories had little to say about young girls, the implications of such an approach are clear to see. Gendered regulation in the family home and school, alongside limited access to public spaces, reduces the possibility of them being involved in criminal or deviant activities.

This issue of social control at the level of social interaction and language was also seen as important (Lees 1986). She focused on the private, as opposed to the public, sphere of social relationships, especially between boys and girls around the discourse of sexuality. This, she claimed could not be added on as simply another dimension in the lives of the young as it was fundamental to their social identity. Sexuality is central to the way a woman is judged and viewed in everyday life, not only by boys but also by all other social institutions. Girls are defined primarily by their sexuality – whether they are 'tartish' or 'cheap', whether they are 'nice', 'respectable' or 'marriable' – which then affects anything they do. It is their reputation around their sexuality that is critical and it is this that shapes a girl's life. Adolescence, according to Lees, represents a crucial phase in the lives of women, and one during which they are increasingly exposed to the controlling discourse of sexual reputation in ways not experienced by boys. The reputation of a young man is even enhanced by reference to his sexual exploits, whereas being called a 'slag' could severely damage a girl's reputation. For young women, being called a 'slag' not only illustrates the unequal power relations between girls and boys, but also illustrates the ways in which sexuality structures young people's lives. Its extensive influence stems from its very elasticity and its application to a range of social contexts and situations, which sometimes goes beyond the immediate boundaries of sexual conduct. The term therefore functions as a way of controlling girls in ways advantageous to boys. It does not define or describe a set of acts, as it covers a multitude of activities, but its significance lies in the ways in which it controls, denounces and challenges behaviour of young women, in what amounts to a process of moral control. Girls also use the term to control behaviour and to encourage conformity of each other. As a result the term 'slag' steers girls into safe environments and encourages conformity.

Social control, conformity and labelling were also important concepts used to understand the lives of 'problem girls'. Girls tended to be treated differently by a range of state agencies. For example, when young women do get noticed by the justice system in that they could be 'doubly dammed' (B. Hudson 1989). Not only were they seen to break social norms but also 'gender norms'. Evidence from magistrates' courts showed that when girls did come before them, little attention was given to their offences (Parker *et al.* 1981). What was examined was their 'moral' character and behaviour, including whom they associated with, and whether or not they were promiscuous. Girls become 'sexualised' (Hudson 1982). Decisions about how they should be treated were then located in questions of whether they were in 'moral danger' and whether they needed to be taken out of the family (B. Hudson 1989). In the 1970s the 'treatment model' that emerged from the 1969 Children's Act expanded the powers of agencies to make decisions about destinations of young people. As a result girls' incarceration in children's homes increased because social workers operated on a model of 'in moral danger' (Thorpe *et al.* 1980). Similar outcomes came with the expansion of intermediate treatment. Early prevention programmes were dominated by services to boys. When girls' groups were formed by social workers, it was as a means of creating a 'space for girls to talk' about issues of sexuality (Bottoms and Pratt 1989). But in doing this they focused attention on girls with sexual problems, reinforcing a model and discourse that saw girls as having 'sexual problems'. The labelling and control of girls who came into contact with the welfare or justice system seemed almost inevitable:

> Social workers are still bound by psychoanalytical imagery of aggression as masculine, passivity as feminine. This imagery, broken adrift from its Freudian moorings and floating freely as the 'common knowledge' and 'popular stereotype' of outrage, is so culturally pervasive that it is difficult to imagine how social workers, or anyone else, could escape its influence.
>
> (Hudson 1982: 13)

These issues were not just about social work. Research showed how gendered difference influenced schools' construction of deviance (Davies 1984). Within pupil culture, teacher management of classrooms, school organisation and the structural order in which education policy and practice were produced, girls tended to be conformists. When they did break rules they were seen as more problematic than boys, the common perspective being 'when she was good she was very good and when she was bad she was horrible' (Davies 1984: 1). Social relationships around deviance were a result of power struggles of social reproduction.

The impact of feminist youth research

Feminism had a significant impact on all the disciplines within the social sciences. It challenged traditional given assumptions over the 'male-as-norm' positionality of mainstream social theorising and research. In cultural studies, criminology, sociology and educational studies, young women are made more visible and given a 'voice' in explaining the forces that shape their present and future lives. This, in itself, is a radical shift that brings a more balanced understanding of the social processes that are at work. But gaps remained which raised future challenges for feminism. By the late 1980s it became clear that research on girls was focused on the private spheres of social life (Griffin 1993). Family relationships, sexual relationships, friendships and private regulation in private spaces dominated how girls' lives were to be understood. Little attention was given to their relationship with the public domain, in areas of employment, unemployment and leisure. The 'gang of lads' model remained central to these research agendas of social science. It is also clear that research was dominated by work on white Anglo-European girls. Little was known about how girls with families from Asia, the Caribbean or Africa, experienced social life or how they encountered racism at school or in their communities (Griffin 1993). Finally, questions were asked about the bifurcation of gender studies, suggesting that to understand how gender divisions exist needed a methodology that explored the processes of masculinity and its interaction with femininity (Griffin 1993) and asked important questions of subjectivity (McRobbie 1994).

As we saw in Chapter 1, the political impact of feminism was enormous, bringing about radical changes in social, economic and political policy especially in the 1970s, yet the inclusion in policy of the work of feminist social scientists, working on girls lives, had little recognition. In fact policy remained focused on problematising girls, regulating their sexuality and punishing them if they stepped outside traditional roles, and limiting their choices in employment (Mizen 2004). Part of the reason for this was the ideological positioning of the New Right government towards the family and its opposition towards feminism (seeing it as a part of the problem). In such circumstances, research evidence that advocated recognition of, and change to, powerful patriarchal forces was not going to be successful.

Conclusion

As we reach the 1990s, youth research has travelled far. New radical movements have challenged traditional understandings of the youth question, giving focus to how the problem is conceived and identified by a range of powerful forces. Models of individual failings are challenged and replaced by theories that recognise the broader social context and processes in shaping social life. Youth are seen as more creative, drawing upon a range of cultural resources to help them manage their everyday lives. Consumption and production are recognised as important sites, where the young find autonomy and engage in creativity, leading to new countercultures being developed. Within these developments feminism is influential in challenging 'malestream' approaches to social research, bringing important insights into how structure, location, language and values can shape the everyday lives of young women.

But there remain problems. Youth are still seen as mainly 'passive' to the processes that shape their lives. There is a feeling of inevitability about social reproduction. Race is also marginalised, with most studies concentrating on Anglo-European white youth. Other differences remain significant in that little is known about 'ordinary youth' or about those not involved in some of the more spectacular public displays. While girls get more attention, work concentrates on their private lives, their relationships and sexuality. Little is said about their relationships with employment, unemployment and leisure. In many areas the 'gang-of-lads' model still continues.

Although the study of youth is more politicised, its influence at national policy level is clearly ineffective. At one level this is because the dominant paradigm of knowledge used by policy-makers in government relies upon positivist traditions and approaches. It is also the time when political ideology is anti-intellectual, anti-social science and is driven by its own political project of social change. This being said, more radical understandings, in certain areas, are generated at the localised level of policy implementation, providing real opportunities for change. A growing radical educational movement puts new ideas on to the curriculum of universities and other training institutions, providing opportunities for professionals to reconsider the youth question.

4 Youth transitions in the age of uncertainty

Introduction

In this chapter we turn our attention to contemporary debates over the youth question. As we reach the early 1990s, the 'crisis' in modernity is being experienced as a period of rapid structural and cultural change, and we are thought to be living in a period of 'late' or 'high' modernity, where uncertainty is shaping social life. The impact of this on the young is a major source of anxiety and concern for adults influencing how the youth question is conceptualised and framed. In this chapter we will focus on how policy has responded to the global changes in labour markets and employment, and the restructuring of youth transitions. We will examine how the changes have been understood, how policy in particular has responded to the 'problem', and what implications this has had for young people. In the concluding discussion we will discuss social science debates that highlight fundamental weaknesses in recent policy approaches, indicating the need for a rethink of what the problems (and solutions) might be.

Changing patterns of school-to-work transitions

By the 1990s the 'crisis' in school-to-work transitions is well recognised. Evidence from around the world shows that major structural changes in labour markets and opportunities have brought about a major restructuring of how young people move from school into work (Bynner 2001; Wyn and Dwyer 1999). In late modernity, global forces have constructed new forms of employment, and training pathways (Raffe 2003). Three major trends exist across developed and developing nations:

- The youth labour market remains stagnant. Limited opportunities exist for young people leaving school to enter paid employment. What work is available for post-16s tends to be low skilled, low paid and located in the expanding service economies.
- Education post-16 has been expanding. Not only have opportunities grown but also the number of young people continuing their

education after leaving school has expanded. Large numbers of young people continue their formal education in further and higher education institutions.
- The training state becomes a major pathway option for young people leaving school. This tends to have a high vocational and skills development focus. National governments around the world expand its provision (although markets are also important) as a way of managing unemployment and skills shortages.

This is not just a Western phenomenon. Evidence from post-communist countries (Roberts 2003), and Asian countries (Lanuza 2004) shows similar major structural changes taking place in young people's transitions from school to work. The impact of these changes has raised new questions about what youth transitions might mean for different social groups in late modernity. For example, across much of the Western world there is an 'academic drift', where young people are more likely to go to university (Raffe 2003). The impact of this on youth transitions is still relatively unknown, although early evidence suggests that this creates new routes out of the family home, improved housing opportunities and better career opportunities for those who are already likely to be the most successful (Rugg *et al.* 2004).

But as school-to-work transitions have been undergoing change, there has been a growing recognition of other important influences on young people's transitions (Jones and Wallace 1992; Coles 1995; France 1996). Youth transitions cannot be understood simply as employment-based. In modern societies, there exists a range of 'markers of status' which help structure young people's transitions into adult life. These can be social, political and economic, and relate to material resources, social opportunities (Jones and Wallace 1992) and public policy (Coles 1995). For example, being in a relationship, leaving home, and being an active consumer, alongside an incremental access to social, economic and political rights, have an important role in shaping a young person's transition into adulthood (France 1996). As late modernity has become more complex, these pathways into adulthood have also been changing. Not only is the school-to-work transition being restructured, but also changes in family forms, as well as political, social and economic rights, are restructuring the 'markers of status'. For example, there is growing evidence of a new boomerang generation that leaves home but then comes back time and again (Wyn and White 1997).

Individualisation in transitions

As social life has become more complex, and major changes have taken place, there is a growing recognition that young people need to act more individually in their transitions (Bynner *et al.* 1997). Life, it is claimed, is more uncertain and becoming a 'biographical project' where individuals (and especially the young) have to plan and navigate their own career and lifestyle directions (Beck and Beck-Gernshein 2002). This is not always a matter of choice, in that late modernity is seen as thrusting upon us a requirement to take control, yet the risks are high:

> The normal biography thus becomes the 'elective biography', the 'reflexive biography', the 'do-it-yourself biography'. This does not necessarily happen by choice, neither does it necessarily succeed. The do-it-yourself biography is always a 'risk biography', indeed a 'tightrope biography', a state of permanent (partly overt, partly concealed) endangerment.
>
> (Beck and Beck-Gernshein 2002: 3)

Individualism is also seen as becoming institutionalised within our everyday lives, being driven by global forces of production and consumption (Beck and Beck-Gernsheim 2002). It is not just driven by neo-liberal politics of self-interest, neither is it about free will. Individualism is linked to the disembedding of tradition and structure and the emergence of the age of uncertainty (Beck and Beck-Gernshein 2002). Tradition and old collective ways of managing these processes are now, in late modernity, not able to help us negotiate a way through and, therefore, individuals have to rely upon their own biographies and personal skills. Class divisions and traditional collective solidarities would have, in the past, offered a source of support, but these have recently been breaking down (Beck 1992).

It is claimed that individualisation is becoming the 'new' social structure, where people seek biographical solutions to systematic contradictions embedded in late modernity. A number of studies have highlighted the increasing patterns of 'choice' being made by the young. Cross-national evidence supports the claim that young people are acting more individualistically, especially in their career choices and biographies (Wyn and Dwyer 1999). There is a growing 'blending' within young people's lives, where they are combining a range of tasks and activities, rather than being singularly focused. An example is the balance between work and study. The young are leading a 'double life', which is radically different from previous generations who saw transition being located in the school-to-work paradigm. Part-time work alongside study is now becoming a choice, and young people are varying their activities over time (Chisholm 1997). This can include the interruption of study or work, and deferral of certain pathways that then become active again in late life (Wyn and Dwyer 1999). Choice is something that the young also have a strong belief and commitment towards, seeing it not only as a critical aspect of their ability to have independence and control over their own lives, but also as real, and something that shapes their own biographies. It is being seen as a major factor in how they get jobs, or get into future training or employment opportunities (Looker and Dwyer 1998). Young people see their own individual choices shaping their own future career directions and identities (Wyn and Dwyer 1999; Ball *et al.* 2000; Thomson *et al.* 2002).

New times and New Labour

In 1997 the arrival of the New Labour government brought with it a new approach to policy, drawing upon the politics of the 'third way'. Influenced by the work of Anthony Giddens (1994), the newly elected government constructed a perspective of social order that recognised 'new' times, seeing existing traditional frameworks of governance and policy as not being able to respond to the changing environment created by late modernity. Society was in a period of rapid change, with increasing pressures from the expansion of globalisation. This, it was claimed, not only threatened to undermine social democracy, but also increased risks, uncertainty and insecurity (Driver and Martell 2000). A government's role in this context was not to use policy to challenge or change globalisation, but to equip its citizens with the new skills and knowledges to prosper in a changing world.

The 'third way' politics of New Labour was underpinned by a set of core values which went beyond the traditional boundaries of 'old' Labour. These included a belief in 'equal worth', 'opportunities for all', the importance of responsibility and 'community' (Driver and Martell 2000). Ideas generated by left libertarians and communitarians such as Etzioni (1995) also influenced New Labour in constructing policies that advocated the formation of a 'new' social contract between the state and individuals (Clarke *et al.* 2000). This included a number of core principles that were to underpin policy:

- a rejection of 'state versus market', and in its place the introduction of partnerships between business, the voluntary sector and the state ('state and the market' in partnership, running the economy);
- government as regulator rather than provider – creating basic standards and monitoring their implementation – not only in the business sector but also in social welfare;
- the creation of joined-up government to tackle 'joined-up social problems';
- the centralising of the 'workfare state' – where social welfare benefits become linked to responsibilities;
- a movement from universalism to targeted social provision in welfare.

While New Labour may not be a coherent ideology, being influenced as much by disagreements and pragmatism (Clarke *et al.* 2000), it clearly starts to reshape how policy in the UK should be developed.

New Labour and managing youth transitions: Tackling social exclusion

During its time in office, New Labour has given much attention to the youth question. It was keen to be seen as the 'youthful party' and one that would create a new future for the young (Mizen 2004). Its approach to youth can be divided into three areas: social exclusion and the policy towards the unemployed; life-long learning; and policies towards citizenship. While all three are interconnected, it is worthwhile examining them separately.

New Labour entered office in 1997 with a strong commitment to address the problems of the unemployed. At its heart was a commitment to increase employment opportunities and improve 'employability'. Its first action, for example, was to instigate its New Deal employment programme. In the election it made a pledge to develop a 'welfare to work' programme that would move a quarter of a million 18–24-year-olds experiencing long-term unemployment into work. This programme, with £2.6 billion in funding,[1] emphasised the importance of the full employment agenda of the incoming government. But as New Labour took more control of the policy agenda, its focus and concern shifted to 16–18-year-olds and the problems they were having, given the changing contexts in education, employment and training. Large sections of this population, it was claimed, were becoming 'socially excluded' and the state, therefore, had to take a central role in helping them avoid it: 'The best defence against social exclusion is having a job, and the best way to get a job is to have a good education, with the right training and experience' (Social Exclusion Unit (SEU) 1998a: 6).

As a result New Labour set up the Social Exclusion Unit. This was aimed at identifying the causes of social exclusion especially amongst the young. In its first major report it indicated that, at any one time, 9 per cent of all young people aged 16–18 were not in employment, education or training, and that periods of inactivity could be as long as 6 months for some (SEU 1998a). Non-participation in education and training of this age group was seen as a good predictor of future unemployment. Evidence suggested that there were areas of high concentration of social exclusion and that spatial distribution was uneven. Such high levels of exclusion were explained by the distribution of acute problems and risk factors such as illiteracy, homelessness, mental illness, drug addiction and 'serial offending' (SEU 1998a), all with multiple causes. It was by policy that the state needed to intervene more in the lives of the young. The SEU produced a range of other reports on young people's experience of exclusion that led them to construct an interventionist policy agenda around education, employment, and training that aimed to get the young back into work (Mizen 2004).

Alongside these reforms has been the increasing use of 'work-to-welfare' type programmes for the unemployed. New Labour was keen to link benefits to work, arguing that this is a part of the new social contract. Young people, who were not willing to take up their responsibilities in trying to find work, or keeping work when they found it, would be penalised (Finn 2003). In 1994 the Conservative Party introduced the Jobseeker's Allowance. This imposed sanctions on those not 'actively seeking work'. New Labour endorsed and supported this approach by expanding it within the 1997 New Deal Programme. Unemployed young people who do not comply with Jobseeker's Allowance or New Deal requirements face sanctions that include the suspension of cash assistance. If a person fails to attend a meeting, is unavailable for work, or refuses a job, a range of penalties can be imposed (Finn 2003). Evidence from previous research suggests that such an approach can cause as many problems as it aims to solve, in that young people can 'disappear', or become increasingly cynical about employment (Mizen 2004), and its positive impact may well be limited, in that those most likely to suffer are vulnerable young people (Finn 2003).

By binding social exclusion to the labour market and constructing a work-to-welfare policy, the 'third way' approach shifted policy to focus the construction of 'progressive competitiveness' for those most vulnerable (Mizen 2004). While the social exclusion agenda has broadened its approach to explore other factors that impact on young people's transitions into adulthood, the major focus has remained on transitions into work. For example, while the Social Exclusion Unit gave attention to the impact of issues such as runaways (SEU 2002), education for young people in care (SEU 2003), and being a teenage mother (SEU 1999), the solutions always returned to the importance of getting a job as a way of avoiding exclusion. This supply-side approach locates the problem in the quality of 'human capital' and has led to the state increasing its investment in training and vocationalism for the over-16s. In the training sector, programmes such as New Deal, Curriculum 2000, vocational GCSEs and the expansion of NVQs have seen vocationalism expand across the entire curriculum, but it has been central for those over-16s who were excluded. Tackling social exclusion, therefore, is about creating skills of 'employability' for the unemployed and 'disengaged'. This links to the overall New Labour objective of creating a new workforce with the vocational skills and abilities to manage social changes, yet it is also encouraging the poor and excluded to take their 'place' within the lower end of the labour market.

While New Labour claims, in its rhetoric, to be championing a positive approach to those excluded, other evidence suggests its approach has both a strong moral agenda and a 'responsibilising' programme (Mizen 2004).

Within this policy framework there is a moral crusade that is 'victim-blaming', focusing on tackling system or social integration failure. Issues of structural inequality or redistribution have, in these discussions, been marginalised (Mizen 2004; Byrne 2005). New Labour, since coming to power, has focused on constructing a policy approach to social exclusion that has its roots in the moral overtones of the underclass thesis of writers such as Murray and left libertarians (MacDonald and Marsh 2005). While New Labour wanted to distance itself from the underclass thesis and, especially, the positioning of the New Right, below the surface of its own policy is a moral position that continues to 'blame the victim' for the present failing situation. Many of the risk factors identified as 'causal' tend to relate to failings of individuals, and therefore the problems are seen as being located in poor parenting, bad influences from peers, and lack of interest in school. The SEU report *Bridging the Gap* (1998a), for example, had, underpinning it, a 'blame culture' that locates the problem of exclusion in the actions and attitudes of young people themselves:

> Overwhelmingly they [young people] are portrayed as deficient, delinquent, or a combination of the two, as are their dysfunctional families and communities. Young people we meet in this report are at best passive victims ... at worst they are deviant perpetrators of criminal behaviour and drug abuse who pose a more sinister threat to the rest of society.
>
> (Colley and Hodkinson 2001: 340–1)

This is not to ignore the positive developments New Labour has brought about in giving attention to the problems of the young unemployed (Finn 2003; Mizen 2004), but underlying much of what is being constructed remains an inherent belief that many of the social problems of the young are caused by individual failings and problems.

While this approach is clearly underpinned by a moral positioning, evidence also shows that, as a form of 'inclusion' for those most excluded, it has had problems. Youth unemployment has fallen to its lowest level since 1975 and the number of 18–24-year-olds on long-term unemployment has also fallen dramatically (Mizen 2004), yet questions have been asked about how much this is a result of New Labour policies. For example, New Labour inherited a period of sustained employment growth, and an expanding economy, and evidence suggests that New Deal had a small impact on reducing youth unemployment (Riley and Young 2001). Participation rates of young people in post-16 education and training have also increased, although these have not been sustained over the full time of office or, equally, across geographic areas (Mizen 2003). Staying-on rates for 16-year-olds have declined since 2001 and 16–18-year-olds in education and training have remained lower than before New Labour.

Other problems also seem to exist. Plans to expand the number of qualifications amongst the young have not materialised. Learning targets for 19–21-year-olds have consistently been missed (DfES 2004a). Rates of truancy and permanent exclusions have also continued to remain high (DfES 2004b). Youth not in education, employment or training have also actually increased, between 1999 and 2004, to levels similar to those under the previous government administration. Over 177,000 young people, aged between 16 and 18 (9 per cent of the total population), still remain outside employment, education or training (DfES 2004b).

But not only are there doubts about New Labour working; evidence suggests that their pledge to youth also hides the reduction of basic rights and rewards of participation, and the continued focus and construction of 'youth as the problem'. Not only have we seen the extension of a stricter benefit regime implemented on New Deal, with penalties and punishments for those who do not comply, but also New Labour replaced the responsibility of full employment for the young with one of 'employability'. In effect, this gives the market a major role to play in determining the levels of youth employment and youth wages, but also, more importantly, in constructing a view that much of the problem of youth labour is a result of individual deficiencies and failings (Mizen 2003).

Life-long learning: Developing an educated workforce

So far our discussion has focused on those groups of young people defined as 'socially excluded'. But New Labour also entered office with a strategic plan to create a new well-educated workforce for the future. This policy was constructed under the banner of life-long learning and was targeted at all groups and ages, yet much of New Labour's policy has concentrated on the 18–30-year-old (Taylor 2005). At the heart of this policy have been two critical objectives. One has focused on increasing the skills base for the UK; the other on widening participation in post-school education.

Since 1997 New Labour has undertaken major policy initiatives aimed at increasing the skills and knowledge base of young people after they leave school (Tomlinson 2005a). A whole range of programmes and legislations have been constructed and implemented.[2] Underpinning this approach have been three core beliefs:

- Education and skills development are essential assets individuals need if Britain is to become a successful and modern economy. This 'human capital' model emphasises the needs of employers and the economy as core motivators to policy.

- Individuals have a responsibility to invest in themselves and their own life-long learning. It is in the individual's interest to be educated.
- Life-long learning is concerned with developing individual skills and knowledge to help with 'employability'.

The emphasis on individual responsibility, choice and employability has remained central to New Labour's policy agenda for the young. Once again this has a strong emphasis on 'blaming the individual' for not taking up opportunities, locating skill deficiencies as individual failings (Mizen 2004). Vocationalism as a solution has also become a major part of the post-16 education programme, and those not entering higher institutions of education or getting high-quality jobs are being trained to face insecure employment futures and changing opportunities (Tomlinson 2005a). Helping the young to gain skills in how to manage risk and uncertainty, and how to get back into work, has been critical to this skills revolution (Mizen 2004). Other problems also exist in how government understands the problem, in that it is seen as the quality of supply (the skills of young people) to the economy and business that is the problem. This fails to recognise the class, gender and racialised dimensions to education and training (Coffield 1997). It blames the young for the problems they have, while also failing to recognise the structural constraints that limit opportunities.

When it comes to the question of widening participation in life-long learning, the central focus has been on attempting to increase the numbers in higher education. Major changes have been taking place in the university sector. Not only has it been strongly influenced by policies of 'marketisation', where market forces are helping shape its development (Tomlinson 2005a), but also it is under pressure to expand and increase numbers participating in higher education. Government recently proposed that 50 per cent of all young people aged 18–30 would, by 2010, have received a university education, suggesting that there is a need to increase the 'intellectual capital' of the nation to help it become internationally competitive (Tomlinson 2005a).

At one level this approach seems to have been highly successful, with universities presently taking over 40 per cent of young people. But this expansion in participation rates has not necessarily widened participation. Evidence from a number of sources, including the government's own figures, shows that 72 per cent of all young people entering university in 2000 were from the highest socio-economic group, and only 17 per cent were from the lowest (Higher Education Funding Council for England (HEFC) 2004). Higher education, in its expansion, retained its class base (Ball 2003; Taylor 2005; Tomlinson 2005a). There is a clear 'postcode' effect, where those in most advantaged areas of the UK are six times more likely to go to university (HEFC 2004). But divisions also exist in what universities different socio-economic groups attend. Those from poorer backgrounds tend to go to the 'new' university sector which are teaching-led and are less successful, while those from the affluent groups go to the old well-established, research-led universities (Taylor 2005), thereby helping to increase their chances of better-paid jobs. The government is aware of these problems and has recently attempted to monitor and regulate universities' recruitment of poorer students, but all evidence so far suggests that 'nothing has changed' and that higher education is predominantly a middle-class pathway to future prosperity (Ball 2003).

The politics of citizenship

While much of New Labour's youth policy has focused on increasing 'employability' and widening access to higher education, there have also been attempts to educate the young in the responsibilities of citizenship. This policy approach has its roots in the Conservative government of the 1990s, which argued for the need to increase young people's 'active citizenship' as a part of the process of becoming an adult citizen (France 1998). The then Home Secretary, Douglas Hurd (1989: 1), suggested that active citizenship was 'the free acceptance by individuals of voluntary obligations to the community of which they are members'.

The concept of citizenship had an appeal to New Labour in the construction of its youth policies. Part of the problem within society is perceived to be the unwillingness of the young to undertake their obligations and responsibilities. Government had also failed because it did not link obligations and responsibilities to individual rights (Etzioni 1995). As a result, the Labour government has given a strong emphasis to citizenship training in its youth policy programmes. For example, concerns have been expressed over the lack of involvement of the young in political processes, suggesting that they are not taking up their civic duties (Advisory Group on Citizenship 1998). Concerns have also been raised over the lack of involvement of the young in volunteering programmes, and their apparent unwillingness to take up roles as 'active citizens'. For example, the new policy on youth (DfES 2005) proposes the construction of a volunteering programme targeted specifically at the young. But, as we have seen, questions of citizenship obligations have also been widened to include a strong emphasis on work. New Labour has claimed it is a central obligation of all young people to seek out and undertake work. Those who do not risk losing benefits and social rights (France 1998).

This approach to citizenship does have its problems. It starts by identifying youth as a special case and in need of specific policies to ensure smooth transition to 'good' citizenship. Apart from uncertainties about what 'good' would mean, it also assumes that young people are apathetic and 'less than good citizens' (Osler and Starkey 2003). Evidence suggests that the majority of young people are already active in undertaking a wide range of obligations and responsibilities (France 1998; Smith *et al.* 2005) and are willing to volunteer for a wide range of activities (Prime *et al.* 2002). Active citizenship is a 'deficit model' that sees the fundamental problems in the individual not taking civic responsibilities seriously. It also gives little attention to the rights of young people (France 1998). The focus on responsibilities reinforces the view that young people are irresponsible and in need of attention. Others have also raised the question of New Labour's narrow definition of what being a citizen might mean. For example, Lister (2001) argues that, as long as family-care work is not recognised or valued in our definitions of citizenship, then it tends to be gender-specific, giving limited attention to major areas of women's activity. A similar picture exists in the definitions used for political participation. If the focus is on the narrow confines of Parliament and elections, then other forms of political participation are marginalised. Activities such as political protest, campaigning and social action groups are not seen as legitimate forms of citizenship (France 1998).

Youth research and transitions into adulthood

New Labour's perception of transitions to adulthood has been dominated by concerns over the school-to-work transition. Even in further and higher education, the shift in emphasis towards 'employability' and vocationalism is built upon models of transitions that emphasise the importance of employment. As we saw above, questions of citizenship have also been of concern, yet the focus is less on transitions to adulthood and more on encouraging the young to be 'responsible', and to volunteer. Yet youth research in transitions has provided a growing body of evidence that shows the importance of building policy on a broader understanding of these processes of transition, beyond purely labour markets (MacDonald and Marsh 2005).

New Labour's notion of citizenship (as work and responsibilities) gives little recognition to issues of family relationships and 'family careers' (Jones 2002), housing transitions (Heath 2002) and personal relationships (Thomson *et al.* 2002). These are all seen by the young as having a major influence on how they move through transitions towards adulthood. Young people identify the importance of social location, personal circumstances, family structures and personal relationships as influencing factors (Thomson *et al.* 2004). No single simple route exists. Different contexts give rise to different understandings and practices of transitions. While getting a job is still seen as a critical process to transition, other factors are also important (Smith *et al.* 2005). Legal, social and economic markers of age remain key in the importance of gaining autonomy (Thomson *et al.* 2004). This is linked to how young people perceive themselves and their feelings of being independent (Smith *et al.* 2005). Young people also recognise that relationships, and feelings of greater responsibility for themselves as they get older, are also important in this process (Thomson *et al.* 2004). To make these transitions, they develop strategies and tactics which are influenced by circumstances and power (Thomson *et al.* 2004). Class and gender also remain important influences on how they experience transitions into adulthood (Jones 2002). These can be determined by the resources available, especially in terms of social, economic and symbolic capital (Bell 2001). In this context young people remain active players in negotiating their pathways into adulthood:

> Attempts at achieving social mobility [require] young people to renegotiate the resources with which they are faced. This may entail rejecting the forms of adulthood they see around them, disentangling themselves from the values of their family and wider community, and propelling themselves into uncharted territory.
>
> (Thomson and Holland 2004: 20)

Youth inequality and transitions into adulthood

Policy has had little to say about youth inequality, yet much transitional research shows that it remains significant to how young people experience social life. New Labour policy has reflected the 'individualisation' position of writers such as Beck (1992) by constructing the problems young people have around individual failings. Issues of class, gender and racial inequality have been given little attention in the policies of late modernity. Yet evidence shows that inequality remains a strong influence. In terms of school-to-work transitions, large sections of the poor remain within the expanding training sector or in unskilled employment (Furlong and Cartmel 1997), while the more affluent and middle-class go on to access higher education (Ball 2003; Tomlinson 2005a). Social class origins remain excellent predictors of outcomes for future employment (Roberts 1997). Even those who support the claims of greater individualisation remain sceptical and cautious, arguing that, while international trends indicate it has increased, there remains evidence that indicates structural factors remain influential in shaping young people's lives. The evidence of change is strong, yet structured pathways still seem to remain:

> Young people can struggle to establish adult identities and maintain coherent biographies, they may develop strategies to overcome various obstacles, but their life chances remain highly structured, with social class and gender being critical to an understanding of experiences in a range of life contexts.
>
> (Furlong and Cartmel 1997: 109)

Inequality, it would seem, still has a role to play in structuring young people's lives, even in the 'age of individualism'. Explaining these patterns of continued inequality has been marginalised within much social science. Class analysis, for example, has been rendered invisible, suggesting that late modernity is the age of 'post-structuralism', where social life is more fluid and in flux (Devine *et al.* 2005). Class theory itself has been in 'crisis' (Devine and Savage 2005), being undermined by the commitment to the aggregates of employment or unemployment that locate class in a purely economic set of relationships.[3] The problems of bifurcation between 'the social' and the 'economic' in how class operates to stratify different groups, fail to address more complex relationships that cut across, and through, the structuring of social life (Crompton and Scott 2005). Attempts to address these problems have turned to theories that want to structure individualism (Furlong and Cartmel 1997), or draw upon 'culture' as a means of understanding the social processes that shape people's lives (Devine and Savage 2005).

'Structured individualism' in youth transitions

While many of the changes attributed to later modernity are seen as creating a greater emphasis on structured opportunities, the levels and long-term impact of such changes remain uncertain (Furlong and Cartmel 1997; Roberts 1997). 'Structured individualism' attempts to reconcile social change and continuity, showing how certain movements towards individualism can be accommodated, while also recognising the continued forces of structure (Roberts 1995). It is suggested that while social background and family histories may not lead to particular forms of occupations and jobs, the types of opportunities available to young people will be limited by the structures around them. In choosing their pathways and routes, young people will have to draw upon their own resources to help them in this process. The types of resources available are clearly linked to their class position, and are seen to limit how they might be able to take up opportunities (Roberts 1997). The discourse of 'choice' and 'opportunity' that permeates both common-sense understandings and political approaches to individualism, alongside the decline of collective social identities, also creates a sense of false reality for the young, in that they believe they are able to take control of their own lives (Furlong and Cartmel 1997). Individualism is portrayed as an end in itself, and a reality that is achievable. This 'epistemological fallacy' forces the young to negotiate their lives as though they have real opportunities, yet, once again, failure to achieve them results in their being blamed (by themselves this time) for their own situation: 'Blind to the existence of powerful chains of interdependency, young people frequently attempt to resolve collective problems through individual action and hold themselves responsible for their inevitable failure' (Furlong and Cartmel 1997: 114).

How this relationship between 'individualism' and 'structure' operates can be seen at the level of the local community (MacDonald and Marsh 2005). Deprived areas, and communities that have suffered from intense deindustrialisation over a long period of time, are creating new types of 'poor' transitions. Local labour markets and state intervention are creating particular types of 'structured opportunities'. In poor areas these tend to be unpredictable, insecure and, in the majority of cases, of poor quality (Webster *et al.* 2004). But individual young people living in such areas feel that they are making clear decisions, reflecting and drawing upon their own agency, yet the choices available are clearly made within the limits of the opportunities that exist in the local labour market and educational and training agencies (MacDonald and Marsh 2005). Structural constraints located in the local context, therefore, have a major impact not only on young people's levels and quality of education, training and employment, but also on their longer-term life chances (Webster *et al.* 2004). Within this context young people still maintain a continued optimism and strong set of beliefs, and positive commitments over life choices (MacDonald and Marsh 2005). Most are making choices, taking responsibility, and acting independently. Yet the extent of 'choice' remains limited and structured by the local context of how local labour markets and state intervention structure their opportunities.

While such a position allows us to understand the impact of local economic restructuring on the lives of the young, it does tend to create a sense of dichotomy between 'structure' and 'agency'. 'Structure' is located in institutions such as the labour market, and in government responses, while 'agency' is perceived as autonomy. Little attention is given to understanding the broader cultural knowledge and understandings that young people bring to their engagements with these wider social processes and practices. There is, therefore, a need to explore the complexity of the relationship between structure and agency, and have an understanding of how local culture is influential in shaping young people's transitions.

Structure, agency and culture

The question of 'culture' in class analysis has more recently replaced approaches that emphasise social reproduction. Up until the early 1990s, this was seen as a major theoretical model for understanding the different class experiences young people had of the school-to-work transition.[4] But with the decline of class theorising, its limitations in explaining social difference and the breakdown of traditional routes into adulthood, it was rejected. In its place we now see the emergence of theories that 'turn' to culture (Gewirtz and Cribb 2003).

At the centre of this 'cultural turn' in class analysis is the work of Pierre Bourdieu (1990, 1991). He argues that a person's economic, social, cultural and symbolic capital shapes their cultural tastes, their lifestyles, their accent, their cuisine and their social networks (Skeggs 1997). This locates them in a certain social space and gives them resources to deploy for further advancement (Devine and Savage 2005). Class is then defined through a set of social relationships in which individuals deploy their resources, which leads to the maintenance of social inequalities. Within this process we also have to understand the importance of what Bourdieu calls the 'fields' and 'habitus'. Fields present themselves as 'structured spaces', which are fluid, exist between individuals, and are shaped by local knowledge. This local knowledge, or 'habitus', tells individuals 'how to play the game', providing them with competences and skills that help them negotiate their way through life. Culture in this context is about social networks and interrelationships between history, tradition and social relationships in social context.

Transitional studies have tried to incorporate such an approach into understanding why certain outcomes of transitions remained fixed in the age of individualism. Ball *et al.* (2000) in their study of youth transitions in London, suggested that the relationships a young person has with the local area and the adult way of life are important in shaping the routes that taken. This provides a 'framed field of reference', alongside their own knowledge and experiences, which then informs them of the decisions they should make to 'get on' (this is then their 'habitus'). Social and economic capital, alongside emotional capital in the shape of friendships and support, operate to help them make this investment in their transitions. This starts to explain the patterns of continuity, even in times of individualisation. For Ball *et al.* (2000) it is this, alongside the influence of the cosmopolitan city of London, that shapes not only the opportunity structures available to young people but also the cultural influences on their attitudes to everyday life. London is a large and diverse economy that requires substantial negotiating. The young have to travel large distances in different forms of transport. They also encounter the city as a social space that allows for different forms of leisure. This, in effect, creates a different context to transition than for those living in more isolated or geographically smaller communities.

The focus on the cultural context of transition has also been discussed in terms of gender (Walkerdine *et al.* 2001). Again, in an attempt to address the ambiguity of the individualisation thesis, Walkerdine *et al.* (2001) suggest that while the notion of class may have changed in late modernity, it still remains a critical influence in shaping girls' subjectivity and transitions. For example, major differentials of outcome exist between middle- and working-class girls (Walkerdine *et al.* 2001). These tended to arise because of the different levels of social, economic and cultural capital held by girls and their parents. Walkerdine *et al.* (2001) draw upon the work of Bourdieu to explain many of the cultural processes that shape young women's pathways, suggesting that they are undertaken not just through relationships with production, but within social relationships in a certain conceptual space.

These approaches open up and intersect the 'structure versus agency' debate, drawing out the micro-processes evident in cultural activity that shape the process of class identity. They also show the importance of the locality, the surrounding space and the influence of social relationships and history, in shaping the cultural context of youth transitions. Yet problems remain in how 'culture' is defined and used. Bourdieu and his followers still have a limited view of culture. It is relegated to 'taste', 'style', 'lifestyle' and 'accent' and is expressed through individual social interactions. In this sense it separates culture out from important economic practices, seeing them as dualistic (Crompton and Scott 2005). Such problems are not unique to youth studies or studies of transitions. Questions of how culture operates to shape class inequality in late modernity remain central to class theorising (Crompton and Scott 2005). What is needed is a fully integrated theory that is able to bring together a unified understanding of these processes, alongside an understanding of the cultural processes that underpin our learning (Cohen and Ainley 2000).

Masculine identities in fragmented labour markets

One area of social reproduction theory that has expanded in the youth transition research has been that of masculinity studies. Youth research has been greatly influenced by broader sociological developments in the embodied construction of identities that are shaped through the labour market experience (McDowell 2004). This work has mainly focused on questions related to changes in employment routes for young men, and its impact on their identities. Previous social reproduction studies concentrated on how working-class young men get working-class jobs (Willis 1977), showing how masculine identities were reproduced within schools preparing young working-class men for traditional manual labour. More recently, attention has concentrated on the impact deindustrialism has had on this process. As employment in traditional forms of production has collapsed, especially for young working-class men, questions have been asked about the impact this is having on their masculine identities.

Much of this work has focused on boys 'doing gender' through the transition from school to work (McDowell 2004). Traditional approaches failed to recognise the complexity, multiplicity of influences, and fluidity of how young men negotiate their embodied identities in different social contexts (Griffin 2000). Work is recognised as an important site, where gender identities are both formed and 'preformed'. Social changes to the youth labour market have deconstructed traditional routes and pathways, especially for young working-class men. As a result, they are encountering new experiences, new institutional practices and structures that are challenging or threatening to their notions of being 'a man' (McDowell 2004).

How young men have managed these has varied by context. Traditional identities of masculinity have not disappeared or been rejected, but reconfigured in the new industrial context (Taylor and Jamieson 1997). For example, in areas such as Sheffield in the UK, the environment of employment has radically changed. As a response young working-class men have reworked nostalgic images of 'maleness' and interwoven them into their everyday lives in different ways. Sheffield is an industrial city dominated by images, myths and folklore associated with working in the steel industry (Taylor and Jamieson 1997). These dominated the industrial landscape in Sheffield's industrial history, providing a hegemonic form of masculinity and a model of behaviour that young men are now unable to aspire to in their search for work. But as these sites have disappeared, young men have expressed these forms of masculinity in other places and parts of their lives. Similar processes are also at work in Newcastle where young men draw upon notions of being 'real Geordies' in acting out their masculinity (Nayak 2003). These are historically and traditionally seen as the 'aristocracy of labour', and inform young men about 'how to be men' in the North East of England. 'Real Geordies' were real men – strong, with a muscular work ethic, and dominant in all aspects of their lives. But for young men in Newcastle 'living out' this ideal in late modernity is increasingly problematic. Many young men in Newcastle still define themselves as 'real Geordies', viewing mental work as 'soft and babyish'. As a result they reject work or education if it offers only a pathway into the service sector or non-manual types of employment. Young men, therefore, 'resist' non-manual work and look for other sites and settings to express their maleness (Nayak 2003).

The local and regional context to how hegemonic masculinity is defined, and the new forms of masculinity being constructed, are clearly important. Other studies have shown how this operates across different urban and rural environments (McDowell 2000, 2002, 2004). This is a complex interplay between changes in the types of jobs available within the local labour market, and the local masculine culture. The shift to service-sector employment has reconstituted and reconstructed traditional notions of 'being male' (McDowell 2004). Much service-sector employment demands particular attributes that are problematic for young working-class men who still desire 'male jobs'. Service-sector employment desires clean, neat, sterile bodies, 'service with a smile' and bodies that are trim, conforming to conventional norms and standards of dress and presentation. To fit into these acceptable versions of 'embodied masculinity', young men's existing notions of masculinity have to change. Old traditional ways of 'being a man' are resisted and rejected by employers, therefore creating major problems for young men in finding work (McDowell 2004). Masculine identities cannot be understood by using theories of social reproduction alone. Becoming a man, for young working-class boys, involves a complex negotiation between traditional, localised forms of 'hegemonic masculinity', changes in the local labour market, and employment opportunities (McDowell 2004).

Conclusion

In the late 1990s, New Labour constructed the youth question in terms of 'social exclusion', life-long learning and citizenship. While there is a strong positive rhetoric within New Labour's language over youth, the youth question itself is still fundamentally conceived and produced as one of 'problems'. Many of the young are seen to lack the skills and motivation to tackle their own exclusion, or are seen to have personal problems and problematic families that limit their willingness and ability to be included. Within this perspective there remains a strong 'victim-blaming' component to policy, which justifies greater surveillance, intervention and regulation of the young. This is aimed at not only ensuring they take up their responsibilities, but also instructing them how they should be 'good citizens'. In the political understandings and constructions of youth transitions in late modernity, the young are still seen as the problem.

But the focus on social exclusion through work, rather than social inequality, has also been problematic. It fails to recognise the broader social processes involved in transitions, and the ways that young people make complex moves from youth into adult forms of citizenship (Thomson *et al.* 2004; Smith *et al.* 2005). Recent social science research has increased our understanding of these processes, yet little recognition has infiltrated policy. The focus on social exclusion also denies, or rejects, the importance of more embedded structural forces that influence the unequal outcomes to youth transitions between certain classes and genders. It also ignores other factors that might influence transitions outside the purely labour market agenda. Social science research has shown how class and gender differences can be reproduced, and how they remain entrenched in the locality, yet political rhetoric and ideology have been unwilling to engage creatively with such findings. Class still remains important to the life chances of many young people. Even in the age of individualism, where 'choice' and 'opportunity' seem to be expanding, some young people find their options limited and their pathways pre-structured, thereby offering no real choice.

This is not to say that social science has been entirely successful in explaining how these processes operate. There is still much to understand about the role of 'culture', but even less is known about how the cultural industries, and the new jobs that are emerging within them, are impacting on the wide range of youth transitions (Hollands 2002). It is also the case that many 'voices' still remain silent. For example, while there has been an interest in how change impacts upon the lives of young men, little research has been done on how girls are experiencing economic and social restructuring. While writers such as Walkerdine *et al.* (2001) have started this process, little work has explored the processes of social reproduction of femininity in the changing context of labour markets in late modernity. A similar issue arises over the impact of these changes on different ethnic groupings, and how new migrant labour forces experience citizenship, transition and inclusion. Only a limited amount of research has been undertaken in areas of racial transitions (Haywood and Mac an Ghaill 2005), leaving a gap in our understanding of how groups, such as young Asian or African-Caribbean young people, make these transitions into adulthood.

5 Youth, education and the politics of inclusion

Introduction

How Western societies engage with globalisation and the restructuring of employment and work has been seen as a central feature of the education systems of those societies. Creating a workforce of highly skilled and knowledgeable workers, capable of facing the challenges, is at the heart of much educational reform. In such a context, the youth question becomes focused on how, in 'new times', the next generation of workers are to be trained and educated. This chapter takes this question and explores how the 'problem' has been understood, and what types of policies and practices have helped shape education policy in late modernity. In this discussion we will also consider what social science has had to say about this development, and how it both challenges mainstream political perspectives while also offering alternative understanding of both the 'problem' and the 'solution'.

Education and the post-welfare society

As was identified in Chapter 3, the post-welfare society had its roots in the economic crises of the 1970s. Since then the post-war consensus formed after the Second World War has been abandoned and replaced by policies that see a core role for the market, and for individual action and responsibility. Nowhere is this more evident than in the development of education policy over the last three decades. The neo-liberal governments of Margaret Thatcher set the tone for what was to come in the 1990s. While the emphasis varied over time, the Conservative governments' approach to education was underpinned by six core developments:

- 'Market forces' should have a critical role to play in education policy. The 1990s are seen as a period of consolidation, where market forces were established as a mechanism to address the failings of previous education policies.
- Under this commitment was the expansion of the 'choice' agenda. Policies were designed to restructure access to schools, allowing parents more choice in selecting schools for their children.

- Schools were given more freedom from local control. Local education authority powers were reduced, while local schools were given more autonomy.
- National government took more control over the curriculum, setting out key requirements. There was also an increase in the monitoring and auditing of schools and teachers, alongside the increased use of league tables.
- Selection was maintained and expanded. Schools were given new powers and opportunities to select pupils on a number of different criteria. 'Ability' is once again central to the new selection agenda.
- The school curriculum for 14–19-year-olds was restructured and saw 'vocationalism' playing a major part in the national school curriculum. New policies were introduced that increased skills training and qualifications that are seen as relevant for employers (i.e. GNVQ).

Between 1988 and 1994 consecutive Conservative governments introduced: ten new Acts of Parliament; four new government quangos, among them the Office for Standards in Education (Ofsted) and the Training and Enterprise Councils; and three national reports that made core recommendations about the direction education should take. This was a period of 'frenzied activity' (Tomlinson 2005a) which saw the transformation of education policy.

After nearly two decades of Conservative rule, evidence showed that the number of young people leaving school with a qualification had increased dramatically (Tomlinson 2005a). But evidence also suggested that Conservative education policy had increased the levels of social inequality between rich and poor, and that education differentials remained (Tomlinson 2005a). Official government sources showed that government policy itself was contributing to the problem through its policy of 'market forces' and 'choice' (Tomlinson 2005a). Ofsted (1993), for example, reported that schools in disadvantaged areas were unable to compete. Schools in disadvantaged areas did not have the resources to tackle the underlying social issues that impacted on learning. Choice policies and access to good schools were also greatly influenced by a family's income (Smith and Noble 1995). Class remained a critical factor in shaping the educational experience of young people:

> Evidence to support the idea that a 'classless' society is emerging is weak. Social class is still central to our understanding of educational outcomes and the advantages of the middle class have been largely preserved throughout a period of rapid change in education and the labour market.
>
> (Furlong 1997: 69)

Throughout this period, Conservative governments also showed little interest in tackling racial inequality within the education system (Tomlinson 2005a), even though inequalities between ethnic minorities and white pupils were seen to be growing (Mamon 2004). The gap between black and Asian pupils' levels of achievement was also widening and there had been an overall increase in qualifications of young black and Asian pupils, but many were still leaving school less qualified than white young people (Mizen 2004). A major cause of this was that large sections of the ethnic minority population in the UK lived in the most disadvantaged urban areas, with the worst schools. Choice policies were also to blame in schools dominated by minority ethnic groups in that the middle class deserted schools that seemed to have 'problems' associated with ethnicity (Tomlinson 2005b).

The Conservative government rejected these explanations of causes for the inequality by blaming others. One approach blamed individual pupils and/or their parents. So, for example, it was claimed that a number of working-class parents, and especially single parents, had little interest in their children's education, and that welfare policy created a dependency culture and an 'underclass' with an increased lack of moral responsibility (see MacDonald 1997). The teaching staff within 'failing schools' were also blamed for their 'failure' to address the performance of children. It was claimed that part of the problem was that the teaching profession was greatly influenced by 1960s liberalism, which was not effective at dealing with discipline or increasing pupil performance. And finally, the Conservative government created a 'discourse of blame' around racial inequality that accused black parents for either their lack of willingness to learn 'British ways' and embrace 'Britishness', or their negative attitudes towards education (Tomlinson 2005b). Even though evidence existed that showed African-Caribbean and Asian families have strong commitments to education, seeing it as a critical pathway into a better life, media and political explanations focused on blaming the failure of black pupils within education on poor parenting and black culture (Archer 2003).

New Labour and inclusive education

New Labour was swept into power, claiming that its priority for the first term of office would be 'education, education, education'. In the early years New Labour had a reforming zeal that matched that of the Conservatives in the preceding era (Ball 1999). This being said, much of this reform retained a commitment to Conservative ideals. Its policy direction focused on market commodification, consumer choice and competition, alongside the use of league tables, increased regulation and control of the curriculum, enhanced inspection, and greater control of teacher training.

Where New Labour differed from the previous regime was in its claims to pursue policies of social justice and to develop approaches that would tackle the problems of social exclusion (Tomlinson 2003). As was outlined in the previous chapter, this approach claimed that large sections of those excluded from the benefits of society were also receiving poor-quality education. A growing number of young people were either excluding themselves from education by truanting, or were being excluded by schools (SEU 1998b). Government evidence suggested that large numbers of young people truanted from school on a regular basis and that numbers of exclusions from school were also highest in disadvantaged areas. New Labour promised to prioritise tackling these issues, as truanting and exclusion from school were seen to lead to further forms of social exclusion later in life (SEU 1998b).

Improving standards

At the heart of New Labour policy was 'raising standards'. This was seen as the best way not only to increase the life chances of young people, but also to improve the economic performance of the UK in the global economy (Tomlinson 2005a). Numerous initiatives have been developed, ranging from the strategic, such as the setting up of the Standards Unit within the Department of Education and Skills (DfES), to the implementation of practical applications, for example, the introduction of 'numeracy and literacy hours' in all primary schools. Government also had a targeted strategy on areas of disadvantage. For example, Education Action Zones targeted 73 disadvantaged communities, with the intention of discovering new ways of delivering education. Other initiatives that had educational targets included: Excellence in Cities; Health Action Zones; Sure Start; and New Deal for Communities. The DfES also set up new advisory bodies that had a specific focus on those groups known to have the most problems in education: they replaced Section 11 grants[1] with the Ethnic Minority and Traveller Achievement Group (EMTAG), and also set up a Special Needs Advisory Group.

Diversity within the education system

At the heart of New Labour education plans has been the creation of a diverse education system as a way of modernising the comprehensive principle (Tomlinson 2005a). Previous Conservative governments had started this process, and New Labour remained enthusiastically committed to continuing the fragmentation of educational choice for parents and pupils. By 2002, 14 different types of schools existed, all with different status, and all with different funding models and opportunities.[2] These included: private and grammar schools; foundation schools; voluntary schools; city academies; community special schools; and city technology colleges. Market forces and parental choice have been (and continue to be) seen as critical mechanisms of ensuring that diversity is achieved within the educational sector. Competition has remained a core principle in New Labour policy, being seen as something that helps school innovate and raise standards. Competition for parent choice between schools would, it is claimed, require all schools to have high standards if they are to be attractive to parents. But competition also removes the less desirable, in that 'failing schools' would either have to address their problems or close.

Selection

The previous Conservative government was strongly committed to the principle of selection, seeing it as morally and ideologically the best way to encourage potential. New Labour, however, has remained, throughout its term in office, ambiguous about its approach to selection. Differences clearly exist within the Labour Party over the acceptability of selection as recent debates about proposed new legislation have shown (*The Guardian*, 25 January 2006). While in opposition, New Labour rejected selection and argued in favour of removing it from the system, but, on entering office, the policy is more about managing and removing only certain aspects of selection (Tomlinson 2005a). Even though selection by ability is not allowed in the comprehensive system, it exists in a number of guises and has remained within the education system in overt and covert ways:

- The retention of the private sector within education has meant that selection on income, privilege and ability remains.
- Under New Labour, the grammar school system remains. Over 36 local education authorities still allow selection by the eleven-plus, and grammar schools can still select pupils in terms of ability.
- Selection *within* schools has also taken place. Government has advocated selection and streaming of the most (and least) able through the construction of programmes such as learning support units (for 'failing students') and the gifted and talented programmes for those identified as potential 'high achievers'.
- Evidence has shown that large sections of the middle class have moved into catchment areas where the best schools are located (Tomlinson 2003).
- The growing vocationalism is leading to an increase in the types of subjects certain young people can take and a diversification of the curriculum between the vocational and academic.

Tackling social exclusion

New Labour's commitment to tackle social exclusion had a major impact on education policy. Those young people living in disadvantaged communities, who had special needs, were excluded from school, or were disaffected and truanting were seen as being most 'at risk' of future social exclusion (SEU 1998b). As a result, the government set about constructing a programme for inclusion. This had a number of components. Firstly, it was felt that it was not only morally, but also economically appropriate that pupils with special educational needs be integrated into mainstream provision. Special schools were to remain, but with a task of increasing inclusion and helping integration. Services for parents were to be increased, alongside increased forms of special training for staff. In 2001 the new Special Educational Needs and Disability Act reinforced this commitment while also ensuring discrimination against disabled students was made unlawful. Throughout its time in office, New Labour has aimed, through this initiative, to bring about a change in the system, ensuring that all children and young people, irrespective of need, have the highest quality of education possible (Armstrong 2005). Secondly, exclusions from school were to be reduced. Evidence suggested that, throughout the early 1990s, school exclusions had increased dramatically, partly as a result of government policy, and partly because it fast-tracked troublesome young people out of school quickly. Concern was raised about the high number of African-Caribbean young people being excluded, well out of proportion with other groups (Tomlinson 2005b). New Labour set about limiting the powers of schools to exclude pupils, and developing guidelines that would make the process more transparent and ensure it was fair and equitable. Finally, New Labour aimed to construct a range of policies that would address the growing problem of truancy. These have ranged from changes in the curriculum, to the introduction of new forms of policing and the use of punitive powers by the courts. For example, in 1998 the DfES increased resources and arrangements for home schooling. They also expanded opportunities for truants to take up vocational training. Schools have introduced electronic registers and new systems of monitoring pupil attendance throughout the school day, while the police and local councils have run 'truancy watch schemes' that stop children who are out on the streets during school hours. More recently, the government has encouraged courts to use powers to imprison parents of persistent truants. For example, in 2002 a mother of two was imprisoned for 60 days for allowing one of her daughters to truant from school. Since then a number of other cases have been taken to court, using powers that have been in place since 1996.

The problem of (with?) social exclusion

An ongoing theme of our discussions is how policy and policy-makers understand the 'problem' of youth. This not only sets down the parameters of the debate but also structures the types of solutions offered. In this context, the youth question in education becomes structured in particular ways, with specific consequences for our understanding of what it means to be young in late modernity. The dominant discourse across education policy on 'social exclusion' once again constructs the problem as individual failings or pathologies of individuals, parents or communities (Alexiadou 2002; Armstrong 2005), therefore 'blaming' them for their own problems. It locates the 'causes' as being the lack of personal traits or the willingness to be included. One example can be found in government policy towards students with special educational needs. While New Labour has actively promoted policies of inclusion, through a range of new legislation (DfEE 1997b; HMSO 2001) and strategies (DfES 2004a), underpinning its construction are assumed models of social development that construct inclusion of people with special educational needs or disabilities within traditional frameworks. This perceives the child or young person as having an impaired pathology (Armstrong 2005). Within the disability movement and social research, this model has been strongly criticised as failing to recognise the 'social act of discrimination embedded in the power relations of society' (Armstrong 2005: 143) and, as a result, policy in this area has focused on removing physical barriers, or assimilating young people with impairments into mainstream schools without tackling fundamental causes of exclusion. Similar conclusions can be made about New Labour policy towards the most 'troublesome', such as those excluded or truanting. Policy has conceptualised the problem on the basis of pathologies and lack of moral responsibility (Parsons 2005). Issues such as educational assessment then become technical solutions that identify 'at risk' populations early, justifying greater early intervention and regulation:

> the idea of inclusive education is used to justify the growth of surveillance and management of troublesome populations based on the assumption that special educational needs are an outcome of dysfunctional individuals and communities and that these individuals can be identified through an assessment process determined by experts.
>
> (Armstrong 2005: 148)

The pathologising of the problem of exclusion has also been operating in policies towards parents and parenting. Recent government initiatives to improve the quality of parenting, and the parent's role and responsibilities in education, have focused on the 'failings' of poor parents in not parenting properly – that is, not providing 'good' (middle-class) forms of parenting. The reasons why the most troublesome young people 'fail' at school are seen as a result of parents in disadvantaged areas not implanting the necessary skills, morals and knowledge for young people to become 'good citizens' (DfES 2005). To ensure a child is included, a parent has to be skilled in managing risk and being able to take opportunities when they arise in particular (middle-class) ways (Gillies 2005).

In this context, inclusion is a 'normative' concept that serves to prioritise the middle-class values of personal responsibility for individual achievement over everything else. It constructs a particular framework for establishing the opportunities to conform (Armstrong 2005). The critical focus of this policy has then been on those parents and young people who are perceived as 'unwilling' to be included. As outlined above, a solution to their 'resistance' is that government policies and practices aim to force them to take 'their responsibilities more seriously' (Armstrong 2005; Parsons 2005). For example, in new legislation being planned, parenting orders are to be expanded and made compulsory for 'problem parents', forcing them to undertake training and to learn their responsibilities:

> Parenting orders, for parents that will not engage with voluntary measures, compel parents to attend a parenting programme and comply with any other conditions imposed by the court. We will extend parenting orders, so that schools can use them to make parents take responsibility for their children's bad behaviour in school and so that they can be used for serious misbehaviour where the pupil has not been excluded.
>
> (DfES 2005: 77)

Social policy in education therefore has taken a regulatory and disciplinary function for those defined outside the parameters of middle-class social acceptability. The 'disaffected', the 'excluded from school', and those involved in 'bad behaviour' in schools, are seen as the problem to be tackled by greater intervention and control (Osler and Starkey 2005; Parsons 2005), which, in effect, justifies policies that are punitive and intrusive (Armstrong 2005). Terms such as 'inclusive education' have then become exclusionary discursive practices that privilege the knowledge of the professional over the views of others (Slee and Allan 2001). Inclusion is about professional power and about assimilation to narrow middle-class morality and sets of values that view 'good society' as unproblematic (Armstrong 2005).

Finally, as a part of the 'responsibilising' agenda, New Labour has also 'blamed' schools for the continuation of social exclusion (Whitty 2001). Government claims that the best way to address social exclusion is to raise the standards and effectiveness of all schools in tackling low achievement (Department for Education and Employment (DfEE) 1997a). Poverty or social disadvantage should not be seen as a barrier to higher levels of achievement amongst disadvantaged populations. It is the school's responsibility to improve and provide the high quality of education available elsewhere (DfEE 1997a). But such a position does not recognise the substantial evidence, from a wide range of sources over a long period of time, that has shown that such a policy is unrealistic. Social class will always stratify achievement (Rutter *et al.* 1979; Thrupp 1999). Even with this conclusive evidence New Labour policy has remained firmly fixed on raising standards in schools as a solution to 'social exclusion'.

The reasons for tackling social exclusion over the problems of class within New Labour's approach to education are twofold. Firstly, New Labour holds an ideological position and vision of society that prioritises both a meritocracy and the creation and expansion of opportunities within a market-based society (Lawson 2005). New Labour's policy towards the welfare state has shifted away from welfarism towards the 'marketisation of welfare', where individuals are consumers who are given opportunities to purchase services to meet their needs (Tomlinson 2005a).

Social justice in this context is then concerned with opportunity, not with tackling the root causes of social inequalities. New Labour, and Tony Blair in particular, believe in a society where merit has a critical role to play. Government must create a 'ladder of opportunity' by which social mobility is achievable for all. It is argued that, if barriers to participation are overcome and new opportunities are constructed, usually through competition and market forces, then ceilings will be removed and mobility will be open to all (Lawson 2005). In this sense New Labour have argued not only for the 'expansion of the middle class' as a core policy objective, but also that, given the right type of opportunities, this is achievable for all. As a part of this argument New Labour see the 'blocks' not as structural, but as institutional, individual and cultural. Schools fail to create the right sort of opportunities for young people or fail to raise their achievement levels, or individuals lack personal aspiration and self-belief, have personal failings or are held back by the 'culture of poverty' and their lack of self-responsibility (Armstrong 2005). Within this argument poverty and structural factors are usually given marginal recognition (Tomlinson 2005a).

A second and related issue is more pragmatic and is related to New Labour's strategy in gaining and maintaining its position in government. In restructuring itself in the early 1990s, the Labour Party 'think tanks' recognised that the Party would need to reject its class-based approach to policy-making for one that appeals more to the middle class (Ball 2003; Tomlinson 2005a). This explains the construction not only of the language and policies under the concept of social exclusion, but also of policies within education that have greater appeal to the middle classes. For example, the 'choice agenda' in the selection of schools is one that was born out of Conservative political agendas of the 1980s and has greater interest in the upwardly mobile middle classes (Ball 2003), a point we shall return to in the next section.

Education and the social reproduction of inequality

So far we have seen how New Labour reconfigured the youth question within education in a particular way, but social science research has provided a wealth of evidence that challenges this particular approach. Much of this work has focused on issues of inequality related to class, gender and race, and those that have not benefited. Evidence in this context offers an alternative perspective of the youth question that could offer politicians a different way of conceptualising (and responding) to the needs of the young.

Class and education

Arguments over the relationship between class futures and educational opportunity have a long and distinguished history within the social sciences (Halsey *et al.* 1997). As we saw in the previous chapter, in more recent times class analysis of social problems has been much marginalised, not only within educational policy, but also within social theorising. For example, it has been suggested that either 'class is dead' (Clarke *et al.* 1993), or that class in late modernity has far less influence in shaping individualised identities (Beck and Beck-Gernsheim 2002). Sociologists at Nuffield College in Oxford have set about challenging such assertions by undertaking considerable technical reanalysis of large quantitative data sets to create a new schema of socio-economic classification of class (Goldthorpe 1996; Marshall 1997). This reclassifies different categories within classes showing the impact on life-chances in a number of diverse ways (Rose and Pevalin 2003). But such work is unable to explore the processes at work in shaping people's choices (Savage 2003; Crompton and Scott 2005). As a result it has had little impact on those who argue that class analysis has lost its significance, or on the educational policies of New Labour (Savage 2003).

Evidence from a broad range of sources supports the claim that class remains a central feature in structuring education and future life chances (Tomlinson 2005a). For example, working-class young people are more likely to leave education at the minimum age than their middle-class counterparts (Furlong 2005). While attainment and the number of qualifications received from school has improved across the board, differentials by class still remain strong (Furlong and Cartmel 1997; Tomlinson 2003). Working-class young people are also more likely to be streamed into poor schools, to be in lower streams within schools (Tomlinson 2005a), and to 'choose' a vocational route, both at school and after school (Archer and Yamashita 2003). As we saw in the previous chapter, they are also less likely to go to university (Archer *et al.* 2003), and, even when they do, the type of institution they go to tends to be regionally based and of low status in the university sector (Archer *et al.* 2003). The types of courses chosen also tend to have a short duration and are targeted on job skills (Furlong 2005).

Within the social sciences and the sociology of education, a new paradigm of class theory has emerged that sets about engaging with social change, while also trying to explain why class differences remain within education. Influenced once again by the work of writers such as Bourdieu and Bernstein, contemporary theorists have attempted to explore the political, the social, the cultural and the emotional forces at play in shaping opportunities and decisions within the educational system (Savage 2003).

The middle class and education

Over the past twenty years, a wide range of research from across the globe has shown how the middle class is able to control and shape the national and local education system (Ball 2003; Devine 2004). International research from the United States, Australia and Europe has been able to illuminate how the middle class is able to reproduce its position of power and authority, not only at a national level, but also internationally, through control and influence of education systems (Brown 1997). These processes of social reproduction are evident at all levels of society, working in the construction and development of national and local policy, and also at the micro level and the interface between parents' actions and teachers' responses (Ball 2003).

As was outlined earlier, the 'choice' policies in the UK emerged in response to middle-class demands (Devine 2004). Middle-class policy developers, with certain values on how society should be organised, designed them (Ball 2003). 'Choice' policies can advantage the middle classes in a range of ways. For example, in the 'marketisation' of education, and selection processes, strong evidence exists that shows the middle classes are able to develop strategies for improving the chances of their children (Ball 2003). For example:

- Those with the power and wealth can purchase the best education. Evidence has shown that those who receive this become part of the global elite moving into world-class education and jobs (Brown 1997; Ong 2004).
- While the claim is that selection in grammar schools and the use of the eleven-plus creates wider opportunities for working-class pupils,

evidence shows that less than 2 per cent of those from working-class backgrounds get selected (Tomlinson 2005a).

- Evidence on selection within schools shows that programmes such as learning support units and 'gifted and talented' programmes tend to be 'class-ridden'. For example, an evaluation of the National Academy for Gifted and Talented Youth at Warwick University showed that it was middle-class students who tended to be selected (Bloom 2004).
- Evidence also shows that the separation of 'the academic' from 'the vocational' within schools has a strong focus on class differences, leading to greater streaming. For example, new policy initiatives within the 14–16 curriculum are targeted on those young people seen as being at risk of future unemployment, the socially excluded and the 'disaffected' (Huddleston and Oh 2004).

But policy only creates the opportunities. What is critical is the way that middle-class parents are able to mobilise their personal and collective economic, social and cultural capital to give their children advantages within the education system (Ball 2003; Devine 2004). The middle classes are good at developing strategies that use resources sparingly when necessary or with abandonment when required (Devine 2004). In terms of mobilising economic capital, evidence shows that middle-class parents are willing to use their finance resources to ensure advantages for their children in the education system (Ball 2003). For example, while private education in the UK has not increased substantially, it is still mainly the upper middle classes who pay for their children to attend some of the best schools in the country. Evidence shows this is a major form of social reproduction for the middle class. Not only does it lead to access to the best universities and job opportunities, but it also schools young people in middle-class values while also giving them social networks that will benefit them in the future. They are not afraid to pay for advantage if it is necessary. Not everyone within the middle classes can afford or wishes to take this route, but many are keen to buy access to the best state schools by moving house into the catchment areas of schools that have the best success rates (Ball 2003; Devine 2004).

When it comes to social and cultural capital, the middle class can mobilise this in a range of ways. For example, parents will ensure that their children engage with the 'right sort of people'. This will involve buying them into leisure pursuits that take place in and around the school, as well as filling their non-school days with productive forms of leisure (Ball 2003). Parents will draw upon their own 'social networks', both at work and around the school, to identify 'best schools' and to find access routes into them (Ball 2003; Devine 2004). It is also the case that underpinning middle-class discourses is a common sense that 'middle class children are bright, clever, and possess potential. It is a common implicit assumption articulated by parents, teachers and children themselves' (Gillies 2005: 844). As a result, middle-class parents are able to invoke a claim to 'the right to be bright' (Gillies 2005) and to receive the best attention within the school. Within this discourse parents are able to negotiate at school level with head teachers, and classroom teachers, over how their children are defined, for example, as 'a problem' or as 'having problems', and ensuring that they get the extra resources needed to increase opportunities (Walkerdine *et al.* 2001).

The working class and education

Much of the research in the area of social reproduction has concentrated on how the middle classes utilise their power and influence within education, showing how this increases their opportunities and possible futures. What is missing in this work is comparative analysis of how these processes operate for the construction of working-class identities and futures (Savage 2003). Work that has been done in this area provides important insights into how young people's attitudes and futures are reproduced, being influenced by the culture and practice of schools, the locality, and parents' experiences and understandings (Walkerdine *et al.* 2001). Drawing upon Bourdieu's notion of habitus, it can be argued that an individual's feelings and responses are in relation to their context. For Bourdieu (1990), the normalisation of behaviour and attitudes, especially towards education and young people's social futures, is greatly influenced by the imposition of cultural norms and values through what he calls 'pedagogic action'. These tend to be identifiable through institutionalised education, family education, and membership of the wider community. Experiences within these three contexts are massively influential in shaping young people's attitudes to education and their career choices (Bourdieu 1990). For example, young people living in areas of high deprivation are influenced in their attitudes to education by the quality of education they receive (MacDonald and Marsh 2004). Schools can be critical in not only offering them limited choices but also 'cooling out' their aspirations (Connolly and Neill 2001). Pupil culture within schools can also be important especially in how that success is perceived and valued by young people. Evidence suggests that the notion of 'being a swot' is still a major risk for lots of working-class young people (MacDonald and Marsh 2004) impacting on how young men, in particular, engage with education.

Localised factors are also influential in reproducing social inequalities amongst young people (Reay 2000; Jeffery and McDowell 2004). Preconceived perceptions of local labour markets, and the types of opportunities available, shape how young people understand locally what is possible within their futures. The global restructuring and collapse of both the youth labour market and regional employment opportunities is a strong indicator to young people about what they can achieve. In depressed and declining communities this reinforces the notion that education is not what gets you a 'good job' (MacDonald and Marsh 2004). As a result attitudes to school and the willingness to engage with the academic curriculum, especially for those on the margins, are seen as 'irrelevant' to the 'real world' futures they face:

> possession of educational qualifications appeared to play an, at best, minor role, by this point in their lives, in the shaping of overall transitions for these young people. This is best explained by reference to the peculiarities of this local labour market and the cultural knowledge, tastes, and aspirations of this group.
>
> (MacDonald and Marsh 2004: 159)

Perceptions of locality can also operate to limit young people's willingness to move into other educational opportunities. For example, evidence from Northern Ireland showed that young people's perspectives on other communities as 'dangerous places' restricted their willingness to take educational opportunities outside their own community (Connolly and Neill 2001). Others have shown how strong localised social networks can actually have potential for negative outcomes. Some can offer transitions into local criminal or drug networks, while others reinforce an insular perspective on the importance of not leaving a particular geographical area (MacDonald and Marsh 2004).

Parental experiences and attitudes to education can also be critical factors in shaping both the experiences young people have of the education system and the values they put on it for their future (Walkerdine *et al.* 2001; Gillies 2005). As we have seen above, working-class parents are often 'blamed' for their children's lack of engagement with education, yet in reality many working-class parents feel undervalued and unable to draw upon appropriate economic, social and cultural capital to enhance their children's futures. Education, built upon the notion of 'personal responsibility', advantages the middle-class at the expense of the working-class parents. Many have found schools are quick to construct the problem as one of lack of 'good parenting' (Gillies 2005). They also find themselves in conflict with middle-class teachers and schools that are unresponsive to their questions or are unwilling to recognise the economic and social context of parenting (Walkerdine *et al.* 2001; Gillies 2005). Others find themselves being patronised and embarrassed by teachers who see questioning by working-class parents as a threat to their authority and power (Gillies 2005). Working-class parents also tend to have negative histories about their own schooling experiences and they lack the time, due to material deprivation, to actively engage with schools. As a result, working-class parents tend to have a more 'bounded' view of what they want their children to achieve at school. For example, they give greater significance to children being able to 'stay out of trouble, get on with others, and work hard' (Gillies 2005: 845), rejecting the importance of their children being 'different' and 'special' or even 'bright'. They also tend to emphasise the importance of their child being happy at school rather than being a high achiever (Walkerdine *et al.* 2001).

Gender and education

So far our discussion has focused on class inequality, yet education research also has much to say about the relationship between education and gender inequalities. Much of this work has been dominated by the growth of masculinity studies. At one level this has seen girls' voices marginalised (Skelton 1998). Studies in the 1990s (Mac an Ghaill 1994, 1996) and early 2000s (Frosh *et al.* 2002) highlighted how schooling had an important role to play in shaping young men's masculine identities. Masculinity studies were able to show how 'being a boy' at school was a negotiated process that was greatly influenced by essentialist models of heterosexuality and the dominant 'hegemonic masculinity' (Mac an Ghaill 1996). Boys had to negotiate and construct themselves either in line with these dominant discourses and positions or in opposition to them (Mac an Ghaill 1996). Being masculine and heterosexual requires young men to distance themselves from women, femininity and gay males, because they have to maintain the superiority of heterosexuality to continue the process of control and domination (Frosh *et al.* 2002).

Boys and 'underachievement'

The issue of boys has remained a centre of attention not only to academics but also policy-makers. Political anxieties and media panics have concentrated on the 'problems of boys' underachievement' (Arnot and Miles 2005). In the late 1990s and early 2000s there was concern about national figures, which indicated that girls were outperforming boys in schools. What we saw was a public outcry by ministers and newspapers claiming concern about 'Britain's lost boys' (Griffin 2000). The 'problem' of boys' underachievement was conceptualised and explained in discourse on education in one of four ways:

- 'Masculinity was in crisis' as a result of deindustrialisation. Boys were aware that their future employment would not be in the male-dominated industries of their fathers. Work was being feminised and their futures were uncertain (Lucey and Walkerdine 1999).
- Boys are victims in the education system. Men have lost control of education, there are more female teachers, and the curriculum has

been feminised, creating problems for young men in relating to education (Lydon 1996)

- Boys are being failed by failing schools. Linked to the school effectiveness debate, it is argued that managerialism shifts power away from professionals, which suppresses anti-sexist work (Davies 2003).
- 'Boys will be boys', in that it is in their nature. Their masculinity incorporates a rejection of schoolwork as being normal for boys. This essentialist position locates the problem in natural differences between the sexes.

Critiques of these four positions have been robust and thorough. For example, it has been shown that the claims about 'underachieving boys' have to be read with caution (Epstein *et al.* 1998; Griffin 2000; Archer 2003; Arnot and Miles 2005). At one level there is a historical continuity in that boys have always underachieved in certain areas compared to girls, but also national figures hide differences between social groups (Epstein *et al.* 1998). Common discourse has constructed the problem as one of *all* boys, but in reality it is working-class boys who tend to be underachievers (Epstein *et al.* 1998). For example, middle-class boys have always had higher levels of achievement than both working-class boys and girls, and, therefore, the problem may not be about 'masculinity in crisis' but more about increased forms of class inequality (Epstein *et al.* 1998). Racial differences are also significant and usually under-reported. For example, Bangladeshi, Pakistani and African-Caribbean boys have low rates of attainment and high rates of exclusion (Archer 2003).

Policies of 'marketisation', 'managerialism' and 'privatisation' were seen as possibly leading to greater social injustice (Gewirtz 1998). The explanation for any difference between social groups of boys' needs to recognise the social context and material conditions of how these inequalities are maintained. For example, working-class boys are pathologised and seen as 'the problem', giving no weight to material conditions or cultural context. Neither is any recognition given to practices that see African-Caribbean boys being eight times more likely to be excluded from school. New Labour turned to the more essentialist explanations, drawing on strong nature and biological explanations:

> The Labour Government fell into the binary trap – a form of categoricalism that relied heavily upon theories of sex-role socialisation. From this zero-sum perspective, girls' successes were interpreted as boys' failures and vice versa. The social-psychological implications of such a policy approach were considerable.
>
> (Arnot and Miles 2005: 178)

Part of the solution, for New Labour, has been the remasculinisation of education (Lingard 2003; Arnot and Miles 2005). Recent policy and practice changes within education have seen a reinforcement of masculine values and beliefs (Raphael Reed 1999). The language of the new managerialism, of technical solutions to complex social problems, and of the importance of performance, draws upon masculine language and understandings of the problem (Lingard 2003). Issues of equal opportunities in training and policy documents have been given little attention, leading to assumptions that gender inequality has been addressed (Arnot and Miles 2005). It is also well recognised that working-class girls fail on a number of critical fronts (Plummer 2000) yet, within the discourse of education, this issue remains of low importance, with boys' underachievement seen as the major problem.

Research has shown us how some of these processes work for girls. For example, we have seen in this and the previous chapter that girls from different classes have different experiences and opportunities within the education system as a result of different levels of social and cultural capital (Walkerdine *et al.* 2001), yet policy continues to see the problem as boys. How girls are dealt with within the education system as 'social problems' has also been greatly impacted upon by perceptions of gender differences. Girls tend to be seen as less of a problem in school exclusions (SEU 1998b). Evidence suggests that this ignores the way that girls' problems are misunderstood and unrecognised by both professionals and policy-makers. Young women tend to self-exclude through activities such as truancy, and skipping lessons through the day, when faced with personal problems and difficulties, rather than expressing their problems in other ways. Boys who are aggressive and loud tend to be seen as 'the problem' and in need of discipline and, therefore, receive more resources and intervention (Osler and Vincent 2003). Girls' needs remain unmet within both policy and practice, leaving them isolated and without help and support in the education system. When they are having problems they devise a range of personal strategies to manage school, but when these fail they exclude themselves (Osler and Vincent 2003).

Race and education

The relationship between education policy, practice and race-related issues has historically been one of tension and problems. In the 1960s and early 1970s the problem was constructed as a lack of assimilation to the British way of life and the refusal of ethnic groups to 'give up' their culture (Rattansi 1992). By the 1980s and early 1990s, the focus was on 'multiculturalism', arguing for the celebration of difference and recognising the contribution ethnic minority culture could bring to British society (Department of Education and Science 1985). Both approaches have been criticised for the limited understanding of the problem, and the potential to blame ethnic groups for their situation or to stereotype them in particularly unhelpful ways (Archer 2003).

In the late 1990s, government policy towards race-related issues in education was silent (Archer 2003). Although New Labour constructed a range of initiatives that aimed to tackle the problems of ethnic minorities within education, little real change has been achieved (Tomlinson 2005b). It would seem that recent policies, rather than tackling the problem, continue constructing the problems in stereotypical ways, and increase inequality. Policies of 'choice' and selection, for example, disadvantage ethnic groups. The battle for access into desirable schools by the middle class is an attempt to move away from schools with high numbers of ethnic minority pupils (Tomlinson 2005b). Evidence has shown that, despite high aspirations amongst black and Asian parents, they are also less likely to get their children into successful and desirable schools (Noden *et al.* 1998). New Labour policy is underpinned by, and normalises, white middle-class values in terms of schooling (Gewirtz 2000), leaving the 'race issue' to be subsumed under the policy of 'tackling social exclusion' (Archer 2003). But this approach reinforces race as a problem of assimilation and a matter of 'inclusion', ignoring reasons why exclusion may happen.

A body of work exists that shows how, at the level of the school, the understanding of the problem is constructed around misrepresentations and misunderstandings of black and Asian culture and experiences of inequality. Teachers, for example, are seen to construct young black masculinity around the body and natural attributes. They are seen as 'naturally' drawn to 'bad' behaviour or involvement in crime while their 'positive' contributions are seen as being good at sport or making music (Sewell 1998a). This is not a simple process of teachers being racist, but a complex interplay between external stereotypes embedded within the institutions of education and wider society, alongside the preconceived ideas of teachers (Sewell 1998a). These preconceived and typically 'essentialist models' of behaviour help frame how African-Caribbean young people are managed, regulated and treated within the education system, leading to negative experiences, exclusion and underachievement (Sewell 1998b).

Others have explored how these processes operate for Asian young people, showing how preconceived perspectives dominate both policy and practice, and how they fail to understand the complexity of the processes that shape the lives of Asian young people (Archer 2003; Shain 2003). Traditional models and perceptions of Asian life construct it as fixed, static and individualistic. It tends not to recognise diversity or differentiations related to concepts such as heritage, religion and language (Archer 2003). Within this modelling, Asian culture is presented as being both positive and negative. For example, it was seen as encouraging strong commitments to education yet it was also seen as oppressive and restricting, especially for girls (Alexander 2000). The discourse around Asian culture also constructs a range of negative pictures of how it understands the problems. Girls are seen as being troubled because of the conflict between their tradition and Western experience (Archer 2003). Similarly, Pakistani and Bangladeshi families are seen as 'inward-looking' and unwilling to participate in mainstream society, forcing young women to conform to cultural practices that are oppressive (Shain 2003). Asian youth had, until recently, been normally portrayed as passive and 'model' students in school (Connolly 1998), being seen as high achievers as a result of parental interest in education. More recently, after the London bombings of 7 July 2005 and the rise of Islamophobia, Muslim youth is being portrayed as the new 'folk devil', being a threat to social order, and being more problematic and difficult to manage in schools. Recognition of differentiation, where Muslim young people are less engaged in education, is 'blamed' on religious fundamentalism and the strong anti-Western values of the Muslim religion (Archer 2003).

Conclusion

Those driving British education policy have argued that, in the modern age, the UK needs a highly skilled and knowledgeable workforce. To achieve this, it is claimed that the education system needs modernising and policy needs to ensure that it is inclusive for all. Yet, as we have seen, policy not only creates exclusion and limits opportunities for many, but also constructs the 'problem' in particular ways that are built upon essentialist understandings of youth, gender and ethnicity. Policy sees the poor, those with special educational needs, the excluded, truants, and different ethnic groups as not engaged in mainstream education due to the influence of pathology, personal difficulties, and a lack of social responsibility and obligation. As a result, many of the policies not only locate the problem in individuals, but also create practices that punish and penalise those defined as 'the problem'.

Policy within education has run counter to much high-quality evidence from a wide range of sources within the social sciences. As we have seen, strong evidence exists that shows that class inequality still exists within the system, and that policies can and do operate to advantage the middle classes while disadvantaging the poor. Place and location are important in helping to reproduce class inequalities in a range of ways, yet little has been done to address the cause of such disadvantage. Similar problems have emerged in relation to gender and race inequalities: strong evidence shows that the problems of 'boys' underachievement' and race inequality are far more complex than envisaged by policy and, in fact, strong evidence exists to show that the lack of understanding leads to increased forms of exclusion, and the remasculising of schools. In this context, the youth question in education, constructed by governments, fails to engage with important critical learning that has emerged from educational research.

6 Threatening youth and risky futures

Introduction

In this chapter we turn our attention to the 'youth crime problem'. In late modernity this has remained a central concern and focus of adult anxieties. The historical durability and fascination, by defining institutions and agencies, of seeing youth crime as a singular but central major problem for society, still remains dominant (Pearson 1994). While anxieties over youth crime have a long history, responses in the present day are usually discussed ahistorically or with 'historical amnesia' (Newburn 2002). But it is these responses and reactions to the 'problem' that are greatly influential in shaping how the youth question is constructed and understood in late modernity. In the first part of this chapter we will explore the political responses to youth crime since the early 1990s, highlighting how policy towards youth justice, and the management of youth in public activities, has unfolded. In the second part of the chapter we shall turn our attention to social science research, exploring how this has understood the youth question and what it has added to our knowledge of young people's encounters with crime.

Youth justice policy in late modernity

In the late 1980s and early 1990s, major changes took place in youth justice. Growing concerns over urban disturbances, and the awareness of 'persistent offenders', led to a campaign by the Conservative Party to be 'tough on crime' in its policy-making (Muncie 2004). The growing anxiety over youth crime was then fuelled by the highly publicised events of 1992 surrounding the abduction and murder of James Bulger, aged 2. His abduction by two older boys was captured on film, which had a significant impact on public perceptions of youth, providing a 'focusing event' (Birkland 1997), and constructing a 'collective agony' (Young 1996) over the state of 'our' youth. The response by the Conservative government was to reintroduce the notion of punishment and prison as a central feature of youth justice. The 1994 Criminal Justice and Public Order Act doubled the maximum sentence available in a young offender institution while also introducing a new secure training order for 12–14-year-olds. To accommodate the expected new inmates the government commissioned five new secure units. The Act also limited the use of cautions, and increased powers to punish parents of young offenders who refused to do their community service. Punishment was to be the main drive to youth justice (Newburn 2002).

The arrival of New Labour saw the emergence of a new form of youth justice (Goldson 2000). Policy became detached from traditional core principles, and priority was given to management and performance (Muncie 2005). In this context youth justice becomes a series of systems that need managing. The introduction of performance targets, risk assessments, and the standardisation of practice, alongside the growth of research-based evaluations and evidence-led policy, created a focus on how the system operates rather than on 'due process'. The emergence of this new form of youth justice is linked to wider political ideologies in which welfarism has been discredited and is being replaced by approaches greatly influenced by neo-liberal politics (Muncie 2005). This emphasis within youth justice is then reflected in more individual explanations of the crime problems:

> The fundamental change in criminal and juvenile justice has been broadly characterised as placing less emphasis on the social contexts of crime and measures of state protection and more on prescriptions of individual/family and community responsibility and accountability.
>
> (Muncie 2005: 37)

Youth justice policy has been reshaped by a number of principles that reflect this neo-liberalist approach. Welfarism has been given limited consideration within the system. Justice has become more important, ensuring that 'deeds rather than needs' are addressed (Muncie 2005). This 'back to justice' campaign has led to what Muncie calls the 'adulteration' of youth justice policy, in which young people are treated as responsible for their crimes and treated more like adult offenders. In the UK this has seen the abolition by the Crime and Disorder Act of the principle of *doli incapax*. This had traditionally protected a proportion of children under the age of 14 from the worst excesses of the law, recognising that under-14s were incapable of criminal intent. The United Nations was critical of this decision, arguing that New Labour was going against the UN Convention on the Rights of the Child. In 2002 they advised the government that it was breaking the Convention by not raising the age of criminal responsibility. New Labour stubbornly refused, arguing that its actions were not in conflict with the Convention. Children, it was suggested, needed to be made more responsible for their own actions, and that preventing offending would promote the welfare interests of the child. As a result children aged 10 and under became a focus of the newly emerging crime policy (James and James 2004). For example, legislation now allows local authorities to set up and enforce curfews for children and young people under the age of 16 in those areas where it is seen they are 'out of control'. This bans all unsupervised children being in specified areas between 9 p.m. and 6 a.m. Interest in under-10s also emerges in new policies focusing on crime prevention. These aim to target children who are most 'at risk' of being future offenders (Hine 2005; France *et al.* 2004).

The issue of crime prevention is a growing area of policy development under New Labour and a site where 'welfare' is to be practised. Historically, social crime prevention has been marginalised, but under New Labour we see the emergence of new forms of prevention, especially the 'risk and protective paradigm', which is aimed at intervening early in the lives of the young (France and Utting 2005). This approach sees a relationship among risk factors such as hyperactivity, the lack of self-control, poor parental supervision, low achievement in schools, community disorganisation, and future criminal behaviour (Farrington 1996). Such a theory does recognise the wider social and economic context to behaviour, yet its main emphasis is on the failings of individuals, their families and communities (France and Homel 2006).

New Labour has also introduced policies that aim to 'responsibilise' others in the process of crime control and management. For example, the Crime and Disorder Act 1998 installed a legal requirement on local authorities to develop a crime reduction strategy that would include a wide range of professional groups and agencies. The core message was that crime, and its reduction and prevention, is a responsibility of us all (Crawford 1998). Policy has also aimed to responsibilise parents and the offender in dealing with youth crime. This approach is influenced by the ideas of communitarianism, where communities, families and individuals are seen as being more responsible for their own problems and solutions (James and James 2001). For example, new penalties, such as restorative justice, have been developed that aim to make offenders feel more responsible for their own actions (Newburn 2002).

Under New Labour the use of penal sentences and punishment for the young has also been expanded. Its policy developments since 1997 have focused on 'toughening up' the custodial system for young people so that, while in prison, they encounter programmes that challenge their behaviour and install discipline and punishment as core to the experience. There has also been a range of policies that increase control and surveillance of the young in their own communities, such as the expansion of electronic tagging for 10–15-year-olds, an increase in the legal powers of courts to name and shame juveniles, and the introduction of final warnings to replace cautions, limiting the powers of social workers and the police to divert youngsters out of the system.

But what has been worrying in New Labour's policy approach to youth justice is their continued commitment to and, in fact, extension of the use of custody for young offenders. They have, for example, remained committed to the expansion and growth of 'boot camp' type institutions for young offenders. While they are less military-based, and focus more on education, discipline and training, they are still high-intensity forms of punishment. However, previous evidence (Thornton *et al.* 1984) showed they were unsuccessful in challenging and stopping offending. New Labour has also continued the previous government's programme of building new prisons for juveniles. They have expanded juvenile secure units, while also giving courts new powers to lock up children under the age of 15. Since 1997 the government has built five of these across the UK, holding up to 200 places. The minimum sentence at these units is 6 months, with a maximum of 2 years. There has also been an increase in the powers of the court towards creating detention and training orders for 12–17-year-olds. Such developments go against the United Nations Convention on the Rights of the Child, which states that custody for children and young people should be a last resort and used for the shortest possible time.

Youth policy and policing of space

Young people also encounter crime policy in other aspects of their lives. Anxiety about their usage of public space has always been at the heart of much youth policy-making (Pearson 1994). The young, while 'hanging about in public places', are perceived as unproductive, potentially threatening and unruly, and at risk of getting up to no good. Explanations for this consistently rely upon 'common-sense' perceptions of youth as a period of natural 'dangerousness' and 'vulnerability', where impulsiveness, immaturity and the lack of regulation can lead them into future criminal behaviour (DfES 2005).

Such perceptions dominate not only public discourses of youth but also many of those agencies responsible for policing and maintaining public order. It has been well documented that policing is greatly influenced by the 'police culture' (Holdaway 1983), which constructs the world into 'us and them'. In this context the police believe it is their role to ensure society is protected from the undesirables. At the heart of this are views of 'respectables' and 'roughs' (Shearing 1981). Respectables are usually the white middle classes, who are upholders and supporters of the police and law and order, and are those who the police 'do things for'. Roughs are usually the excluded and social disadvantaged and the ones who they 'do things to', being 'police property' (Shearing 1981). Loader (1996) suggests that the popular discourses of 'youth as trouble', as a problem and as roughs, put them into the frame for being defined as 'property', which consequently structures the way they are policed.

Yet the streets and public spaces are important to the young. They may be the only spaces they can use outside the family home and school. Limited free youth provision, cost of leisure activities, and age restrictions leave them with limited choice but to use the streets in local neighbourhoods. As a result, they are publicly visible, and seen by many as a threat to personal safety (Loader 1996). Adults consistently want their own worlds made safe, and the 'tidying away' of the young off the streets is one such strategy that appeals (Brown 2005).

Youth contact with the police has, therefore, never been very positive. It has been well documented that the young get more attention than any other group in public spaces, and most of this is negative (Smith and Gray 1983; Anderson *et al.* 1994). Black youth also receive far more attention than warranted, in that they are more likely to be stopped and searched for drugs or on the assumption that they are involved in illegal activities (Bowling and Phillips 2002). More recently, as a result of the introduction of new immigration policies around asylum seekers, anti-terrorism legislation, and anxiety about the 'Asian gang', there has been a considerable increase in the levels of 'stop and search' for a wide range of Asian groups (Alexander 2004).

But public space is not neutral or without its relationships of power (Malone 1999). Recent changes in public space, and its redefinition towards privatised space, are also creating greater tensions between the young and the police (Loader 1996). For example, with the growth of out-of-town shopping malls, private housing estates, and the selling-off of public land, young people are consistently seen as 'the problems' to be removed (McCahill 2002). As Malone (1999) suggests, this is related to a range of changes taking place in the reconstruction of public space, where young people are 'designed out' of certain spaces, which can then have serious consequences for their feelings of inclusion.

As a result we start to see spaces being closed down for the young. It is not just 'unruly' groups of young people who are seen as problematic but young people *per se*, as they are seen to threaten normal family space (Sibley 1995). Public spaces are being replaced with 'pseudo-public spaces' such as shopping malls, where commercial imperatives rule who is watched and who is excluded (Reeve 1996). Similar trends are now taking place within town centres, where space remains 'public' yet under greater surveillance (McCahill 2002).

The policing of the young, in public and private spaces, has taken new turns in late modernity. Throughout the 1990s there was a sustained moral panic over what has been labelled 'yob culture'. As a way of tackling this, New Labour's youth policy has aimed at targeting 'anti-social behaviour'. This concept has its roots in American research (Millie *et al.* 2005), being associated with the work of Wilson and Kelling (1982) and their thesis on 'broken windows'. Low-level incidents of disorder or incivility are seen to damage public confidence in community life, leading to increased fear of crime and a withdrawal by 'community guardians' from community life. Over a longer time period this can lead to opening up public spaces in which criminals, drug dealers and other 'undesirables' can take control (Skogan and Hartnett 1997). But such claims are contested. Not only is there a problem with the claim that anti-social behaviour has increased, as evidence is unreliable, but also the causes of anti-social behaviour cannot simply be 'read off' as the 'breakdown' of community' (Millie *et al.* 2005). Wider structural factors have to be recognised in any explanation surrounding anti-social behaviour. For example, evidence shows that levels of anti-social behaviour tend to be the highest on disadvantaged council estates and other low-income areas (Thorpe and Wood 2004).

Concern over anti-social behaviour has led to new legislation. In 2003 the Criminal Justice Act provides the legal framework for local authorities to implement programmes that tackle anti-social behaviour. The police and local authorities have the powers to arrest a wide range of people who might be acting 'anti-socially'. The police may disperse intimidating gangs of youths and take home unaccompanied young children who are out late at night. The Act also provides the legislative framework for the emergence of community police, who have 'special powers' that help them deal with localised incivilities in neighbourhoods (Crawford 2002). But New Labour has gone further by developing what is called the anti-social behaviour order (ASBO). This was created under the Crime and Disorder Act 1998 but has only recently become used more by the courts as a mechanism of tackling local problems of anti-social behaviour.[1] The ASBO is seen as blurring the boundaries between civil and criminal law, inasmuch as local people and professionals can have a major role in their usage. The local authority or police can give an ASBO to anyone over the age of 10 who is thought to be causing alarm, distress and harassment. It lasts for a minimum of 2 years but can be imposed for longer periods of time. Breach of the ASBO can lead to up to 5 years' imprisonment. The standard of proof required for giving a person an ASBO is less than in a criminal action (Blake 2002), therefore giving substantial powers to professionals working in the police, housing and other local authority agencies. It has been suggested the ASBO has given new powers to 'social landlords' to label and criminalise groups and individuals who are perceived as problems, thereby increasing the intrusion of the state into the lives of the poor and deprived (Brown 2004). ASBOs are not concerned with causes of crime but with individual behaviour. In this, they have real potential for net widening, as they are not based on criminal evidence, but rely heavily on hearsay and popular perceptions of 'the problem'. They tend also to represent the interests and voices of the powerful within community settings (Brown 2004). Evidence from recent research supports such claims, in that over 4000 ASBOs have been used by local authorities and, out of these, a third are breached and two-thirds result in jail sentences (Youth Justice Board 2005). This can increase the number of young people going to prison, although research shows that a large number of those who breach their ASBOs were already at risk of being imprisoned (Home Office 2005). While such legislation provides another quick route into prison for persistent offenders, it also opens up the possibility for an increase in the number of lower-end offenders being criminalised and propelled up the justice system (Muncie 2004).

New technologies have also been created that increase surveillance, and monitor the young in both public and private spaces. Closed-circuit television (CCTV) has a long history in the UK.[2] Government is using it as a tool against high crime in late modernity (McCahill 2002). But, as researchers have identified, such technology is not neutral or unproblematic, especially in terms of how certain groups are put under surveillance (Norris and Armstrong 1999). Operators of CCTV tend to target the young and, in particular, the young black male. This happens for no other reason than that the operators think they are potential criminals (Norris and Armstrong 1999). CCTV surveillance is also being increasingly used in privatised spaces, such as shopping malls and town centres (McCahill 2002). Such observation, while not guaranteeing criminalisation, does increase the risks of this taking place.

The politics of youth crime

The intervention into the lives of the young, who are seen to be offenders or have the potential to become future offenders, has therefore increased under recent governments. This is usually justified by claims of the growing 'youth crime wave' that is forever spiralling out of control. More recently it has been suggested that young people are not just becoming more criminal but more anti-social and problematic in their communities. Yet when we explore the evidence, problems emerge that suggest not only that we are *not* witnessing a 'youth crime wave' but, in fact, that we have been seeing a decline in youth crime since the mid-1990s. While evidence in this area is always problematic, official sources support this claim. For example, between the 1960s and 1970s juvenile crime increased markedly. In the 1970s it started to drop but then increased again, and by the 1980s it had reached previous levels. Between 1985 and 1993 we see a major decline, with figures dropping from 172,700 young men, aged between 10 and 17, being convicted or cautioned to 100,200 by 1993 (Newburn 2002). A similar conclusion was found in the Youth Lifestyles Survey. In this repeated self-report study of youth offending, the authors concluded that no significant differences existed between the findings of the 1993 and 2000 surveys (Flood-Page *et al.* 2000). Minor variations existed between ages but, in general, youth crime remained consistent over time.

Similar conclusions can be made over the claims over anti-social behaviour. The British Crime Survey suggested that the British public's anxieties over anti-social behaviour grew in the second half of the 1990s, but by 2003 concern was on the decline (Finney and Toofail 2004). Where problems did seem to exist was in high-deprived areas or 'hard-pressed communities' (Wood 2004). While it is important not to deny the problems this may cause for such communities, the evidence does suggest that anti-social behaviour remains a contentious and problematic mechanism of understanding youthful behaviour, and that uncertainty remains over how much it is a problem for large sections of the adult population. While it may well be a specific local problem to certain poor areas, it is by no means a problem for all. So if there is no youth crime wave and anti-social behaviour is of limited importance, why is it that youth remains a focus of adult anxieties?

Popular punitiveness' in youth policy

Youth crime has always been of great interest to politicians. It is mobilised on a regular basis as showing signs of 'social disintegration' and 'moral decline', acting as a major barometer of society's social ills (Pitts 2001). Politicians have also used it as a means of deflecting attention from other types of problems, such as economic decline, unemployment and questions of legitimacy (Hall *et al.* 1978). Since the early 1990s youth crime has also acted as the 'electoral glue' that provides political parties with opportunities to be 'tough on crime' and to be seen as the party of 'law and order' (Pitts 2001).

In this there is constant reference to tradition, making continual repeated connections with the need to install discipline, respect and understanding of what is right and wrong in our young people. The construction of young people as 'outsiders', as 'others' threatening the stability of our nation, is continually employed as a means of showing the need to be tough on crime (Brown 2005). But part of this durability of the 'youth crime problem' is that it would seem that, regardless of the effort or resources put into the problem, young people are immune to attempts to keep them away from criminality, thus justifying ever-greater intervention (Mizen 2004). In this context, government draws upon a form of 'populist punitiveness', as a strategy. It can use the 'youth and disorder card', claiming the need for more and more intervention. Youth crime policy in late modernity is, therefore, not only to do with tackling offending and reducing crime levels, but also about gaining political credibility with the electorate (Newburn 2002). Youth crime, therefore, has been repoliticised and young people are being demonised in the process (Goldson 2000).

Youth crime and the media

To understand the growing anxiety over youth crime, we also need to recognise the role of the media. This relationship as we saw in chapter 3 has been generally discussed through the notion of 'moral panics' (Hall *et al.* 1978; Cohen 1980; Pearson 1983). But questions over the reliability and usefulness of this concept have also dogged discussions about moral panics (McRobbie 1994; Jewkes 2004).

Since Cohen's (1980) work on *Folk Devils and Moral Panics*, and Pearson's (1983) hooligan study, the notion of moral panic has become mainstream not only in criminological discourses, but also in political and everyday usage. As a result, the notion of moral panic has become seen as a weak conceptual tool that lacks real depth of understanding (McRobbie 1994; Kidd-Hewitt and Osborne 1995). Part of the problem is that the concept itself has a number of significant weaknesses that have never been fully addressed. Questions over its limited definition of deviance, its lack of understanding of morality, its lack of attention to questions of source and purpose, and its limited understanding of audience responses remain fundamental problems (Jewkes 2004).

The media itself has also undergone major changes, which is reshaping how moral panics are constructed and understood (McRobbie 1994). In these 'new times' the speed and growth of the media, the fragmentation and expansion of interest groups who are sophisticated media users, suggest that there needs to be a greater appreciation of how these factors might impact upon moral panics. There is also a more diverse body of media opinion. It is no longer appropriate to speak of a 'right and left' dichotomy but a new and fragmented set of values in which a diverse set of concerns operates. While the Labour Party is becoming indistinguishable from the Conservatives, new pressures groups, which are highly sophisticated media users, have emerged to defend the marginalised (McRobbie 1994). So while concerns over morality have become more acute, single concerns come and go much more rapidly.

While the notion of moral panics has its weaknesses and limitations, we cannot underestimate the influence that the media has on shaping our everyday understandings of the youth question, particularly in relation to youth crime (Critcher 2003). Across the media, negative images of the young dominate both news stories and pictures (Muncie 2004). Crime is always newsworthy and a core value to reporting (Brown 2005), and youth crime in particular is given prime position in reporting (Neustatter 1998). This representation of young people's involvement in crime is now being presented more constantly as a growing problem to society (Muncie 2004). While youth crime is less of a problem, the media continue to provide a growing picture of it being on the increase and spiralling out of control. Such representations outweigh the evidence of reality. But it is more than this. In the rapid turnover of images, youth as a social category is becoming associated with a large-scale moral panic about the state of a generation. This image of youth, symbolised by anxieties over youth crime, is said to be a reflection of the state of the nation, an indicator of the fact that it is in moral decline:

> Dangerous youth is the cornerstone of a number of key concerns about a disorder present. Are the streets safe? Are schools too permissive? Are parents failing to exercise proper control? Is television a corrupting influence? Are the courts too soft on young offenders? And so on.
>
> (Muncie 2004: 9)

Young people are carrying, symbolically, the burden of the health of the nation and of its future (Cohen 1997). Across the majority of news stories, then, the message is clear: young people today 'lack morality and discipline' and are a 'danger to themselves and others'; being young in itself is 'dangerous'; and there are a growing number of young people who can be deemed as 'evil' and 'demons'. As a result, society needs protecting from such problems, which then gives justification for greater forms of control and surveillance (Jewkes 2004). The classic representation of the 'evil' child or young person is reflected in the case of the murder of James Bulger (Scraton 2002). This led almost immediately to a growing consensus and moral outrage – a growing belief that the young were out of control and needed more control and regulation (Jewkes 2004). Since then, the Bulger case has been consistently referred to by the media as symbolising an example of moral decline of our youth and as justification for increased intervention, regulation and control (Scraton 2002).

Social science and the youth crime question

In late modernity youth crime research has been dominated by administrative criminology. Much of this work is focused on either the measurement of youth crime or on the application and administration of youth justice (Tierney 1996). Funding for criminological research has always been a major influence in defining the discipline of criminology. By the early 2000s government became obsessed with assessing its own impact on youth justice policy and its (cost-)effectiveness (Pitts 2001). As a result, criminology was brought into the frame to contribute to the growth of this knowledge base, with much of the work focused on large-scale programme evaluations and policy assessments (Downes and Rock 2003).

The delinquent or 'criminal career'

Alongside the growth of policy evaluation we have also seen the emerging influence and dominance of 'criminal careers' research. Longitudinal studies are seen to be able to provide insights that 'cross-sectional' research cannot (Farrington 1994). One such famous work is West and Farrington's (1977) Cambridge study. This has followed 440 boys from the East End of London for over 50 years, collecting data at different intervals. A criminal career approach is defined as being a course or progress of an individual emphasised by offences rather than purpose: 'A 'criminal career' describes a sequence of offences committed during some part of an individual's lifetime, with no necessary suggestion that offenders use their criminal activity as an important means of earning a living' (Farrington 1994: 515). The Cambridge study aims to understand the causes of offending and its relationship to developmental process of careers, exploring issues of onset, persistence, escalation and, of course, desistence. At its heart is a concern with the linkage between human developments and offending. Longitudinal work is claimed to be able to capture the influences and process of a person's criminal history over time (Farrington 1994). It also creates the opportunity to explore the relationship between age and offending, highlighting variations that can exist between different ages (Smith 2003).

This approach has also been called a 'life history perspective' (Rutter *et al.* 1998). It has a strong emphasis on trying to understand the underlying origins and causes of criminal behaviour, suggesting that early onset of anti-social and problem behaviour in children as young as 2 or 3 can give rise to the offenders of the future (Rutter *et al.* 1998). This approach is underpinned by evidence that points to a range of overlapping risk factors for adolescent problems that include offending, drug misuse, school-age parenthood, poor mental health and failure in school (Farrington 1996; Anderson *et al.* 2001; Bynner 2001). Although they are statistical 'predictors', these risk factors do not *predict* future behaviour in the commonly recognised sense. However, it is suggested that where risk factors cluster together in children's lives, the chances of later problems and problem behaviour increase disproportionately (Rutter 1980; Farrington 2000). Risk factors can arise as a result of problems in the community, in schools, in individuals (such as hyperactivity and impulsiveness), through involvement with negative peer groups, and through family problems.

The limitations of 'criminal career' research

Criminal career research has a number of limitations. It starts from a premise that criminal behaviour is linked, in one way or another, to biological or psychological dysfunctioning (Bessant *et al.* 2002). The problem is seen as an individual problem of maladjustment and is, in some way, a failing of the individual to adapt to modern society. Across the breadth of the research, individualistic models of behaviour are dominant. Even though ecology and peer influences are recognised, the core focus is on personality or biological disorders. For example, Moffitt (1993), in trying to explain the differences between 'life-course-persistent' and 'adolescent-limited' anti-social behaviour, draws not upon evidence but on her own assumptions about what influences behaviour for the adolescent:

> Just as the childhood onset of life-course-persistent persons compelled me to look for casual factors early in their lives, the coincidence of puberty with the rise in the prevalence of delinquent behavior compels me to look for clues in adolescent development.
> (Moffitt 1993: 686)

Her starting point assumes that the explanation of adolescent offending must be located in the rise of puberty. Such a position fails to recognise the lack of evidence and uncertainty over the linkage between puberty and behaviour (Springhall 1986).

A second issue is that criminal career research has its roots in neo-positivism (Tierney 1996), where it is claimed that there are 'offenders' and 'non-offenders' and where levels of delinquency or 'careers in delinquency' can be measured by adding up, over time, the number of offences a person commits. Crime is, in the Durkheim sense, a social fact that can be measured. For example, in their work on community risk factors, Wikström and Sampson (2003: 122–3) argue that, in explaining criminal behaviour, 'we do not necessarily need to be concerned with questions of why an act is considered a crime' or 'whether it is morally right or wrong that the particular act is criminalised'; however, as Armstrong (2004: 107) argues, these issues are in fact very important:

> the reasons why particular acts are criminalised or not are themselves part of the social context that not only frames individual choices but is part of the process by which the social world is individually and collectively negotiated and contested.

A major limitation, then, to criminal career research has been its lack of attention to issues of social context (France and Homel 2006). There is little recognition of the complexity of how social life is shaped by external forces (Goodnow 2006). In criminal career research, wider social and economic structures tend to be relegated to the background (Armstrong 2004), leaving explanations to emphasise the individual characteristics of the offender. For example, Farrington (2002) and Wikström and Sampson (2003) fail to incorporate into their analysis the influence of the youth justice system and its potential criminalising process (France and Homel 2006). History shows us that youth crime and criminal careers can arise as a result of complex interactions between young people, the criminal justice system and professionals. This can result in pushing the young further into criminal careers (Becker 1963; Cohen 1985).

New directions in criminal career research

There has been a growing recognition that criminal career research has limited understanding of the social world and how the young engage with crime (France and Homel 2006; Goodnow 2006). More recently, writers such as Laub and Sampson (2005) in the United States and Williamson (2004) in the UK have undertaken retrospective analysis of young people's pathways, showing how these are fragmented, unpredictable and influenced by a wide range of external factors. Issues of social context have been recognised as important to understanding social action and criminal behaviour. In response to the failings of previous criminal pathways research, it has been proposed that a broader definition of pathways needs to be developed that recognises social processes and context as important influences (France and Homel 2006).

It is also the case that young people themselves have much to tell us about their understanding of crime (France and Homel 2006). Choices to be involved in crime are a complex process where the young themselves are active but are also influenced by a range of external factors (France and Homel 2006). For example, crime for young people in many deprived communities is a 'normal' part of everyday life (Armstrong *et al.* 2006). Being 'witnesses', 'victims' or 'perpetrators' is normal and not something they see as unusual. Crime is important in that it impacts on their lives in ways that are negative, yet it is just something that they see as a part of the everyday. Young people's levels of social, economic and symbolic capital help them manage crime in their lives (Armstrong *et al.* 2006). 'Routine', 'tradition' and history shape 'the way things are done', influencing their decisions to be involved in crime or not. Criminal activity can also have a positive role to play in their lives, offering either a form of 'social inclusion' or providing pleasure in a world devoid of excitement (Armstrong *et al.* 2006). The notion of pathways 'into and out of' crime is, therefore, problematic as it indicates a structured linear trajectory. In reality young people move in and out of crime (and back again), and in many cases actively seek routes out of offending (Armstrong *et al.* 2006).

The criminalising process in late modernity

In the 1990s, labelling theory was criticised for its failure to recognise the important contribution those labelled had to make to our understanding of the criminalising process (Tierney 1996; Downes and Rock 2003). Since this acknowledgement, there has been limited work on how the labelling processes work and what the young themselves have to say about them. While there has been a growth of research on youth perspectives of youth justice, few seem to have engaged with the question and process of criminalisation.

Young people's assessments of youth justice tend to be atheoritical. For example, Home Office-funded research on young people in prison showed how adults working within the criminal justice system had given them little respect or opportunities to influence their routes towards prison. No one listened to them or was willing to 'take their side'. Once in prison, young people felt scared, intimidated and dehumanised (Lyon *et al.* 2000). Similar issues came up in discussions with young black male prisoners (Wilson 2004). They have to play the 'game' as a strategy of managing prison life. Other examples exist (see Newburn and Shiner 2005; Squires and Stephen 2005; Gray 2005), and while they make a contribution to commenting on policy and practice, little analysis is made of the impact they may have on young people's identities and criminal careers.

One study that has explored these questions shows how certain groups of young people, who are defined as a 'social problem' in education and criminal justice, encounter institutional responses (Armstrong *et al.* 2006). The processes of criminalisation within these contexts are not always straightforward or inevitable. Young people's social identities are negotiated and they have strategies for exiting or resisting negative labels and possible criminal futures (Armstrong *et al.* 2006). For example, young women who encounter the care system show how labels around them construct the context of their behaviour, yet, while internalising these labels, they also resist them and create alternative strategies for the future. How far these are effective over time remains uncertain, but it highlights that the labelling process is not inevitable or unchallengeable (Armstrong *et al.* 2006).

The criminalisation of Asian masculinity

One area where processes of criminalisation have been explored is in relation to issues of race and social disorder. From the middle of the 1990s, a range of incidents of public disorder took place in cities and communities in northern England with high concentrations of Asian young men. Historically, Asian youth have been perceived as both homogeneous and passive (Goodey 2001), having their criminal or anti-social behaviour mediated by religion (Mawby and Batta 1980). Recent research suggests that these disturbances and outbreaks of disorder have challenged this image of 'passivity', suggesting that Asian young people (men in particular) are resisting or 'fighting back', being more willing to break the law to deal with their sense of injustice (Webster 1997; Alexander 2000; Goodey 2001). Asian masculinity is becoming associated with the criminal 'other', creating stereotypes of whole communities willing to break the law (Webster 1997). Part of this reconstruction of Asian identity is developed through perceptions of the Asian gang: 'The Asian gang has particular potency, fusing longer established fears of "the underclass" and the "fundamentalist / terrorist" with the physical presence of young men on the imaginary landscape of the city' (Alexander 2000: 229). But the Asian gang is a myth and is used symbolically as a 'folk devil' indicating that Muslim identities are a threat to mainstream Anglo-Saxon society. Research into localised disturbances in Sheffield and Bradford showed how Asian youth became criminalised in this process. Locally they were constructed as the 'other' and as a threat to stable order. While the local disorders involved only a small number of young men, they were used to define and demonise the Asian way of life (Goodey 2001).

Political and media explanations tend to see the 'problem' of Asian youth in a variety of ways. These range from a form of social and economic exclusion to 'cultural dysfunction' or processes of 'cultural differences'. Arguments that emphasise social and economic exclusion tend to construct the problem as one of a growing 'underclass', in which Asian young men are seen as self-segregating and lacking social and cultural capital to adapt to changing economic conditions (Alexander 2004). Cultural dysfunction is seen as an individualised failing, locating the 'crisis' not in the social and economic structures or institutional racism, but in the failings of the Asian community itself (Alexander 2004). 'Cultural differences' emphasise 'foreign cultures' and 'alien' ways of life and the failure of 'outsiders' to integrate (Alexander 2004). This focuses mainly on Muslim communities and reflects the growing Islamophobia in the media and mainstream society. All these explanations construct Asian masculinity as being seen as in 'crisis' and becoming a major problem in late modernity.

How young Asian men respond to these labels and discourses varies. Young Asian men are not passive receivers of such labels (Alexander 2000). Neither are they able (or even always willing) to challenge and resist the dominant discourses being constructed of them. These constructions of Asian youth are misconceptions of how they live (Alexander 2000). Much of life for them is mundane and ordinary, and a large part of their time is spent managing everyday life. Young Asian men are passionate about defending their community and, while many of their everyday activities cannot be simply read as forms of resistance, they are unwilling to be passive receivers of either tradition, culture, labels or a perceived future (Alexander 2000).

Gender and crime

Involvement in youth crime is predominantly a male activity (Newburn 2002). It is unsurprising, therefore, that youth researchers have become interested in the relationship between crime and the masculine identity (Messerschmidt 1997; Connell 2002; Laidler and Hunt 2001). As we saw in Chapters 2 and 3, criminology has always had a major interest in young men's engagement with crime and the emerging masculinity studies of post-structuralism have offered new ways into theorising this relationship. The relation between masculinity and crime offered a 'possibility of a critical illumination of troubling public issues' (Newburn and Stanko 1994: 1). It was seen as a new way of exploring gendered crime (Brown 2005). This became known as the 'masculinity turn' (Collier 1998). Similar to labour market studies, much of this theorising has focused on the claim that there is a 'crisis' in masculinity caused by a breakdown in traditional routes of 'being a man' (Messerschmidt 1994; Laidler and Hunt 2001). Campbell (1993), for example, in her journalistic study of riot-torn areas in the early 1990s, suggested that the problems were caused by unemployment and deindustrialisation. Traditional sites where men learnt to be men had collapsed. As a result, boys attempted to express or 'do' masculinity through crime (Campbell 1993). While there has been much theorising of this relationship and interest, little empirical research has followed. If masculinity studies are to have an impact in criminology and sociology, they need to undertake more detailed research on how these processes shape the lives of young men.

When it comes to the question of girls and crime, again little contemporary analysis has taken our understanding forward. As was outlined in chapter 3, girls' involvement in crime has traditionally been seen as 'doubly deviant', breaking the codes of femininity as well as the law. Yet evidence suggests that their involvement in crime is not about 'being male' but about constructing particular forms of femininities in different social contexts.

> Given that gang girls realize that their behaviour is accountable to other girls and boys in the gang, they construct their actions in relation to how those actions will be interpreted by others in the same social context. These girls are doing femininity in terms of activities appropriate to their sex category, and in specific social situations. Accordingly, violence by young women in youth gangs should not be interpreted as an attempt to be 'male' and 'pass' as the other gender.
>
> (Messerschmidt 1995: 183)

Similar to studies of masculinity, we cannot talk about just one form of femininity. For example, girl involvement in gangs is a way of girls constructing themselves as 'bad girls', creating a reputation and status that will act as a form of protection (Laidler and Hunt 2001). Alternatively, girls in this context also act out and draw upon other forms of femininity, concentrating on appearance and relationships as important to their social identities. Femininity can therefore be contradictory and greatly influenced by social setting and context (Laidler and Hunt 2001), being shaped by the constraints of a larger social structure and discourse on what it means to be a girl. Involvement in girl gangs in America shows how femininity is a fluid and negotiated identity that is influenced and shaped by the need to have a good reputation and have respect (Laidler and Hunt 2001). Having this is seen as essential to feminine identity in tough neighbourhoods. Crime becomes one route into getting a reputation and the respect needed, especially in the context of needing to protect themselves. 'Doing gender' and crime therefore is shaped very much by the local context of these girls' lives. Of course work on girls involved in gangs does not provide all the answers for us in explaining girl crime (Miller 2002), but it does give us some insights into how femininity is a negotiated term structured by broader social structural influences and how it is also shaped by how girls try to mange their lives on a day-to-day basis.

Conclusion

The youth question has always been associated with youth crime, but in late modernity its intensity and dominance seem to have expanded. If we are to believe the rhetoric of politicians and the media, we live in times where youth is increasingly more 'dangerous' and 'out of control'. Of course, what is ironic is that over the past decade, youth crime has been declining and, although some high-deprived areas still suffer from high levels of crime, the majority of us are unlikely to be touched by it in our daily lives. Youth crime is a political issue and one that constructs, alongside the media, youth as a major problem. It is also the case that in late modernity criminal behaviour of the young has been increasingly presented as individualised and driven by 'rational choices'. State policy has taken these conceptions and ideas and constructed policies that see punishment, surveillance and control as rational responses to the 'problem'. Alongside this we once again see the impact of a 'responsiblising' agenda, where parents and young people are blamed for the problem. A wide body of non-law-enforcement professionals are also encouraged to take more responsibility for tackling the problem at source, leading to the increased possibility of net widening.

Social science research has not been very effective in providing alternative understandings of youth crime. Neo-positivism, along with administrative criminology, through criminal career research, has dominated the theorizing and old explanations of youth crime. Its influence on policy has been enormous, shifting the focus away from exploring how and why the young might engage in crime or how the state might be criminalising the young. Criminal career research aims to measure pathways into and out of crime, looking at 'what works' in terms of desistence. It has a limited understanding of complexity, of social context and of structured action, leading us to believe that choice is rational and desistence is something that the right kind of intervention can stop. Alternative and new research areas have, in a limited sense, emerged. We see the extended interest in questions of social context, in the processes of criminalisation, especially of Asian youth, and the influence of gender. Yet, in reality, research in this area has been limited and not very progressive. Even work on masculinity and crime has become marginalised after much had been made of it in the late 1990s. Youth crime is still an area of research we know little about.

7 The marketisation and commodification of youth

Introduction

One of the major characteristics of late modernity is the growth of consumption and consumer culture. At its heart are the development and expansion of new commodities, new services and new ways of marketing and selling goods. Consumption infiltrates all aspects of the everyday, and has become a major influence on our lives. Such developments have significant consequences for the young. They are seen as driving this expansion, being major purchasers and creators of fashion, style, commodities and cultural practices. In recent times the young have become a significant target for the purchase of new technologies such as mobile phones, Internet access and gaming consoles. They are also a major target group for the expanding clothes industry, magazine producers and leisure providers. In the first part of this chapter we will explore the impact of consumption and its associated consumer culture on the youth question, highlighting how it has been understood and responded to by government and the market. We will then conclude with a discussion on how these processes might be influencing young people's identities.

Consumption in late modernity

Consumption in late modernity has become a major part of our everyday lives. It frames and influences our daily practices, shaping how we live (Paterson 2005). Its arrival is closely associated with the emergence of industrial capitalism. Consumption, as a significant aspect of everyday life, can be identified with the 'invention of new desires' (Humphery 1998: 25), which are important to the creation of industrial capitalism. It produces not only new material goods but also a 'consumer culture' (Featherstone 1992), which is closely associated with the availability of commodities, goods and services that are being produced. Consumer culture is also concerned with the media and its associated technologies and the meanings that are produced as a part of the process of selling products:

> Yet consumption is far from being just the consumption of utilities, which are addressed to fixed needs. Rather, consumer culture through advertising, the media and techniques of display of goods, is able to destabilise the original notion of use or meaning of goods and attach to them new images and signs which can summon up a whole range of associated feelings and desires.
>
> (Featherstone 1992: 114)

Consumption and consumer culture have continually changed over time (Kenway and Bullen 2003). From the early part of the nineteenth century until the middle of the twentieth century we see the growth and expansion of the 'mass market' aided by the development, within industrial capitalism, of new technologies and Fordist types of production. New goods and innovations are brought into individual lives and lifestyles. These include the car, new fashions and clothing, new forms of foods, and the growth of electrical white goods and inventions for the home. As innovation within capitalism becomes more sophisticated, it is able to mass-produce a wide range of goods and services to sell (Harvey 1989). We also see the development of new forms of media, such as newspapers and magazines, followed by radio and then television, all contributing to the advertising and marketing of new goods and services (Kenway and Bullen 2003).

By the middle of the twentieth century, major changes in production and consumption are taking place. There is a shift from industrial to 'post-industrial' society where new production practices are being introduced. Industrial capitalism embraces and constructs 'post-Fordist' forms of production (Harvey 1989). This involves a shift away from mass production to 'niche marketing' that emphasises choice and individualism in consumption. Production is decentralised and spreads across national borders where 'just-in-time' and 'flexible working' patterns help maintain new forms of production (Kumar 1995). A range of factors drives these changes:

- The processes of globalisation and the breakdown of traditional barriers to trade and production – for example, the collapse of the East–West conflict in the late 1980s, and the emergence of China and other Asian nations in the late twentieth century.
- New innovations in technologies and, in particular, new media hardware, such as video players and music stereos in the 1970s, followed by CD players, computers and MP3 players.
- The emergence and growing relevance of a service economy that both supports new forms of consumption and also creates them – for example, the growth of the shopping mall, the fast food restaurant, and theme parks. Services and leisure become a commodity and a central aspect of consumption.

- New media and information technologies creating new forms of marketing and media opportunities such as the Internet, cable television and mobile phones.

The emergence of the young consumer

The impact of these changes on the lives of young people cannot be underestimated. Consumption is a major force that socialises children and young people for future adulthood (Kline 1993) and 'invades' their everyday lives. We cannot, therefore, ignore its significance for how the youth question has been constructed. Youth as consumers have a long history (see Kenway and Bullen 2003). In the early stages of modernity children and the young were excluded from consumption (Kline 1993). It is not until the late nineteenth century that we see the growth of a specialised market for youth. Advertising did not 'talk' to them directly, talking to mothers and guardians instead (Kenway and Bullen 2003). It is at this time that we see the arrival of toys, specialised food and clothing that were distinctive to children and young people. This was the age of 'medicalisation', where infancy was seen as a medical problem that mothers needed to manage. Therefore we also see the growth of purifying goods such as soaps and self-help magazines giving health advice (Kenway and Bullen 2003). These trends intensified throughout the early part of the twentieth century.

After the Second World War we see the emergence of the affluent teenager who was to become the new consumer (Abrams 1959). Youth was seen as a market to be targeted (Hebdige 1988) with a large disposable income (Lee 1993). This is also the time of 'market segmentation', where industry, and advertising in particular, moves from trying to understand the ordinary consumer to focusing on the lifestyle activities and consumption practices of different social subgroups (Leiss *et al.* 2000). As a result, there is differentiation of commercial products, and encouragement to target goods at certain groups. It is at this point in the 1960s that we see the emergence of marketing that directly 'talks' to the young, through the development of children's television and advertising (Kline 1993; Leiss *et al.* 2000).

The levels and types of consumption amongst the young vary over time, and between different social groups. Youth incomes in the 1960s expanded by nearly 50 per cent, thus creating a consumption boom (Miles 2000). By the 1970s and early 1980s economic decline and high youth employment hit the spending power of the teenager (Stewart 1992). In this context 'shopping around' and 'hanging out' in places of consumption become as important as the act of purchasing the goods themselves (Miles 2000). By the 1990s the spending power of the young is seen as significant. Although the youth population is in decline, its spending power increases by over 40 per cent

(Gunter and Furnham 1998). As Miles (2000: 114) suggests, 'teenagers take it for granted that they were "born to shop"'. As the market further fragments and grows, it is claimed that by 2004 the spending power of 11–16-year-olds is worth over £2.6 billion a year. The largest areas of spending are recognised as fashion, magazines, and records, tapes and CDs (Mintel 2003).

As consumer products and services within these industries become more complex and sophisticated, the marketing industry recognises that the youth market is not homogeneous. Age and gender become important categories for understanding consumption behaviour and marketing (Kenway and Bullen 2003). Knowledge of the target audience, and their preferences, starts to dominate how marketing companies construct their product and brand it. For example, recently the marketing industry has constructed youth into six different profiles and categories: 'the Now Crowd', 'the IO Crew', 'Alter-ego.com', 'Misinsulars', 'ChicGeeks' and 'Hubs'. All are profiled by age, spending power and attitudes towards consumption (Geraci and Nagy 2004).

Youth, new media technology and consumption

While the dominant areas of consumption have historically been fashion and clothing, major changes in consumption patterns have been taking place. It is now well recognised that technological changes, especially within media products such as computers, digital TV and mobile phones, are now a major part of our lifestyle: 'As we enter the twenty-first century, the home is being transformed into the site of a multimedia culture, integrating audiovisual, information and telecommunications services' (Livingstone 2002: 1). Media ownership and usage amongst the young have seen a massive growth of information and communication technology (ICT) in the home. Almost all families now own traditional media such as televisions, videos, radios and telephones. But there has also been a large expansion over the last decade in new media. Over 75 per cent of children and young people aged 9–19 now have access to the Internet from a computer at home (Livingstone *et al.* 2005). School access is also nearly universal, and only 3 per cent of all young people have never been on the Internet (Livingstone *et al.* 2005). Other new technologies, such as the Xbox and PlayStation, have also grown in significance over the previous decade (Livingstone 2002). For example, spending on home-based video and gaming activities in the USA has grown from $2.6 billion in 1996 to $7.4 billion in 2004 (Entertainment Software Association 2006). Similar trends can be identified in the usage of mobile phones, in that 80 per cent of young people aged 11–19 own a mobile phone and use it on a regular basis (Mintel 2003). These patterns of use should not be seen in isolation. What we are seeing is the growth of homes that encase a media environment that integrates many different forms of technology and forms of communication (Livingstone 2002).

The net generation and the digital divide

At the forefront of the new media 'revolution' have been the young. It is claimed by some that in this context we are seeing the creation of a new generation of young people that is the driving force of social change, able to adopt and integrate new technologies into their lives far easier than others. Digital technology is seen as bringing about a 'net generation' that will overthrow traditional hierarchies of knowledge and power (Tapscott 1998). Others have defined this as the 'Y generation', born between the 1980s and 1990s, who are skilled practitioners and consumers of the new media (Kenway and Bullen 2003). This 'new' generation are also seen to have considerable influence over how their households spend their money on technology. In marketing terms this has been used as a justification for targeting the young (Geraci *et al.* 2000).

Of course, as we saw in Chapter 2, constructions and analyses based upon notions of 'generation' can be problematic. Tapscott and others tend to generalise both usage and users of new technology, giving little attention to divisions and differences and to the complex relationships the young may have with technology: 'Young people are seen as monolithic social entity and the relationship to technology is seen as sequential and unidirectional, rather than complex and co-constructed' (Lee 2005: 316). In reality, a 'digital divide' exists. Questions about how different social groups might benefit from the ICT revolution have been asked (Servon and Nelson 2001; Selwyn 2004; Livingstone *et al.* 2005), raising concerns over how certain groups are being excluded and denied access to the new technology. This is not just a simple question of the 'haves' and 'have nots'. Issues of the quality of relationship a person has with technology are also important: 'access to a personal computer does not guarantee a connection to the Internet, any more than "access" to the Internet is a guarantee of effectively accessing every available website and online resource' (Selwyn 2004: 348). Research has shown that general access and usage are greatly influenced by a number of structural differences (Livingstone and Bovill 2001; Buckingham 2002). Internet ownership is greater amongst middle-class children than working-class children. But more importantly, middle-class children have more access points in the home, quicker access through broadband and access points within their bedrooms, creating more Internet literacy and confidence amongst the middle classes (Livingstone *et al.* 2005). Gender is also important. Although the difference between boys' and girls' usage is getting smaller, the quality of use and amount of time on the Internet are greater for boys than girls (Livingstone *et al.* 2005). Age is significant here too: 9–11-year-olds and 18–19-year-olds are less likely to have access to the Internet (Livingstone *et al.* 2005). Finally, other factors such as regionality and issues of deprived geographical areas, ethnicity and disability, can all be seen to impact on the levels and quality of everyday usage by the young (Livingstone *et al.* 2005).

We cannot therefore simply assume the existence of a 'net' or 'Y' generation. Neither can we construct essentialist and static notions of concepts, such as class or gender (Livingstone 2002). For example, the complexity of gendered differences in the ownership and control of gaming media suggests that digital gaming is more popular amongst boys than girls. The structure and production of these games are seen to exclude young women's active and regular engagement (Crawford and Gosling 2005). Only about a third of women are believed to be 'active gamers' (Krotoski 2004). But while these trends seem to establish girls as excluded, girls do use digital games, but this tends to be through mobile phones rather than computers (Crawford and Gosling 2005). The gaming industry itself recognises this, and is producing games that appeal more to girls than boys as a way of increasing sales (Buckingham 2002).

'Inclusive' consumption of new media?

Unlike other domains of youth activity, consumption is an area of limited governmental intervention, seen as being best left regulated by the markets. But anxieties have existed and do exist over 'unfettered capitalism' and the vulnerability of youth, leading to government historically taking a stronger regulatory role in areas such as advertising and censorship. In more recent times government has seen a greater role for intervening in the new forms of media and technology, arguing that it is for the 'good' of society that such technology is integrated into mainstream life. This being said, an uneasy relationship remains over government's interference in the marketplace.

New Labour has been driving a modernising agenda, arguing that Britain and its citizens need to actively engage with the new 'digital age', and that the 'digital divide' needs to be addressed for reasons of economic growth and greater social inclusion (Phipps 2000). Problems of the divide between those consumers 'connected' and 'disconnected' were seen as key challenges to New Labour's agenda of tackling social exclusion (SEU 2000). The government's approach to this was to get the UK 'online' by widening access. This policy intended to increase the usage of media technology, aiming to get 70 per cent of the population 'wired up' and able to use, with confidence, all forms of new media. Its main thrust is on building up capacity by establishing new online centres in deprived areas, new learning colleges, new public libraries, an information technology network and greater access to public services through the Internet (Selwyn 2002). This policy also aims to educate the young, ensuring they have the skills to use the new technology. Under the National Grid for Learning initiative and the New Opportunities Fund the government has provided resources of over £1 billion to support and connect all 30,000

UK schools to the Internet, while ensuring that teachers are also fully trained and equipped to teach ICT skills (Selwyn 2002).

While the resources and approach to ICT provided by New Labour are unprecedented, there are some fundamental problems. For example, the notion of access is seen to be too narrow (Selwyn 2002). The issue of the 'context' to the experience is also ignored. Divisions between groups do not exist simply as a result of having limited access through economic positions and locations alone. The quality and context of technology is 'socially shaped' by a range of critical factors which policy does not address (Livingstone 2002). Understanding young people's media use has to move beyond a simple value of access to recognise how it is appropriated and embedded in everyday life by the users themselves. There is a need to understand how new media are integrated into different environments and the impact of the 'culture of use' in the home (Livingstone 2002). This will shape the experience the young have of technology. Similar issues exist around schools. 'Use cultures' are constructed by schools, governed by the type of resources available and the quality of personnel managing the resources (Lee 2005). Schools may seem to create open access (and also have the resources to do so), but internal forms of regulation and control will have an impact on the student experience of the new technology. Government policy fails to engage with these complexities, seeing the problem as one of providing access at the point of delivery (Lee 2005).

But not only does policy fail to fully engage with these questions, it can also create further divisions and tensions. The failure to deal with fundamental social and economic divisions between 'media rich' and the 'media poor' households means that certain groups are unable to maintain the power to purchase new evolving technology (Livingstone 2002). New media technology is constantly evolving and developing, and families with limited resources are continually unable to keep up, creating tensions within poor families, reinforcing feelings of inadequacy and self-blame (Holloway and Valentine 2003). Public policy does not deal with this question. Parents are held responsible for providing adequate technology, and leaving the 'gap' between groups to be resolved by provision of public services such as libraries and Learndirect centres. These can be inferior, and may not have the same status or value as owning and consuming the hardware itself (Selwyn 2002). Policy has also emphasised 'inclusion' that is underpinned by anxieties over 'economic competitiveness'. It defines the problem as a lack of individual skills and competences, especially amongst the young (Selwyn 2002). ICT policy is therefore targeted at questions of 'employability', rather than learning or inclusion. In this context, New Labour's policy towards getting the young online reflects the wider 'new work ethic' agenda underpinning policy towards the young, and is aimed at increasing participation in the labour market, especially for those on the margins or the social excluded (Selwyn 2002).

Moral panics, new media and technology

In late modernity the growth of young people's use of new technology and media is creating a range of anxieties. Such concerns about new technology are not new. In fact contemporary moral panics around technology tend to be ahistorical, failing to recognise that similar concerns have been raised at different historical times over different forms of 'new' media. For example, moral anxieties were expressed over the introduction of the cinema in the early part of the twentieth century, the television after the war, and video technology in the 1980s (Drotner 1992). Unlike in the area of crime, modern risks associated with technology are focused on the danger *to* the young rather than the dangers *of* the young. Across new media, we can see a range of fears and anxieties:

- Fears over sexual exploitation – especially over the young gaining access to pornography and/or being groomed by paedophiles over the Internet.
- Concerns over the effects of 'new' technology on a young person's personality – especially the dangers of being corrupted (for example, the dangers of violence on television and video).
- The impact of 'new' technology on family life. Media such as computers and video games are seen as undermining traditional family activities and morals. Young people spend time isolated at computers rather than being integrated into 'normal life'.
- The negative effects of new media and technology on young people's health (for example, fears around mobile phones and their impact on brain development, or suggestions that computers are creating lazy and unfit young people).

While we should not discredit such fears without caution, we do have to recognise that many of these have limited evidence to support them. Research in this field has failed to provide reliable proof that new media have damaging or negative influences (Buckingham 2002).

Limited evidence supports the argument that family life is being destroyed, or that the young are becoming more isolated and unhealthy (Livingstone 2002). In fact there is a body of research that starts to highlight how new media technology increases forms of interaction and participation, not only in family life, but also with peers and friends and with social activities that might be healthy (Brown 2005). Even when we explore the evidence on pornography and sexual grooming, we can see that young people are in many cases fully aware of the dangers and risks they encounter on the Internet, and take precautions as necessary (Livingstone 2002). The majority of young people are able to understand the dangers and find ways of managing them. While we cannot deny that real risks and dangers exist around grooming for sexual exploitation, we have to recognise that such dangers are more likely to happen in their own homes and families (Brown 2005).

Why, then, do we have such moral panics about young people's usage of the new media? In this area it tends to be a struggle of generations, and adult anxieties over power to control the future (in which technology is seen to be critical), although it is also about fears over young people's autonomy and about them being unregulated in new (cyber) spaces:

> Both the efficacy of regulation (of content) and governmentality (of use), the traditional comfort blankets in relation to television, are challenged by the internet because children and young people are theoretically free to roam anywhere in the places and spaces of the cyber.
>
> (Brown 2005: 151)

It is this fear of the unknown spaces and places that young people enter, and the autonomy that they have in this process, that drives attempts to regulate the new technology. Regulating this space and youth autonomy has become a major problem for national governments, in that the Internet is seen as global, and cuts across national boundaries. Watchdogs, voluntary organisations and industry, government guidelines and, more recently, new laws restricting the production and storage of pornography have been the main forms of regulation of the Internet, yet this is 'government at a distance' (Brown 2005: 172). It is, in effect, also a part of the 'responsibilising agenda' and where new forms of governance encourage (enforce?) individuals to police themselves (and their children). This has seen the 'lessening of either the will or the ability of the state to "protect" young citizens; and a concomitant responsibilization of policing through the family or industry' (Brown 2005: 174). The main responsibility then lies with parents, who are expected to construct safety systems in the home that act to protect their children. But parents are not always competent at managing the new technology; neither are they aware of all the safety measures they need to take. As a result, regulation of the Internet can vary in how it is monitored and controlled in the home (Holloway and Valentine 2003).

Youth consumption identities

So far, in our discussions, we have focused on how youth consumption, especially in new technology and media, has expanded and been responded to as a part of the youth question. But social science research has also been exploring the impact of consumer culture and consumption on youth identities. This type of approach has its roots in the work of the Birmingham School (CCCS). Young people's leisure activities, such as the music they created and listened to, the clothes they wore, and where they 'hung out', were seen as cultural expressions and ways of dealing with their changing material circumstances (Hall *et al.* 1978). The idea that young people are 'cultural innovators' and 'creators' has since become an important part of the contemporary literature on youth culture (Bennett 2005). Young people's acts of consumption are therefore seen as an important source of individual activity, not simply passivity, and ones that offer a number of possibilities for their identities.

Post-structuralism and 'identity work'

A good early example of this approach is Paul Willis's work on *Common Culture* (1990). He goes beyond the confines of a class or structuralist analysis to identify how the act of consumption can help produce a wide range of youthful subjectivities and identities. Willis shows that young people consume commodities in creative ways having little or no meaningful relation to the 'original' role of that commodity. They are always involved in creation and recreation of their own cultural life. Through their daily interaction with each other and the market, young people engage in a process of symbolic exchange that continually defines and redefines what it means to be young. Their identities are derived primarily from the creative ways in which they consume, not how they produce. Willis (1990) sees the young consumer as bringing certain knowledge to a commodity and not accepting as given what that commodity is said to represent. People have to 'do things' with commodities since they are the only things most people possess, and it is in doing things with these commodities that young people generate their own peculiar experiences of consumption, leisure and lifestyle. Being young, therefore, is constituted through a constant process of interaction and borrowing, and is constantly creative in refashioning what it actually means to be young. A similar position is taken by Bennett (2000) who, in researching the role of music in the lives of the young, wants to argue that music and the activities that surround it are of critical importance to young people's identities:

> On the one hand, music informs ways of being in particular social spaces; on the other hand, music functions as a resource whereby individuals are able to actively construct those spaces in which they live. Thus, in a real sense, music not only informs the construction of the self, but also the social world in which the self operates.
>
> (Bennett 2000: 195)

Within this process, it is the negotiation between the products of the global music industry, individual biography and locality that 'bounds' the process of identity construction. Music, therefore, is a critical feature of both the everyday lives of the young but also of their identity construction.

New opportunities for this form of identity work by the young are also emerging in the usage of other forms of technology. For example, the Internet is seen to be allowing young people to create virtual identities (Bassett 1991). Who you are, where you live and what you like can be reconstructed through the invisibility provided by the Internet (Jones 1997; Wilber 1997). As this technology has expanded, young people, it is claimed, reconstitute how it should be used, finding opportunities to enter 'other' worlds and spaces. Within these young people are able to create new identities. Being online creates the opportunity for the young to hide their real identities and create new ones:

> Both S. and Fg.[1] illuminate how their local, physical identities can be hidden in online spaces and the different parameters of interaction can be used to challenge assumptions, gain confidence or just play ... they become used to seeing multiple perspectives, engaging in multiple interactions and experiencing multiple ways of being.
>
> (Maczewski 2002: 124)

Young people are able to be 'someone else' and create 'multiple' identities. This form of disembodiment, separation of the body from identity work, offers young people the opportunity of stepping out of their 'real identity' and creating a 'new' virtual identity through play (Heim 1998).

The importance of 'difference'

The notion of 'identity work' has also been influential in shaping discussions on gender and race. Angela McRobbie, writing in the 1980s, demonstrated how girls do not just passively accept the dominant culture and ideology of femininity, but attempt to appropriate it to give it new meanings. Thus she interprets girls' reading of *Jackie* magazine as a way of taking a commodity and giving it new meaning, to generate their own sense of what it means to be a girl and to actually empower them. Reading a magazine is, therefore, not just buying a commodity and passively absorbing the intended content and messages, but is an active process of engagement and creativity. Other examples would be around shopping (McRobbie 1994) and advertising. For example, they do not just receive advertising messages, they decode and deconstruct the cultural messages around the product. They do not merely absorb their messages but become discriminating consumers, able to articulate what they like about some and what they dislike about others (Nava and Nava 1992).

More recent work has seen new technology creating 'new spaces' and opportunities for girls to experiment with their identities. Davies (2004), for example, shows how young girls, interested in *Babyz* web pages and products, construct alternative usages and understanding of the product. *Babyz* is a software programme that provides 'virtual' children for young girls to care for online. Owners are required to name them, dress them, feed them and take on parental roles of responsibility. By interacting online with other girls over the Internet they are able to challenge traditional perceptions of girlhood and experiment with new identities:

> Participants become involved in interactions that seem at once both private and public, a forum for confidence and disclosure, as well as public displays of feminism and/or rebellion ... girls use the *Babyz* media as channels through which they can present multiple identities.
>
> (Davies 2004: 36)

Girls online are therefore able to construct new forms of resistant feminism, and challenge traditional notions of what it means to be a girl.

The question of difference has also increased analysis on issues of racialised identities. Gilroy (1987) and Hall (1992) have suggested that what is fundamentally different in terms of race is that the structural component of social relationships has to be understood not only in class terms, but also in terms of colonist history, institutionalised responses to race, and global forces. Black youth can only be understood in this context. The new cultural politics of difference is shifting and displacing the hegemonic cultural norm from 'high' (i.e. American) to more popular and diverse cultural activities (Hall 1992). New technologies and opportunities are creating ways of expanding and sharing varied and diverse black cultures. The global world is a world of diverse cultural practices that can be transported, via new communication mediums, between the First and Third World. The focus on local or national identities alone, and cultural practice as a set of local practices, is now inappropriate:

> Culture does not develop along ethnically absolute lines but in complex, dynamic patterns of syncretism in which new definitions of what it means to be black emerge from the raw materials provided by the black populations elsewhere.
>
> (Gilroy 1987: 13)

What we start to see is a stronger focus, within cultural studies, on how black youth construct themselves through drawing on both local and global content, form, expression and dissent. Black youth are therefore critical producers (as well as consumers) of their own culture. This has seen the emergence of what have been called 'new ethnicities' (Back 1996) that recognise this context to youth identities. This is therefore a process of negotiation, where new ethnicities are actively produced, consumed and transformed by young people themselves through different cultural practices such as dress, styles, listening to music, and watching television. Dwyer (1998), talking about young Muslim women, suggests they are active producers of new forms of identity that have to engage with historical traditions and new social changes taking place. These 'hybrid' styles help young Muslim women take more control over their lives and to 'resist' dominant discourses about what it means to be Muslim women.

Cultural and media studies, therefore, have constructed an approach to understanding youth that rejects the traditional view of seeing young people's lives as most vividly constituted through the production, state and objective structures of modernist social theory. Instead, they are arguing for a position that recognises that young people construct their own distinctive subjectivities through the use of the market as a source of creativity and freedom and which has no set meaning. In one sense this is a 'celebration' of the creativity of the young, and their ability not only to resist social structures but also to challenge and change them.

The political economy of consumption

Such a position has not been without its critics. One major issue that post-structuralists fail to address in detail is the interrelationship between the political economy of consumption and the process of identity formation. The innovativeness of some aspects of youth activities is difficult to deny. Music would be one particular example, but the debasing and emptiness of much youth culture is hard to escape. In this way, young people are continually subordinated to the market, and only the market has got better at presenting things as new, different and innovative. Thus, instead of seeing young people's lives as constituted in consumption, we cannot divorce them from patterns of production (Frith 2004). The sphere of consumption is not some autonomous sphere free of the constraints of production. On the contrary, consumption is a fundamental aspect of capitalist social relations, in which labour not only is replenished, but also gives rise to a whole host of new consumption pursuits, which have involved the further commodification of social life.

'Girl power' and feminism

One important area of research that has explored this commodification of social life is an analysis of 'girlhood'. Use of the body, and the sexual form of the different genders, has always underpinned advertising and marketing strategies towards girls. Marketing tends to build on female hegemonic discourse (Kenway and Bullen 2003). Girls draw upon these images (and stories) to understand the role of make-up and clothing in how they present themselves, thus creating new spending patterns and opportunities for manufacturing (Greer 2000). For example, women are positioned within advertising, as commodities that are dehumanised. As a result, womanhood tends to be constructed from commodities such as make-up, hairstyles and clothing. Much of this is built upon making girls feel discontented with their bodies, seeing them as being in need of repair, or alteration, or transformation (Frost 2001). How girls receive these images and use them in their everyday practice of identity work has been the focus of much discussion. Most magazines and television adverts construct femininity as being concerned with beauty. The maintenance of this beauty becomes a normal part of 'being a girl'. Similar processes are seen to be at work in television soap operas and television adverts. If the range of cultural messages that girls receive in the diverse areas of their everyday lives emphasise the 'perfect body', then it is highly likely that these messages will impact on choices and consumption practices of girls (Frost 2001).

More recently 'girl power' has come to be seen as significant. While there is much uncertainty about its meaning, it has had major cultural impact on notions of girlhood (Aapola *et al.* 2005). Although its 'arrival' was credited with the teen pop group the Spice Girls, it has, in fact, a longer history, being associated with Riot Grrrls in the 1990s. These were seen as a more radical movement of girls who rejected the notion of femininity as passive (Harris 2003). Girl power has become a mainstream term that has been appropriated by the cultural industries and national governments, symbolising new forms of femininity (Aapola *et al.* 2005). Within popular culture it has been massively influential. Films such as *Charlie's Angels* and *Crouching Tiger, Hidden Dragon,* alongside TV shows such as *Buffy the Vampire Slayer, Sabrina, the Teenage Witch* and *Xena: Warrior Princess,* have all drawn upon representations of the 'new girl' as being in control and all powerful (Aapola *et al.* 2005). It is also commonly used by the media around stories about girls especially when they are seen as challenging the mainstream or behaving outside cultural norms. Governments from around the world also use girl power to encourage greater self-reliance, autonomy, self-control and responsibility amongst young women over how they conduct their own lives (Aapola *et al.* 2005).

Girl power constructs and positions girls as 'feisty, ambitious, motivated and independent' (Aapola *et al.* 2005: 26), creating a new form of feminism that challenges more passive models of girlhood. This has been seen as a positive development, in that it has brought feminism into the mainstream, and been used to touch and influence the lives of girls worldwide (Driscoll 1999). Characters such as Buffy the Vampire Slayer and the Spice Girls have provided girls with positive images and models of what it means to be a girl in late modernity. Girl power challenges sexist stereotypes and tells young women that they have the power to change and influence the world (Projansky and Vande Berg 2000). Icons such as the Spice Girls are seen to create a dialogue about feminism in a popular discourse, therefore creating opportunities to engage young women in discussions about what being a girl should mean in late modernity (Driscoll 1999).

But is this a new form of feminism? What we are seeing is a commodification of girlhood, by the powerful cultural industries, which is depoliticising girls and reinforcing traditional models of girlhood. Girl power is seen to construct girlhood as non-political, making girls think about how to be a girl in a cultural rather than political way (Taft 2001). In this context it depoliticises girls and does not challenge the status quo. It tends to construct girlhood as a reflection of white middle-class values and of personal individualism and responsibility over collectivity, seeing consumption as an active form of citizenship (Aapola *et al.* 2005). Many of the cultural icons and images created by the consumption industries also reinforce traditional values of girlhood. For example, in the TV sitcom, *Sabrina, the Teenage Witch*, girlhood is created in a contradictory way. On the one hand Sabrina is portrayed as independent and in control of her life, being encouraged to make decisions about the things she wants, yet on the other hand she is constructed as a confused teenage girl, driven by female desires and uncertainties, playing out traditional feminine roles (i.e. chasing boys and looking beautiful) and relying upon cultural consumption as a means of exercising her middle-class privilege. This then reinforces a normative femininity of the importance of beauty, the body and dress as critical symbols of 'being a girl' (Projansky and Vande Berg 2000). But it is also important to recognise that this age group of young women has an enormous amount of spending power, estimated to be over £1.3 billion in the UK alone (Mintel 2003). As a result, the marketing industry has seen this as a lucrative market to enter, providing opportunities for large profits. Its interest is not in the promotion of a new form of feminism, but in selling products associated with cultural icons and movements that young girls are attracted to. Within this process, it recognises the importance of reflecting the core images and values of individualism, while also celebrating feminism, but its main objective is to capture the shopping power of girls (Aapola *et al.* 2005).

It is advantageous for the consumption industry to get the young consuming early. It is well recognised that, once a young person is tied into a brand loyalty, it can be maintained and built upon. In fact whole lifestyles can – and are – created around particular brands and certain pursuits (Russell and Tyler 2002). While young people may be becoming more skilled consumers, the leisure and consumption industry is becoming more skilled at getting people to buy their products (Mansell 2004). We like to think that we make choices and are not greatly influenced by advertising, but in reality advertising, and marketing, is a powerful medium that is driven by profit. It will analysis and follow taste, but also construct it in ways that bring the greatest financial gain to producers. For example, young girls may be aware of the targeting strategies of the media, they may also be astute and disconcerting in their consumption practices, yet the industry is highly skilled at producing a perception that young girls can identify with, thus increasing their profits (Russell and Tyler 2002). To argue, therefore, that young people are creators of their own culture, or are able to differentiate between products without recognising the broader social forces within the advertising and marketing industries, is naïve of writers in cultural studies.

The importance of structural positions and locations

Similar problems exist over how other structural understandings have been theorised and empirically explored within this approach (Hollands 2002). The theoretical framework of post-structuralism does not explore and understand how youth might be differentiated, not only by the power of the cultural and media industries, but also by young people's economic, domestic and geographical positions. As Hollands (2002: 158) suggests:

> So, while it is clear that hybrid symbolic and lifestyle aspects of consumption are critical for an understanding of contemporary youth culture, it is equally obvious that existing social divisions and transitions, locality and corporate ownership are also important and provide a context for understanding consumption 'choices'.

In fact, in many senses it is not surprising that post-structuralists have little focus on these broader processes, as they are not looking for these connections (Cohen and Ainley 2000).

As we saw earlier, the digital divide reflects structural divisions in society, with those in poorer communities and households having less access and opportunity to engage with the new media technology. Class, gender and race, therefore, become important economic, as well as cultural, divisions that shape how young people encounter the market (Livingstone 2002). To see these divisions as 'performance' or 'textual reproductions' is to fail to recognise the structural influence and forces that limit choice and opportunity.

If we return to the work of Dwyer (1998) we can see how these fundamental problems exist in post-structuralist approaches. In her study on Muslim girls' identity work, we are left unclear about who these girls are, what their family backgrounds are, and what their economic relationship is to both production and consumption. We only know them through their cultural practices of dress and style. Identity is seen as being 'in flux' and these young women 'change faces', dependent on the situation. What we are led to believe is that this post-modern practice of 'pick and mix' is within the control of the girls. In other words, there is no real identity, only a mix of identities to pick from. Race and gender are equated with textual performance and given equal importance to the material positions of class relationships. Even racism is not recognised as a potential influence on the life-worlds of these girls. Their identity is constructed in their everyday social interaction and practice with items of consumption, but there is no recognition of the power of the cultural industries to represent and reproduce the identities of young Asian women, or of the relationship of this media to the post-Fordist reordering of production. Girls are seen as 'in control' and able to resist or accept representations at will. Little attention is given within this analysis to the power of these images to shape how girls' culture is constructed, and how this may be inclusive or exclusive.

This is not to say that the creative nature of consumption by the young is not or should not be important in our understanding of youth in late modernity. Clearly, consumption practices have become more important in their lives and we have to find ways of understanding this. Yet how we theorise them and investigate them shapes how we understand social life. For example, historically, class analysis has always recognised the importance of culture in the lives of the working class (Skeggs 1997; Savage 2003), seeing it as an important contribution to our understanding of social divisions. But traditional theories of class culture, while being historically linked to notions of production, have either not engaged with the massive growth of consumption and its impact on everyday life, or been unable to incorporate such changes into their analyses (Cohen and Ainley 2000; Savage 2003). Much, then, still needs to be done to understand the interaction between consumption, culture and youth identities.

Conclusion

It is clear that in late modernity youth consumption has become a major site of youth activity. Fashion, magazines, mobile phones, games consoles and the Internet have become everyday products of young people's lives. The net or 'Y' generation is seen as a new phenomenon associated with late modernity, although, as we saw, evidence suggests we need to accept such claims with caution. While New Labour has been advocating an expansion of a 'knowledge and information' based society, policies have not been successful in either understanding the problem or providing solutions. Panics over youth being at risk have seen New Labour increase its expectations of parents to be the key regulators of 'cyberspace', even though many have limited skills and resources.

While New Labour has focused on increasing access to the new technology, youth studies have been investigating the impact this technology has on the identities of the young. It has successfully shifted the research focus away from 'youth as a problem', seeing them as leading the technological drive. For example, cultural studies have shown that, in fashion and clothing, it is now well recognised that the young are not 'cultural dupes', just receiving messages and responding accordingly. They are disconcerting consumers who are reflexive and able to transfer goods in ways that go beyond the original usage of the product. Similarly, in new media young people are taking the product and using it in new and creative ways. Much of this work is also innovative as it starts from an epistemological position that emphasises the importance of human agency. As a result, we see a wide range of studies that prioritise the voice of young people and draw upon their perspectives in understanding their cultural activities.

But there are important points here that we need to consider. While cultural studies have brought positive images and the creativity of youth to the forefront of youth research, we also have to recognise it has a tendency to overread it. Having an active and engaged consumer is also critical for the maintenance of profit and production. Consumption amongst the young has grown and, with it, we have seen the emergence of new marketing categories and strategies that target and construct certain groups in particular ways. While a concept such as girl power seems to offer an element of empowerment, we need to be aware of the power and influence of the media and marketing to use it to reinforce traditional gender roles and notions of femininity. The lack of recognition within cultural studies of the political economy of consumption, and its powerful influence in the processes of buying goods and the limited interest in more fundamental problems of structural differences, leaves us with a one-sided perspective that sidesteps important questions about processes of difference in late modernity. One final, but important, point is the limited active engagement with the political debates about youth and the youth question. Apart from a few limited studies,[2] youth cultural studies fail for the most part to engage constructively with policy-making. This polarisation of research and policy is a fundamental problem that leaves policy-makers unaware of more positive images and understandings of youth.

8 Youth culture and the growth of the 'risk-taking generation'

Introduction

The youth question has always been shaped by anxieties over young people's use of leisure and their cultural practices. In late modernity, there has been a range of moral panics over new forms of cultural practices, such as those of New Age travellers, raves, clubbing drug use and 'binge drinking'. In the first part of this chapter we will examine the development of these new cultural practices, highlighting their history, and their impact on the reconstruction of the youth question, showing how they have been understood and how governments and the media have responded to the 'problem'. In the second part we will turn our attention to how these have been explained and theorised by social science. The study of youth has a long history in researching youth leisure and its cultural activities, and such a tradition still remains strong.

New Age travellers and eco-warriors

By the early 1980s, the youth counterculture movement discussed in chapters 1 and 2 seemed to have fragmented and almost disappeared and it is at this point that we see the emergence of New Age travellers and the eco-movement. Both have their routes in the radicalism of the counterculture movement, being linked to activities such as the free festival movement, the growth of an alternative radical press, the anti-nuclear weapons movement, and the squatting movement (Osgerby 1998). Early groups of New Age travellers had radical utopias that rejected urban living for a more rural nomadic lifestyle (Hetherington 1998). They also rejected materialism in favour of a simpler life that celebrated tradition and nature above all else (Hetherington 1998). But the New Age traveller movement was not homogeneous. As the economic landscape of Thatcherism, and the attack on rights for the young, took its toll, many young people found themselves 'economic refugees' who were both homeless and jobless. As a result, many found refuge in a traveller lifestyle that offered inclusion (Martin 1998).

Their resistance to the conformity of rural life, and their desire for an alternative way of life, brought New Age travellers into direct conflict with the police and the state. They became the moral panic of the 1980s, threatening the peaceful tranquillity of rural life (Hetherington 1998) and the hegemonic project of the Thatcherite government (Hill 2002). They were seen as the polluters of the familiar and a challenge to the powerful hegemonic order of rural life. As a result the 1994 Criminal Justice and Public Order Act gave the police new powers to limit the movement of New Age travellers, especially on historical sites. In effect, the new legislation criminalised their nomadic lifestyle. Yet, in reality, by the time the legislation came into being, the New Age travellers were already being dissipated across the UK, replaced by groups such as the 'anti-road programme' movement and The Land is Ours campaign groups, that were more willing to take direct action on specific individual political issues.

Rave culture and the arrival of ecstasy

But not only are the 1980s and 1990s linked with the growth of alternative political movements, we also see the 'arrival' of the rave. Its history has been well documented (see Critcher 2000), showing how 'acid house' music, combined with ecstasy, created a new youth cultural phenomenon that became known as 'rave culture'. Underground music from the USA, and new styles of record mixing, transformed not only the music industry but also dance culture. Ecstasy became known as the new 'recreational drug' having a close association with particular dance and music. This created a music industry that aimed to construct a total experience, drawing on the needs and wants of ecstasy users. Venues and producers created lighting and sound systems that played on the pleasure-seeking sensations of the drug experience. Ecstasy increased the sense of community and sociability where dancing, rather than romance, was to become the major pleasure. A whole new industry and lifestyle emerged that replaced the individualism of Thatcherism with a collective sense of being (Hill 2002), while also celebrating hedonism and pleasure-seeking as core values to youth culture (Collin and Godfrey 1997).

Rave was a hugely popular activity amongst the young, being seen as the second coming of the 'summer of love' (Osgerby 1998). In its early years, the rave was perceived as representing an 'enemy within' that needed close attention and regulation (Hill 2002), but major difficulties existed in control. As parties in abandoned warehouses became larger, and more people became involved, the police struggled to control them. Once a party was happening, the best the police could do was turn new people away. A number of large-scale events were organised by new entrepreneurs who exploited this principle, ensuring that the illegal event was unstoppable if organised quickly

(Saunders 1995). But as interest by the state and others grew, many entrepreneurs saw the opportunity to make huge profits by mainstreaming raves into a major leisure industry. By the middle of the 1990s the rave had become more respectable and was incorporated into legal venues and clubs. Clubbing became the popular activity of the new youth generation of 'ravers' (Critcher 2000).

The rise of clubbing

By the middle of the 1990s, attention had shifted from illegal raves to the growth of legal clubbing venues. After the Second World War, nightclubs had become important venues for the young, but in the 1990s major changes started to take place in these structures. Instead of being venues for late-night drinking and sexual encounters, they became venues that catered for rave culture, alternative music and the taking of ecstasy. This became big business and, by 1996, it was thought the industry was worth over £2 billion, with every large city seeing the expansion of new clubs (Malbon 1999). Clubbing became an urban pastime that attracted large sections of the youth population. For example, Mintel (1996) suggested that over 42 per cent of young people went clubbing, or to a discothèque, at least once a month – an increase of 9 per cent over five years (Malbon 1999). Clubbing as a route into sexual relationships was seen as low priority, especially among girls (Henderson 1997), and involvement was more about enjoying the atmosphere of late-night dancing and music (Release 1997). Clubbing was closely associated with ecstasy, being tied into the 'oceanic experience' of the night out, giving value and meaning to a seemingly meaningless activity (Malbon 1999). The club scene grew at a fast pace with between 400 and 500 venues available in and around London, while cities such as Manchester, Sheffield and Leeds used local clubs within cultural districts, seeing it as an important aspect of economic, as well as social, regeneration. But clubbing also became an international phenomenon, with clubbing holidays to places such as Ibiza, Goa and the Caribbean being seen as an extension of the new cultural lifestyle associated with dancing (Malbon 1999).

Fears for (of?) the 'E' generation

Major anxieties focused on drug use, especially on the extended use of ecstasy. Even though evidence suggested only a small proportion of young people were regular users, government and the media collapsed a minority activity into that of the many (Brown 2005). This experimentation led to them being labelled the E generation (Collin and Godfrey 1997). Large numbers of young people were perceived as being actively engaged in taking large quantities of E, and spending most of their weekends, (and later weekdays), 'out of their heads' while going clubbing. Debates concentrated on questions of safety and risk, suggesting that the long-term impacts of such activities remained unknown, and that a whole generation was putting itself at risk of harm. A major focus concentrated on girls (Blackman 2004). The media has always used girls as a site of moral panic, and the death of a number of young women generated media interest (Blackman 2004). One such example can be found in the death in 1995 of the schoolgirl, Leah Betts. She was described as a middle-class girl, who was not a regular user, and who died after taking one ecstasy tablet at her birthday party. These events led to substantial media attention to the dangers and risks to a whole generation (Collin and Godfrey 1997). The campaign following Leah Betts's death concentrated on showing her dying in hospital and on messages that advocated total abstinence rather than safe usage (Blackman 2004). These images were then used by the media to show that E was 'taking our children away from us' and creating a loss of childhood and youth amongst the E generation.

Raves, and then clubbing, replaced New Age travellers as the new moral panic of the 1990s. Both were symbolised as representing the moral and cultural decline of the young in Thatcherite Britain (Hill 2002). The young were claimed to be 'out of control' and involved in 'dangerous' activities. Their 'creativity' and their 'hedonism' in rave music and dancing were used, by the press and government, as symbols of an immoral society, where social order was threatened, and respectability was seen to be in decline (Blackman 2004). Youth was being commodified and portrayed within the media as the 'mindless hedonism' of lost youth (Brown 2005), 'out of control' and 'out of their heads'. The hedonism of youth was symbolic of a generation that seemed to have little responsibility, little care for others or for principles, but was willing to spend its money on activities that enhanced its pleasure-seeking. It was a careless generation that was only concerned with seeking pleasure and satisfaction from personal risk-taking and drug-taking (Brown 2005).

The regulation and control of raves and ecstasy use was problematic. Government realised that trying to remove raves would cause major difficulties. The Entertainment Act 1990 gave police new powers to restrict raves by punishing organisers with heavy fines and the confiscation of equipment. Other forms of control were also included in the Criminal Justice and Public Order Act 1994, which again increased the powers of the police to stop people travelling to open-air raves and limit the use of land for such events. When it came to ecstasy, regulation and control was limited to legal enforcement procedures already in place, and condemnation in public. Governments have always struggled to regulate drug use (Blackman 2004), and it would have been virtually impossible for the police to suppress the growth of ecstasy.

Government would have had to mobilise huge resources against a minority youth population to have any real impact (Critcher 2003).

'Risk-taking' in late modernity

More recently, anxieties have shifted from rave culture to 'risk-taking' (France 2000). The focus has broadened to suggest that the young are willing to take more risks in their leisure (France 2000; Mitchell *et al.* 2004). This suggests that the young are involved in a range of cultural practices in their leisure time that are driven by hedonistic and self-centred values, first displayed in rave culture. Much of this recent concern has focused on binge drinking and the 'normalisation' of drug use in young people's lives. Both developments suggest that youth have become greater risk-takers, seeing substance abuse as a form of pleasure-seeking activity (Plant and Plant 1992). While the concept of youth has always been associated with risk-taking and pleasure (France 2000), evidence suggests that the youth of today are drawing upon illegal substances and dangerous activities as ways of taking more risks, and are becoming a 'risk-taking generation', where leisure is only pleasurable if risks are increased.

Binge drinking and risk-taking

Images of drunken youth staggering around our high streets late at night, out of control, involved in fighting and conflict with the police have recently been common images on our television screens. Urban life has seemingly been transformed by the growth of a 'culture of intoxication' (Institute of Alcohol Studies 2005), where the young seem to be involved in 'unbounded hedonistic consumption' of alcohol (Brain 1998). Yet evidence is unclear about the extent of the problem. Alcohol consumption is claimed to have been on the increase since the early 1990s and large numbers of surveys have shown that young people have increased their alcohol consumption (Richardson and Budd 2003; Alcohol Concern 2004; Fuller 2004) and the range of drinks they take (Fuller 2004). While it is recognised that problems of measurement exist, it is claimed that in the UK binge drinking accounts for 40 per cent of all drinking episodes amongst men, and 22 per cent amongst women (Cabinet Office Strategy Unit 2004), that 16–24-year-olds are more likely to binge drink than any other age group (Richardson and Budd 2003; Office for National Statistics 2004), and that involvement in this type of activity is likely to increase with age (Beinart *et al.* 2002). Concerns have also been raised over young women. It is suggested that the number of girls involved in binge drinking has increased more than the number of young men. For example, Sweeting and West (2003) found that between 1987 and

1999 levels of drinking among girls 'caught up' with those of their male counterparts. Questions have also been raised about the impact binge drinking has on other forms of risk-taking. It is suggested that, as a result of binge drinking, there has been a growth of street violence, fighting and other criminal activity, especially amongst young women (Richardson and Budd 2003), and that they are more involved in unsafe sex, greater risk of 'date rape' and taking risks such as getting into strangers' cars (Richardson and Budd 2003). Binge drinking is therefore seen as the catalyst to other forms of risk-taking and risks.

The 'normalisation' of drug usage

Similarly, it is claimed that risk-taking with drugs amongst the young has also increased (Beinart *et al.* 2002; Fuller 2004). Drug-taking is now seen as a normal part of youth leisure (Parker *et al.* 2002). While problems of measurement persist (Shiner and Newburn 1997), it is claimed that the growing body of national and international evidence confirms that drug-taking, especially of cannabis, is becoming a normal and accepted part of young people's everyday lives and a major leisure risk-taking activity. Evidence to support this is shown in five areas:

- Access to and availability of drugs are increasing. While difficulties of understanding these issues still exist, evidence indicates that large numbers of young people have access to drugs.
- Drug-trying rates are also increasing. Many national surveys show that between 50 and 60 per cent of young people have tried drugs at some point in their life and that, amongst certain groups such as students and clubbers, it is seen as a core part of their lifestyle.
- Drug usage rates have also increased. National studies suggest that between 20 and 25 per cent of young people are regular users. A survey by Parker *et al.* (2002) found that 31 per cent of young people had used in the previous month.
- Attitudes of 'sensible drug use' have been changing. It is claimed that there is growing social acceptability of sensible drug use. Young people are clearly aware of the dangers, but are willing to accept drug use (either as users themselves or by their friends) as long as it is sensible and undertaken as a 'normal part of life'.
- There is a growing cultural accommodation and acceptance of drug use. It is argued that there is enough evidence across the media to show that drug use is becoming more tolerated and acceptable. Public opinion seems to be softening and less interest is being taken in key people who 'out themselves' as drug-takers, past or present.

Risk-taking, moral panics and governance

While it has to be recognised that the evidence indicates a growth of risk-taking through binge drinking and drug-taking, we should be cautious about accepting such claims uncritically. Evidence in this area is not always clear-cut, and how such concepts are defined and measured can be misleading. For example, in the Home Office Study on alcohol abuse and crime, binge drinking had a wide-ranging definition that included getting really drunk once a month (Richardson and Budd 2003). Similarly, the definition of 'normalisation' of drug use is accused of overestimating the claim (Shiner and Newburn 1997; Blackman 2004). It is important to recognise the evidence of increased risk-taking, such as drug usage, is contestable. While drugs may be coming more available, and young people may have more contact with them, evidence on 'takers' as the 'norm' exaggerates the real position. What are ignored are the attitudes of the young themselves. A large section of young people, while aware of drugs, and in possible contact with people who take drugs actively and consciously, choose to reject drug-taking as a leisure activity. Even though evidence shows an increase in drug usage, what we have to recognise is that large sections of the youth population have never tried or used drugs and, even amongst those that have, only a small proportion of young people are still using drugs on a regular basis (Shiner and Newburn 1997).

We need to recognise that both the media and government have been influential in fuelling and reinforcing perceptions of 'problem youth' taking risks and being out of control. Binge drinking is constructed, in policy documentation and the media, as nihilistic, irresponsible, irrational, lacking respect, self-interested, immoral and, therefore, in need of greater regulation and control. Media representations of the problem have linked the binge drinker to a new image of uncaring, hedonistic and self-centred youth, who are symbols of 'tasteless Britain', and youth at the leading edge of a new form of lifestyle that is devoid of morality and responsibility.

Young people are perceived, with their anti-social attitudes and actions, to be focused purely on their own interests. Young people associated with high levels of binge drinking and risk-taking are normally constructed as representing 'all that is bad in society'. They are seen as being an outcome of parental failings and 'bad' communities, where regulation and informal controls have been removed. Government has therefore constructed a policy agenda that aims, as Tony Blair put it, to 'reclaim the streets for the decent majority' (Hansard, HC vol. 434, col. 48: 17 May 2005) by being tough on those groups and communities involved in binge drinking. This has been linked, by New Labour, to their 'respect agenda', which suggests that the 'problem' lies in the lack of respect the young have for society – in a speech outside 10 Downing Street on 6 May 2005, marking his return to power in the general election, Tony Blair said: 'I want to tackle this [lack of respect] and prioritise for this government how we bring back respect in our schools in our communities, in our towns and our villages.'

New Labour has argued that its policy framework should aim to create a 'culture of respect' for adult society. But how far the issue is about education, and cultural change amongst the young, remains unclear, as policy is focusing on tackling this through increased forms of punishment and governance. In 2004 the Licensing Act created the legal framework for flexible drinking and extended opening hours for public houses and clubs. This was greatly criticised for its failure to tackle the problems of the binge drinking culture, but also for its potential to increase opportunities for excessive drinking. As a result, the government is planning, through new legislation, to give stronger powers to the police (Home Office 2005) as a way of tackling binge drinking. The plan is to create alcohol disorder zones where the selling and drinking of alcohol will not be allowed, and new civil orders, not dissimilar to ASBOs, called 'drinking banning orders'. These will give powers of arrest, and exclusion, of people identified as problems (or potential problems). Once again, the method of dealing with youth is to grant further powers to regulate and punish them by excluding or criminalising them.

Within these discourses, there is a limited understanding of the broader processes at work (Brain *et al.* 2000), or the cultural significance of this activity in late modern society (Brain 1998). For example, social context and cultural values can be important factors that underpin the growth of drink-related violence in bars (Graham and Wells 2003). Similarly, drinking behaviour of the young can be greatly influenced by the cultural context and meanings of consumption. Issues such as image, style and preconceived cultural boundaries of drinking shape how the young engage with and use alcohol. Within this context, 'rational choices' are being made (Brain *et al.* 2000). But policy does not see the problem in this way, emphasising instead the need to create 'responsible drinking' by force if necessary.

A similar position exists in the ways in which the government and the media have responded to the question of drug use amongst the young. Since 1997 the government has created a wide range of policy initiatives to 'tackle the drug problem'. These range from the reclassification of cannabis use from class B to class C, and large public spending programmes aimed at educating the young in abstinence from drug use. For example, the government recently launched a website, 'Talk to Frank' (*www.talktofrank.com*), that has been specifically designed to inform young people of the dangers and risks of drug-taking. Debates have raged over approaches that encourage 'harm reduction' or 'total abstinence', with the latter dominating government policy (Blackman 2004). Such an approach has historically been limited in its effectiveness (Blackman 2004), as it lacks an understanding of cultural and structural influences that can shape how decisions are made around health-related matters (Cornwell 1984). The recent emergence and belief in the notion of 'normalisation' has also been used by the powerful agencies of government and the state to construct a discourse on 'respectable fears' in relation to drug use, which in turn is helping to justify increased forms of regulation and control:

> 'The drug consumer is categorized as a delinquent threatening society, whereby government can exercise legitimate power to regulate whole populations; normalisation is thus concerned with conformity and prescription'.
>
> (Blackman 2004: 143)

Drug users are described in policy as 'delinquent' and as 'others'. Not only are they seen as responsible for their own actions but they are also blamed for being irresponsible, untrustworthy, working against the interests of the community in general, and being seen as acting to destroy community cohesion (MacDonald and Marsh 2005). Underpinning the government position towards drug normalisation is the influence of powerful hegemonic institutions, such as medicine, psychiatry and law, all holding strong 'scientific beliefs' about drugs and drug usage (Shiner 2003). The impact of these dominant discourses is that they 'create' an 'objective' and 'scientific' base for a moral stance. Young drug users are constructed as a threat, as not normal, and as a sign that society is in moral decline, thus requiring government intervention and an increase in mechanisms of control.

Youth culture and social research

The understanding of changes that have been taking place in youth culture has been greatly influenced by the emergence of post-structuralist and postmodernist thinking.[1] Social theorising (and empirical research) in modernity has been challenged. Post-structuralists reject modernist claims of structural dominance in shaping people's lives and emphasise the importance of subjectivity, agency, diversity and difference over the objectification of the individual, through concepts such as class, gender and race. They also reject grand theorising, as well as 'totalising discourses' that claim to be able to construct coherent patterns and 'truths'. They see social life as more complex, and being able to understand and theorise it in simplistic ways fails to grasp this complexity. Post-structuralists are keen to emphasise the importance of discourse, language and representation. They would claim that we only understand ourselves, and the world we live in, through our relationships with others and the broader discourse of power. The development and expansion of these ideas has had a major impact on how youth culture has been theorised and researched in late modernity.

The relevance of subcultural theory in late modernity

Cultural theorists argue that what it means to be young has to be viewed in the context of its cultural significance. It is this that makes being young so distinctive, not the structural focus of society. Indeed, post-modernists, such as Redhead (1990, 1993), argued that the attempts of subcultural theory to 'read off' the real meaning of youth, post-war, and British subcultures by reference to some underlying structural determinations were misplaced.

For Redhead, the advent of rave culture showed up the fundamentally mistaken approach of the previous subcultural perspective, because it had little to offer in understanding the significance of rave. Rave culture represented a fusion and eclectic mix of pre-existing youth cultural forms that made it impossible to connect it to any number of underlying structural determinations. Cultural artefacts were borrowed, repositioned, realigned, juxtaposed and given new meanings at such an alarming rate that the attempt to look for their underlying meanings was bound to fail. For example, rave appropriated the 'smiley face' of the hippy movement and the clothes of the sports generation; held its gatherings in warehouses against the backdrop of the disintegration of much of British industry; took a new generation of designer drugs and mundane items, such as Lucozade and lollipops, as its accessories; flaunted sexuality, yet often appeared highly asexual in the sense that people went to dance and not to chat others up; and involved highly socialised gatherings, yet turned inwards to celebrate the individual experience of dance, drugs and music. It borrowed its music from the ghettos of Chicago, the 1970s discos of East Coast America, Northern soul, and funk; it mixes white culture with black culture; and it uses state-of-the-art technology to create ever more eclectic sounds which draw from a vast array of cultural resources. The sheer eclecticism of such a cultural form and its rapid tendency to shift, change and reconstitute itself in new ways, for Redhead defined the subculturalists' attempt to reveal its hidden meaning. Thus, rave culture had no real meaning or underlying significance that we could read off from its structural determinations. Rather, contemporary youth culture is best understood as a series of discursive formations that use symbols, images and language to create new and innovative ways of life and to step outside of traditional representations of normality.

Others have developed this approach and expanded it to talk not just about rave culture but 'club culture'. Here it is argued that the notion of subculture has also lost its significance and relevance both theoretically and analytically (Thornton 1995). Youth in the 1990s is becoming more fragmented and diverse. Club cultures are 'taste cultures. Club crowds generally congregate on the basis of their shared taste in music, their consumption of common media and, most importantly, their preference for people with similar tastes to themselves' (Thornton 1995: 3). Club cultures create a community that cuts across class, gender, racial and status lines having fluid boundaries. They can contain their own hierarchies of what is authentic and legitimate in popular culture. For club cultures are riddled with these cultural hierarchies, covering the authentic versus the phoney, the hip versus the 'mainstream', and the 'underground' versus the media (Thornton 1995). For example, the authentic was being reconstituted, moving from 'live' music to a new emerging 'disc culture', where new heroes, such as sound-productionists, remixers and disc jockeys emerged, as opposed to guitarists and singer/songwriters. These new taste cultures are important in shaping what it means to be young (Thornton 1995).

'Neo-tribalism' and 'hybrid' cultures

Similar to discussions in previous chapters, cultural theorists have raised questions about the relationship between structure and agency. In the context of youth leisure, traditional subcultural theory, as an analytical tool, is seen as flawed and lacking the ability to understand the complexity of youth culture in late modern life (Bennett 1999; Miles 2000; Muggleton 2000; Chaney 2004). In its place, notions such as 'neo-tribes', 'hybrid cultures' and 'lifestyles' are seen to offer a more useful set of tools for understanding youth culture. Muggleton (2000) claims that subcultural theory, in the rave era, has lost its usefulness, with youth culture becoming blurred between 'elite' and 'popular' culture based upon hybrid nostalgia. Young people have become more creative agents, making choices that cross not only class and gender lines, but also subcultural boundaries of old. The notions of rules have become irrelevant, with the young depoliticised and involved in seeking pleasure. Others (Bennett 1999) have agreed, arguing that the concept is too rigid, too focused on the influence of structure over agency, while also over-reading activities of the young as being about resistance:

> In my view the term 'subculture' is deeply problematic in that it imposes rigid lines of division over forms of socialisation which may, in effect, be rather more fleeting, and in many cases arbitrary, than the concept of subculture, with its connotations of coherency and solidarity, allows for.
>
> (Bennett 1999: 603)

Subcultural theory is also seen as excluding large areas of commonality between groups, ignoring the connections that might exist between different youth activities (Bennett 1999), and as not being able to engage with wider cultural changes that are taking place (Chaney 2004). In its place Bennett (1999) argues in favour of 'neo-tribes'. This is seen as a group gathering or event that is less structured and more diverse in its relationships. It refers more to 'a certain ambience, a state of mind, and is preferably to be expressed through lifestyles that favour appearance and form' (Maffesoli 1996: 98, quoted in Bennett 1999: 605). Such a concept offers a more fluid understanding of youth culture, providing a framework for understanding choice and individualism that reflects the temporal nature of identities and their construction, and of the broad range of influences that can contribute to subjectivity. In this context, concepts such as class, gender and race are some of the many factors, but not the only ones of importance, that young people draw upon to define who they are. In late modernity these structural influences are seen as being relegated to the background, with notions of consumption and lifestyle being more important. This can emphasise the importance of lifestyle, suggesting that it is something that is 'a freely-chosen game and should not be confused with a "way of life"' (Bennett 1999: 607), being linked to patterns of consumption and cultural resources rather than structure. In this context, the local becomes a critical resource, as it is where young people appropriate and transform cultural commodities to construct their own lifestyles.

Others have wanted to talk less about 'neo-tribes' and more about 'hybrid cultures', especially in relationship to Asian and black youth (Back 1996). As we encountered in the previous chapter, theories and research on youth culture and consumption practices highlight how ethnic identities are being reconfigured and negotiated within a local context. Back (1996), for example, has argued for an understanding of how new ethnicities are constructed, where the cultural boundaries between different groups are becoming increasingly difficult to identify. Similar arguments unfold in Pilkington's (2004) analysis of Russian youth culture. She argues for the importance of 'youth cultural strategies' that mobilise both the 'global' and 'local' as a way of young people positioning themselves within the youth scene. Youth subculture loses its significance, as does the notion of 'post-modern lifestyle'. Pilkington suggests that this relationship is fundamentally interconnected with and central to how the young construct themselves as cultural:

> 'young people do not live in the shadow of globalisation, but rather ... the "global" and the "local" are resources drawn upon, differentially, by young people in the process of developing youth cultural strategies that manage "glocal" lives.
>
> (Pilkington 2004: 132)

In defence of subcultural theory

Historically, subcultural theories have had a major impact on youth studies (Blackman 2005). They have been used, in many areas, as benchmarks for identifying social change (Blackman 2004; Frith 2004), and their ability to explain youthful behaviour has been brought into question many times (Frith 2004). But they remain powerful analytical tools, even in late modernity. Post-structuralist approaches overemphasise the diversity and lack of rules and boundaries of youth cultural activity. They become enthralled and sucked into the notion of 'free-floating' choice as a normal part of youth culture. Yet evidence suggests we should not abandon subcultural theory altogether. Hodkinson (2002), for example, shows, in his analysis of Goths, that the concept still has a use. His research showed the existence of a subculture which was clearly identifiable. Values and tastes within the Goth culture were identified as distinctive and consistent to participants. Being involved brings a shared sense of affiliation and collective identity. The British Goth scene tends to operate relatively autonomously and, in this context, a subcultural infrastructure exists around goods and services, which helps generate and facilitate a 'Goth scene' (Hodkinson 2002). This is not to say that problems with subcultural theory do not exist. For example, involvement in the Goth subculture is not borne out of a collective structural experience of contradiction. Neither is it about resistance or political motivations. Evidence suggests it tends to have stronger ties to wider cultural processes and notions of consumption (Hodkinson 2002). This being said, the value of Hodkinson's analysis is that it shows that subcultural theory, while having to recognise social change and new contexts, does still have an analytical role to play in explaining certain forms of youthful activity.

Others have wanted to suggest that the contribution that subcultural theory has made, and continues to make, is that it highlights the importance of a need for a more critical reading of youth culture. Blackman (2005), for example, wants to critique the new forms of 'post-modernist subcultures', of 'neo-tribes', and lifestyles, suggesting that they fail to recognise that subcultural analysis is not simply about structured differences between social groups, which draw upon different cultural resources to present themselves. Historically, subcultural theory emerged out of attempts to understand the structural contradictions of the young, recognising that class, gender and race are important factors in shaping the lives of young people (Blackman 2005). While consumption was, and is, important, there needs to be an understanding of structural forms of power (Frith 2004). In this context, choice, especially in terms of consumption, is always limited and structured (or 'bounded'). Subcultural theory has also brought to our attention the importance of the notion of resistance. While its precise meaning remains contested, and still in need of defining (Raby 2005), subcultural theorists have shown that not only do young people exert agency, but also they can be politically motivated (Blackman 2005). In more contemporary terms, we need to recognise that youth movements such as New Age travellers, free festivals, eco-warriors, and anti-capitalist movements are not just free-floating, pleasure-seeking activities, they have strong elements of being late modern forms of subcultural movements that have been performing rituals of resistance (Blackman 2005). In this context subcultural theorising still has something of significance to offer.

Understanding 'risk-taking' in late modernity

These debates over youth culture remain important, yet a major problem is that they fail to explore and explain the role of risk-taking in late modernity. Post-structuralism, neo-tribes, youth strategies, and subcultural theories focus on 'celebration' of specific types of youthful activities at the expense of other forms of cultural practice. Admittedly, they are less about 'problem youth' and more about pleasure-seeking and creativity, but youth research has taken less interest in risk-taking as a cultural phenomena.

How risk in late modernity is influential in everyday life has become important to much social science (Adam *et al.* 2000). Late modernity has been understood as the 'risk society' (Beck 1992), yet social theorising has concentrated on understanding how risks are constructed or responded to. Lupton (1999), for example, highlights three epistemological positions towards risk: a realist position where risk is objective and measurable; a weak constructionist position where risk remains objective but is mediated through social and cultural processes; and a strong constructionist position where nothing is risky, being a product of history and social political forces.

Much social science research on the youth question has been dominated by the realist position (France 2000). This has its roots in the realist epistemological approach of science and, especially, in statistical modelling and mathematics. Young people's decisions to take risks are seen as rational calculations, shaped by psychodynamic processes based upon traditional assumptions of adolescent development (France 2000). Such a position is fundamentally problematic, in that it fails to either recognise the broader societal context that can underpin the reasons why young people engage in risk-taking, or that risk itself can be a social product (France 2000; Kemshall *et al.* 2006). Such a position shifts the emphasis towards the need for a more social understanding of risk-taking (France 2000).

One important influence in shaping young people's understanding of risk and risk-taking is the local context. The types of risks young people encounter, and take, can be structured and shaped by factors in the locality. Some of these are structural, while others are cultural, and risks can be both real and perceived. Young women, for example, can be fully aware of 'dangerous spaces' in their communities and make calculations and changes to avoid them on a routine basis (Seabrook and Green 2004). Similarly, young men can draw upon local understandings and values of risk-taking as a mechanism of being socially included, seeing 'being different', or a 'non-risk-taker', as problematic (Williams *et al.* 2003). Such issues can be important in understanding drug-taking and excessive drinking in local areas. For example, drinking styles and images are structured by cultural norms and beliefs at the local level. Certain drinks reaffirm masculine identities and are given cultural value in certain local settings. Lager and high-alcohol-content drinks, for example, can have greater status for young men in deprived areas: 'Lager is not only a masculine drink; premium bottled lagers have become the drinking symbol of young affluent males in the 1990s. Clutched against designer shirts, there is nothing more required' (Brain *et al.* 2000: 14).

Similar patterns emerge over drug use. Local context defines boundaries of usage and the type of drugs that are acceptable (MacDonald and Marsh 2005; Parker *et al.* 1998). Notions of 'problem' and 'recreational' use are in many senses local constructs that are dependent on local cultural norms (McDonald and Marsh 2005; Shildrick 2002). But what is acceptable as a form of risk-taking in a geographical area is also influenced by wider changes taking place in local communities. MacDonald and Marsh (2005), for example, show how this process in a deprived community in the North East of England impacted on young people's involvement in risk-taking behaviour, moving them from cannibals to crack cocaine consumption. Similar claims can be made over the expansion in the late 1990s of 'illegal' imports of alcohol and cigarettes, after the removal of personal limits on what could be brought into the UK. Local illegal markets, especially in deprived areas, with cut-price goods, blossomed and increased the availability of cheap alcohol and cigarettes to the young.

Similar to evidence in the previous chapter, we can see how risk-taking is being commodified and shaped by the cultural and corporate industries. Evidence, for example, shows a growing linkage between youth culture, drugs and consumer capitalism, that not only commercialises drug-taking but also gives it fashion status and credibility (Blackman 1996). Drug images have become popularised by consumption, so that certain clothes with certain symbols are seen as 'cool'. For example, the 'Spliffy' logo is a case in point. He is a small cartoon character worn on clothes, baseball hats, and bags, and is clearly identifiable with cannabis smoking. Wearing 'Spliffy' is a marker of being 'cool' and a fashion item (Blackman 1996). It does not represent a desire to support drug use so much as a desire to fit in and to be part of the current fashion scene. The idea that drugs and risk-taking are a normal part of youth culture is reinforced by the marketing of a 'drug culture' as a desirable symbol of 'coolness'. Similar findings can be found in the advertising industry. Evidence shows that the advertising industry is using drug culture as a means of selling its products (Taylor 2000). It is seen as a lifestyle choice, like many other consuming activities, and it is being 'naturalised' by commercial interests within youth culture. In other words, advertisers and producers benefit by the construction of a culture that 'popularises' drug use and constructs it as 'hip' and 'cool', as it helps the selling of the product (Taylor 2000). Risk-taking, such as drug use, is then a commodity that helps sell other consumer products.

Similar patterns exist in the production of a night-time entertainment economy (Hollands and Chatterton 2003). This is big business and a major contributor to the cultural industry's profits. Over recent years, there has been an expansion of new leisure, especially around the night-time economy. The creation of nightclubs, themed pubs, casinos, new music venues and café bars, has seen the night-time economy restructured (Hollands and Chatterton 2003). Ownership of the cultural industries has also been concentrated in the hands of large conglomerates, away from small-scale entrepreneurs (Hannigan 1998). Similarly, the brewing industry has recognised the need to find new ways of engaging young consumers. This has taken place through the remarketing of old products with new brands, and creating new goods and services, such as alcopops and 'happy hour' drinking times, that target the young (Brain 1998). As a result, consumption capitalism has transformed the urban night scene and leisure framework for youth. While much of this has tried to gentrify urban centres, nightlife continues to be dominated by industries trying to increase alcohol consumption by the young (Hobbs *et al.* 2000). Themed bars are now the new palaces of drunkenness, promoting loud music, excessive drinking, and cheap meal-and-drink deals (Newburn and Shiner 2001). The restructuring of urban spaces in such ways can have an influence on how young people engage in the leisure industry and the types of risks that they take. It creates new, segmented spaces, which are being inhabited by a wide range of youth groups. Alongside this is the formation of new cultural practices that are interconnected with excessive drinking and risk-taking: 'Mainstream nightlife is generally characterized by smart attire, the consumption of commercial chart music, circuit drinking, pleasure-seeking and hedonistic behaviour framed within largely corporately owned bars and nightclubs' (Hollands 2002: 163). Such nightlife activity is appealing to working-class youth who are on insecure incomes, low pay or are unemployed (Hollands 2002). While subdivisions exist, large sections of working-class youth find pleasure and status in forging some form of 'civic' identity or sense of community. Risk-taking, therefore, is constructed within a culture of urban consumption as acceptable and normal, bringing profits and benefits to an expanding cultural industry.

While risk-taking is strongly influenced by local context and the political economy of consumption, we should not ignore the influence of society-wide developments. Risk-taking is seen as a normal part of everyday life and, in many cases, is seen as positive. For example, babies, in moving from crawling to walking, have to take risks. Risk-taking is also seen as a positive attribute to development in adolescence. Different government programmes have been devised that encourage risk-taking as part of personal growth and development (Nichols 2002). Risk-taking is also perceived as an important part of adult life. Being an entrepreneur and inventor of new products and commodities is connected to being a risk-taker. To 'make it' in industries such as financial investment and property development requires individuals to be good risk-takers. Rewards can be substantial, with success bringing large bonuses. In this context, taking risks, and winning, is seen as a positive attribute to both personal development and society, and something we should see as a normal part of 'successful' life. The 2006 television programme, *The Apprentice*, sets potential future business entrepreneurs tasks to achieve. Participants are rewarded for skills in winning and risk-taking. Similarly, gambling is also about taking risks. As a form of leisure it is legitimised and encouraged, seen as positive when people win, unproblematic when it is irregular and for fun and pleasure, yet negative when obsessive and addictive.

One important discourse around risk-taking that gives it legitimacy as a social activity is the notion of pleasure. Risk and pleasure-seeking have become closely associated in broader political and cultural discourses (Lupton 1999). Across society, high-adventure holidays such as swimming with sharks, climbing dangerous mountains, bungee jumping and skydiving, are given much more credence. This form of 'edge work' and pleasure-seeking has become acceptable and implied as a cultural norm to mainstream society (Lyng 1990). Seeking, and finding, pleasure is given credibility, as it offers ways into a communal spirit for those taking part while helping personal growth (Lupton 1999). As Featherstone (1995) argues, for young people, this is becoming the 'heroic life' that helps many transcend the everyday. This is especially relevant in those communities where pleasure is hard to find (Brain *et al.* 2000; France 2000; Mitchell *et al.* 2004). Searching for pleasure can, in a world where there is little opportunity for pleasure, shape how 'risk-taking' is constructed. For example, chasing around in stolen cars, petty thieving, and shoplifting activities can help manage boredom for some groups of young people (Parker 1974; MacDonald and Marsh 2005). Searching for the 'buzz', 'getting wrecked' or 'getting out of your head' can be a mechanism for managing problematic lives (Parker 1974; Brain *et al.* 2000). Getting drunk can, in some cases, be the only pleasurable way of taking alcohol (Brain *et al.* 2000), and mixing drugs and alcohol gives a 'buzz' and leads to greater pleasure than single usage (Parker *et al.* 2002). But this type of activity cannot always be seen as unbounded, unstructured or irrational. Risk-taking and pleasure-seeking can be structured and influenced by other factors, such as needing to get up for work, the danger of negative effects on future prospects (Brain *et al.* 2000), or not wanting to damage sexual reputations (Bunton *et al.* 2004).

Conclusion

Youth culture in late modernity has been fragmenting and fracturing. Modernist contradictions, alongside the growth of consumption and leisure interests, have created new forms of cultural activities that challenge traditional understandings of youth. In late modernity, youth culture is being expressed and conducted through alternative social movements. Alongside this, we see the emergence of new levels of risk-taking, which is being normalised, suggesting that youth of today are becoming the 'risk generation'. Within this discourse, youth is proclaimed to be at 'the leading edge', being a creative and innovative force that is challenging traditional boundaries, while also constructing new forms of identities. But media representations and political perceptions construct this new 'post-modern youth' as hedonistic, self-interested and irresponsible. Youth have seemingly lost their sense of purpose, their political nature, and their connection to the 'common core values' of a 'good society'. As a result, they also generate fears and anxieties that have consequences for all, leading to governments creating greater forms of regulation and control. Once again the youth question is then being shaped around the actions of the few, which are limiting and controlling the many.

Youth researchers have been partners in the process of constructing perceptions of youth as 'free agents', although without much influence on political understandings. Raves, club cultures and risk-taking are seen as new forms of cultural sites for youth identities. Old theories and models of understanding are seen as limited, being replaced by new models of analysis that argue for more flexibility and the recognition of diversity. Young people are seen as active players in the process, and creative consumers. But dangers exist in that, in proclaiming 'new times', we fail to recognise old processes and practices that are still influential in late modernity. While changes are taking place in the social structure, and the sites of leisure young people engage in, structural influences and location still remain powerful influences. Similarly, while consumption may be a significant aspect of young people's lives, the cultural and marketing industries cannot be ignored as powerful shaping forces in these processes. We need to remember that identities are not created in a vacuum. Social, political and economic forces remain of central importance to the process of identity formation.

9 The changing nature of youth in late modernity?

Introduction

In setting out to understand the changing nature of youth and the youth question in late modernity, I have argued the importance of locating such an analysis within a historical framework. Over the previous two centuries the youth question has always been seen as a matter of serious concern, being used to symbolise wider social problems and difficulties. We should not, therefore, isolate contemporary developments and understandings from historical continuities. The discussion has also concentrated on the important relationship between broader societal developments associated with the economic, political and social ordering, and also the evolution and expansion of ideas and theories of youth. Within these processes I have shown the close connection and relationship between them in constructing our modern knowledge about youth as a phase of the life course.

In this final chapter I want to return to the critical question of the state of knowledge about youth in late modernity. While I have emphasised the importance of historical continuity, we also need to recognise changes in the youth question. In the discussion that follows I want to turn my attention to these issues, drawing out the implications they have for our understanding of youth. But it is not enough just to review what has already been discussed. I also want to propose how we, as researchers of youth and the youth question, might be able to make a wider contribution to contemporary debates over the condition of youth in late modernity.

'Political discourses' and the youth question

Our starting place needs to be on the political processes. As we saw in Chapter 1, political discourses of the youth question have a close relationship with social order, in that it has symbolically reflected wider political concerns about the state of the nation:

> Over the last century, the 'condition of the youth question' has assumed increasing importance as being symptomatic of the health

> of the nation or the importance of the race, the welfare of the family, or the state of civilisation-as-we-know-it.
>
> (Cohen 2003: 43)

The concept of youth has, then, continually been drawn upon to reflect on the state of civilisation at particular moments in time. In pre-modernity this was constructed around anxieties over the transitional processes of children into adult forms of independence. It took place in the locality and was policed by local forms of governance. In modernity the focus shifted between anxieties over delinquency, integration and unemployment. Notions of 'dangerousness' interplayed with concerns about 'vulnerability', leading to a range of national interventions being put into place by the state. These either increased the control and governance of the young, or provided powers to a wide range of professionals to intervene as a form of protection. As a result, youth was formally constructed by the state as a stage in the life course that requires attention. While this universalised youth, a wide range of contradictions exist in how this phase is experienced by different groups.

In late modernity these processes continue, but under new conditions and with new forms of governance (Rose 1999). Global and economic restructuring has a major impact on national economies, and especially on labour markets and patterns of employment. Young people's transitions from school to work collapse, and new challenges face governments over how to manage the increased youth unemployment. Family forms are being restructured, and relationships between the young and their parents are changing. By the 1990s new technology and media are also becoming more influential in the everyday lives of the young. Within these processes, anxieties and 'problems' remain centre stage. Unemployment, educational failure and youth crime are still seen as fundamental, with problems being constructed around a number of specific anxieties such as employability, educational exclusion, underachievement, anti-social behaviour, binge drinking, drug-taking and risk-taking.

Evidence to suggest that these anxieties are justifiable is thin. While we should not deny that there are worrying trends, many are questionable and challengeable. As we have seen, anxieties are far more complex than presented in mainstream policy and the media. They cannot simply be 'read off' as 'problems', yet they can still hold central place in the policy-making process. Policies of late modernity have become framed around notions of the 'underclass' and 'social exclusion', and both locate the 'youth problem' in families and individuals, not structures and processes (Byrne 2005). The young are seen as being in a 'stage of deficit', where they lack morality, skills and responsibility. The causes of 'problems' are seen as pathological and 'blamed' on genes, the lack of cognitive development, poor parenting, or poor 'culture'. Although inclusion is claimed as a core principle of policy, the young, and especially the poorest, are still very much excluded and blamed for their own circumstances (Byrne 2005).

Policy across a wide range of areas has also been greatly influenced by attempts to increase young people's sense of responsibility. This is part of a broader agenda, driven by New Labour's interest in creating a form of citizenship that insists upon the linking of rights and responsibilities. How this has been experienced varies by class, in that those young people who are most vulnerable have been forced to conform by the tying together of social benefits and work responsibilities. We also see increased forms of surveillance and governance, which limit young people's use of public space and increase the possibility that they will be further 'problemitised' or 'criminalised'. Policy increases the 'disciplining' functions of the state for the young unemployed and especially the working-class school leaver. While middle-class youth have entered higher education, the working class have encountered poor work with few opportunities, and increased training in vocational skills, as a response to the 'problem'. The youth question in late modernity therefore remains fixated with 'youth as a problem' that still needs fixing. What seems to have changed is the way policy and the state might go about this process.

Responses to the youth question

But why do such negative views of youth still hold centre stage in political thinking? One explanation lies in the fact that the state itself has been in 'crisis', having to manage major fundamental restructuring (Garland 2000), and its policies and practices of 'responsibilising' and 'blaming' are methods of detracting attention from its existing problems (Hall 1988). Such claims remain strong and should not be discounted. In late modernity, nation states find it increasingly difficult to manage globalising processes. Unemployment has been growing across the world, populations have been getting older, and families have become more fragmented. There have also been greater movements of populations, and terrorism and security have become major anxieties. The state's authority is continually under question, and new ways of governing have had to be constructed (Garland 2000). Resources are also more limited. Global competition, and ageing and transient populations, impact on the resources available to spend on welfare. The state, therefore, needs to find new ways of managing social life and its resources. One solution provided by the politics of neo-liberalism is to limit the role of the state in everyday life. In the 1990s New Labour constructed policies that, while rejecting the 'no such thing as society' mantra of Thatcherism, instigated policies that located the 'problem of youth' in the actions of individuals, the failings of communities and the poor parenting skills of working-class families.

But we also need to recognise that the politics of late modernity is strongly influenced by a moralising agenda. Youth is constructed as the lack of individual morality, especially amongst the poor. New Labour mixes the moral position of 'underclass theory' with that of the views of communitarians constructing the 'problem of youth' as one of a failure of the young working class to hold middle-class values and morals. There is also a pragmatic aspect to this process that continues to contribute to the 'problematising of youth'. As we saw in Chapter 6, youth crime is mobilised and used as 'electoral glue' at general elections, or times of crisis, as a means of emphasising policy plans that will be 'tough on crime'. Popular punitiveness constructs youth as the 'other', and as a threat to the existing security of middle-class life, therefore justifying greater intervention, surveillance and control of vulnerable populations. Within this process we should not forget the critical role that the media can, and does, play in shaping not only 'common-sense' views of the youth problem but also political understandings. Even though major structural changes have been taking place in how the media is organised, youth is still very much portrayed as a problem. In fact, in late modernity moral panics over youth have become what Brown calls a 'total panic': 'This vista – in so far as people take it on board – precisely subsumes "young people" as one problematic entity' (Brown 2005: 64).

One final factor that we should recognise is that of the continued assumptions about the meaning of youth that are inherent within political and professional understandings of the youth question. As we saw in Chapters 2 and 3, developmental models of youth as a biological and physiological stage in the life course have always infiltrated and influenced political, and especially professional, thinking. Puberty, and 'storm and stress', have been continually drawn upon as possible explanations for the 'causes' of young people's 'bad' behaviour. In late modernity these models are as strong as ever and remain a major influence on how policy is shaped.

Youth research and the youth question

In Chapters 2 and 3 we saw that youth research was historically shaped out of concerns over 'youth as a social problem'. This focus remained throughout the twentieth century. Much social science research constructed youth as 'passive' victims of either their biology or their social circumstances. From G. Stanley Hall (1903) onwards, studies of youth were also dominated by concerns over 'problem' boys. This tendency concentrated on the more spectacular and visible activities of the few, those who seemed to be the most troublesome and the most problematic. Notions of difference and diversity, alongside the everyday and ordinary activities of the young, were marginalised and given less significance. Girls tended to be ignored, although when they were included they tended to be sexualised and linked to biological dysfunction, this being seen as a driving force for their behaviour. But as we have seen, in late modernity such an approach has been challenged. Social science research has evolved and developed a body of diverse but important new knowledge improving our understandings of youth and the youth question.

Challenges to the 'youth as a social problem' paradigm

New studies and research have emerged that give stronger attention to the problems young people face in late modernity. Studies on social change have given a major focus to how the young cope with the everyday aspects of life. This is increasing our understanding of the complex problems young people have to manage. For example, the broadening of the simple notion of the school-to-work transition to one of 'transitions to adulthood' highlights how social change is impacting on young people's lives, and the difficulties and multiple challenges they face. Studies have also shown how policy itself, in trying to resolve and deal with the 'youth problem', can create further difficulties. In Chapter 6 we saw how policy on immigration and the policing of Asian communities has created 'new' fears and anxieties that are leading to the increased 'problemitising' of some of the most marginalised groups of young people.

This movement away from the dominant paradigm in studying youth has also been greatly fuelled by the emergence of cultural studies. Not only has it increased the focus on fields of study, such as consumption of music, new media, technology, and youth cultures, but also it has concentrated on the creative and positive contribution young people can make to everyday life. This is not to say that youth research has rejected the 'youth as a problem' paradigm. A strong stream of research, especially that supported by government, still concentrates on trying to find 'solutions' to problem youth. As we saw in Chapter 6, criminological research is still dominated by the search for causes and associations. Of course, we should not be surprised that the emphasis remains so great in discussions over youth and crime, yet the dominance is all embracing, with alternative understandings and explanations marginalised. As we saw, little work has explored the everyday notions of crime and its context, or young people and risk, as victims and witnesses of crime, or even the impact of services and processes on young people's criminal identities. Such a narrow focus of social science research has therefore limited our understandings of the role that crime plays in shaping young people's identities. Similar problems have existed over how 'social exclusion' has been understood and researched. Much mainstream governmental research has concentrated on measurement and monitoring of exclusion, constructing indicators of its extent amongst certain groups. Such an approach categorises individuals as 'excluded' or not, and imposes the classification upon their lives. It tends to be one-dimensional and static, unable to explore the social processes and movement in and out of exclusion that shape people's life chances. A more dynamic approach is one that is able to link the processes to wider contextual developments, showing that people's lives are not to be separated from important global, local and system-wide developments (Byrne 2005; MacDonald and Marsh 2005).

Youth, subjectivity and identity

Interest in notions of subjectivity and identity is not unique to youth studies, yet it has had a major and significant influence on how the youth question, and youth itself, is understood in late modernity. Within these developments, 'agency' has been given a new ascendancy, recognising that social actors are important producers of subjective identities. These are recognised as flexible, negotiated, and self-constructed through a wide range of social processes and experiences. Psychology, alongside the body, is not rejected but incorporated into an analysis that sees that the construction of youthful identities cannot ignore the physical and mental processes young people experience in growing up. This has been most influential in discussions about diversity and difference, especially around gender. Notions of 'girlhood', for example, are seen to involve the interplay of physical changes, consumption practices and culture. But as we have seen, there remain gaps in our knowledge. Much research on 'girlhood' is focused on the private activities of 'doing girl', in friendships and families, in private spaces (bedrooms and chat rooms). Labour market relationships and the formal processes of transition into adulthood remain under-researched. With the growth of training and education for post-16s, we also need more research on how girls' identities are socially reproduced in the new structures and processes that have emerged under late modernity.

Similarly, research on young men has expanded. It has been greatly influenced by developments in the theorising of masculinities. Young male identities are perceived as a negotiated process between the 'hegemonic masculinity' and notions of 'otherness'. Sexuality and body changes are not exempt from these processes, suggesting that what it means to be a boy in late modernity is greatly influenced by a range of social relationships and physical developments. This being said, the original enthusiasm in subjects such as criminology and cultural and media studies over the relationship between masculinity and identities has since dampened. As a result there is limited contemporary work in areas such as 'doing crime', 'taking risks' and the use of new media technology. Even though we know these activities are male-dominated, research on young men's masculine identities in other social contexts is lacking.

We have also seen the emergence of research that takes seriously the question of racialised identities, recognising the interplay between tradition, religion, globalisation and structural inequalities. Being black or Asian in late modernity is a complex process that requires an understanding that recognises the multiple influences at work. Apart from a diverse body of research in education, much of this work does tend to be interested in the cultural activities of young black and Asian youth, especially about the 'mixing' of tradition with Western culture, and about community conflict and tensions. Questions have to be asked about where the studies are on the impact of labour market changes, and on changes to citizenship status, and even on their usage of new media and technology. If we are to fully understand racialised identities, more work needs to be done in these areas.

One final point concerning youth subjectivity is the interplay between global and local influences in structuring the context for young people. In recent times globalisation has been perceived as a major aspect of late modernity, being a significant economic and cultural driving force to social change (Giddens 1991). As we have seen in the previous discussion, global forces can influence the structural 'bounding' and opportunities of the young. For example, international capitalism operating at the global level can structure and influence local labour markets and job opportunities. It can shape the organisation of cultural practice through the structuring of 'night-time economies' and leisure opportunities. Global forces can also set the limits on policy and resources available to national governments, structuring 'what is possible' as a set of responses to young people's needs. The globalising of the cultural world is also opening up new sites and opportunities for the young to gather understandings about other cultural forms and practices. Youth culture is seeing a 'meshing' of the local, the traditional, and the global as ways of being creative in cultural practice. New technologies open the window to 'new' worlds and understandings that are then shaping how young construct themselves as 'cultural'.

Yet as our discussions have shown that the 'locality' still remains a critical site for the young. At one level it is the 'lived' experience of the everyday that is important in giving meaning to social life. For example, how work is to be reconstituted for the young takes place at the local level. Responses to deindustrialisation are, in the main, local and regional decisions. These shape the opportunities available to the young and construct the types of employment and training pathways available. The local can also influence the quality of education and the opportunities for transitions into adulthood. It is also important in giving meaning to cultural activities such as risk-taking in drinking and substance usage. It can shape the cultural responses to the future and values concerning how things are done. The local is also where young people experience public policy and especially policies of crime control, surveillance and regulation. The locality then remains an important site in shaping young people's sense of 'place' in the world. If we are to grasp the complexity of young people's lives and the choices they make we therefore need to understand the influence and interplay between the local and the global.

Questions related to subjectivity and identity have also brought with them new methodologies and approaches that emphasise and respect the important contribution that young people can make to our understanding of subjectivities. Across the disciplines in social science, we see the growth of rich 'thick' data that either complement large-scale samples, or bring in new knowledge about how the world works for the young. This has seen a growth of localised school or community-based ethnographies and detailed case studies of everyday life. In this context, young people's 'voice' is given a privileged position, ensuring that the world in which they live is brought into focus. Of course, questions of giving 'voice' raise as many questions as they solve, and reliance upon one method over another can bring other sets of problems. For example, 'generalisation' remains a distinct problem for qualitative research (Payne and Williams 2005), in that it assumes that readers are equipped to make the assessment themselves (Lincoln and Guba 1985), yet major problems still exist in communicating findings to wider, and more diverse, audiences outside of disciplines such as sociology (Commission on the Social Sciences 2003; Payne and Williams 2005).

Theoretical challenges remain. As we have seen, there is a tendency, especially within the work of post-structuralists, to overread and overemphasise 'agency' over 'structure'. In their enthusiasm to assert the importance of agency, post-structuralists limit the impact of wider structural influences on youth subjectivities and identities. Much of this work is relegated to 'style and dress', with identity work as a form of 'pick and mix' process. Little attention is given to wider political and economic activities that structure inequalities. In a sense, the problem lies with a lack of understanding of the linkages between different spheres of influence. Understanding the cultural cannot be detached from the forces and influences of the cultural industries, and 'choices' cannot be detached from location, opportunities and heritage. Greater attention, therefore, needs to be given to the interconnection of influences and how they operate to help generate young people's sense of selfhood.

The importance of class

The study of class in youth studies has always been important. As a site for exploring the transference of class identities between generations, the youth phase has always been recognised as significant. In late modernity the study of class lost its influence. Post-structuralism challenged the relevance of class, arguing it was either 'dead' or 'withering away', having limited significance to the lives of individuals. Individualism, agency and choice are given prominence in social theorising and research, leaving class, as an analytical tool, a poor relation. Yet, as we have seen in the previous discussion, class does still make an impact on outcomes.

More recently class has re-entered the debates over youth. Class theory is being used once again to consider the processes of how certain patterns of social life are reproduced. Byrne (2005) for example, wants to highlight the dynamic nature of British society in reproducing class divisions, even in times of major social and political change, while MacDonald and Marsh (2005) highlight the entrenched class divisions between geographical regions where local circumstances shape life chances. As we have seen, class theories have struggled to explain both social change and continuity in divisions within youth. Notions of social reproduction have been rejected for 'structured individualism', while 'culture' has been given a new status in trying to understand the gaps between structure and agency. Such concepts are much debated, and youth studies remain an ideal place in which to explore such questions further. Opportunities exist to develop research that examines the interrelationship of structure and agency in a more holistic and dynamic way.

Further research that would enhance our understanding of how class operates to influence life chances is needed. For example, Ball (2003) undertakes an analysis of how the middle class are able to draw upon their own capital to ensure their children benefit from the formal educational system, yet we know little else about how these processes operate away from the school in other locations (in communities, in youth services, in post-16 training and labour markets). More research that explores the relationship between different classes of young people (and their parents) and how they manage themselves within other organisations and systems would also enhance our understanding of how these processes operate to create inequality in other domains of social life.

Little research has also been undertaken on the class differences in transitions to adult citizenship. Most work on this subject has so far concentrated on generalised understandings of the definitions and social processes, yet, given the major changes that are taking place in how different classes make these transitions (i.e. training verses higher education), we need to know more about how they socially reproduce different outcomes for different classes in adulthood. Similar sets of questions remain unanswered in terms of youth culture, risk and risk-taking. It is seen as a growing activity of the young, yet again little research addresses the class differences of youth culture or the role that risk and risk-taking might have in shaping not only present class identities but also future pathways and opportunities.[1]

The social science and policy nexus

So far our discussion has concentrated on discussing the ways that politics and social science have understood and theorised the youth question. As we have seen, significant differences exist in late modernity between how the policy discourses construct the 'problem' (and the types of solutions necessary), and the new knowledges that social sciences have brought to bear on our understandings. In this section I want to explore a range of ways in which youth researchers might be able to ensure that new learning, and knowledge about youth, is more influential in the field of politics.

Evidence-based policy

Social science has always had a precarious relationship with politicians, policy-makers and policy implementers (Sanderson 2004). Under modernism, the Enlightenment movement saw a distinctive role for social science in helping shape the 'new' emerging order. The effectiveness of this influence, especially in the youth field, was limited. In the early stages of modernity, disciplines such as psychology and criminology gained substantial influence. By the 1960s, other disciplines started to gain ground. Bulmer (1987) argues that the take-off point for the expansion of social science influence in policy came in the 1960s, with the establishment of the Social Science Research Council, which became the Economic and Social Research Council (ESRC) in the mid-1980s. But this relationship has always been problematical, in that the political culture has been resistant to 'rational knowledge', and therefore little progress was made (Bulmer 1987). In the 1990s, New Labour changed this. Social science was given a major role in public policy-making (Naughton 2005). Such a position was reinforced in 2000 when the then Secretary of State for Education and Employment, David Blunkett, claimed in a lecture to the ESRC that the 'anti-intellectualism' of previous governments was 'laid to rest', and that the future of government policy embraced social science as a partner (DfEE 2000: paragraphs 35–8).

Evidence-based policy (EBP) has been at the forefront of this development in youth policy (Coles 2000). It has been influential in debates about the shape of youth justice, education and health policies, and social prevention strategies with vulnerable groups (Coles 2000). Yet, as we have seen, how the youth question is framed, and the types of interventions that emerge, have remained located in negative conceptions of youth. Given the expansive knowledge recently generated by social scientists about youth and social change, why has this not infiltrated policy and practice?

The limits of EBP in youth policy

Evidence-based policy has been at the centre of much debate within the social sciences.[2] It has been recognised that it is fraught with problems and uncertainties (Naughton 2005). Some of these problems are seen as technical – for example, how to communicate messages (Nutley and Webb 2000) – and others are more fundamental, related to problems of what constitutes evidence (Klein 2000). In terms of youth research, there have been a range of problems that have dogged the amount of influence that new social science knowledge has had on the policy process.

One critical area is that of the relationships between political ideology and evidence. Social science evidence is but one source of information that politicians and policy-makers draw upon in making decisions about what 'needs to be done' (Sanderson 2004; Wiles 2004). Research 'is not always influential, supplanted by the powerful political forces of inertia, expediency, ideology and finance' (Walker 2000: 62–3, quoted in Sanderson 2004). Research can be used to legitimise policy, rather than direct or guide it, and used when it supports politically driven objectives (Sanderson 2002). As we have seen, youth is a politically contentious issue that acts as a metaphor for 'dangerousness' and threats to the existing 'social disorder'. In this context, the policy-making process is driven by wider imperatives that have little to do with evidence and more to do with ideology. For example, the new youth green paper (DfES 2005) is driven by the political desire to 'responsibilise' the young, and encourage their greater involvement in volunteering as a form of active citizenship. The green paper is less to do with young people's needs and more to do with the political values of New Labour. But the issue is not just one of how evidence is to be used in deciding what policies are best to tackle what problems. Social science research has been marginalised from debates about what problems policy needs to address (Sanderson 2004). So, for example, as we saw in Chapter 5, the entrenched nature of class differences in education remains well established in youth research, yet the unwillingness to draw upon this evidence in framing the problem creates fundamental weaknesses in how policy then tackles educational problems.

In a similar vein, we see that political discourses are still greatly influenced by developmental models of youth that locate the problems in particular ways. Youth, as a biological and psychological stage in the life course, still holds centre stage. Such 'common-sense' perspectives remain a powerful framing context for how policy understands the 'problem of youth', and how it responds. In our discussion on transitions, we saw that policy is still greatly influenced by models that see the process of transition to adulthood as linear and one-dimensional, and related to employment. Little acknowledgement in policy is given to the complexity and changing nature of transitions for the young (Skelton 2002). Similarly, in the new youth green paper (DfES 2005), the problem is defined as the lack of meaningful leisure activities for the young, leading to 'idle hands'. Youth are seen as inherently 'bad', or 'at risk' of being corrupted, or drifting into anti-social activities if left without regulation. The policy solution is to increase (and enforce) leisure opportunities and volunteering, ensuring they are kept 'busy' and out of sight.

The notion of evidence that politicians and policy-makers draw upon in the process of policy-making, and how and when it is used, is another source of difficulty. Policy-makers generally perceive policy-making as a 'rational' process, where research and evaluation findings are used to improve, instrumentally, the effectiveness of their actions (Sanderson 2004). In this context, the ideal form of knowledge is seen as quantitative, experimental (or quasi-experimental) data (Shaw 1999). EBP has given new interest in methodologies that 'prove', without doubt, 'what works'. Questions of reliability and validity are paramount concerns that shape how knowledge is then understood (Shaw 1999). This has focused on developing more efficient scientific methodologies, statistics and models of analysis, such as multivariate analysis (Cabinet Office 1999). In this context more diverse forms of knowledge are marginalised in the process. For example, in our discussion in Chapter 6 on youth crime, we saw how developmental criminology has dominated the political agenda of New Labour, and limited the influence of more diverse forms of knowledge and evidence. In a recent Home Office workshop discussing the future of research into youth crime,[3] the questions raised by civil servants were framed around how to improve our understanding of different models of risk and protective factors, and how to improve the science. Little importance was given to alternative ways of understanding young people's encounters with crime in their everyday lives or of their experiences as victims. Other contemporary examples are evident again in the new youth green paper (DfES 2005). In this we see a very small evidence base to justify the core argument. What evidence is used is taken from a small quantitative sample (Park *et al.* 2004) of 663 young people from across eight years of the life course (12–19-year-olds). This 'snapshot' evidence then underpins and justifies a whole range of policy initiatives. The quality of the data is unquestioned and alternative evidence is ignored.

What is to be done?

There is clearly much to be done in trying to bring some of the more positive messages to the forefront of our everyday thinking about youth. Part of the problem is that youth research has been too narrow in its focus of how to disseminate and share its new knowledges, and has struggled to find ways of communicating the messages. As we saw from the previous discussion, the concentration on EBP has had limited influence in bringing about changes, especially in how policy discourses perceive the problem and feel the need to act. This is not to reject our active involvement in this process, but rather to suggest that we need to rethink what our relationship should be with policy discourses, and how we should be contributing to wider debates about the youth question. We should, of course, still 'speak out' to policy-makers about the importance of new knowledge to our understanding of the 'problem' (Lather 2004), but we also need to recognise that policy is not the only way we can have an influence:

> Policy alone cannot bring about social change. Rather, the participation and empowerment of individuals as agents of change within the lived realities of their everyday lives is critical to the successful of achievement of meaningful social outcomes.
>
> (Percy-Smith and Weil 2003: 69)

National policy may be an important arena, where social change is targeted as an outcome, but it is in the everyday practices and activities of individuals at the local level that real change takes place. National policy may set the context but it is not necessarily the only facilitator of social change. As a result, our active engagement in EBP needs to be focused on engaging with youth issues at the local level, in the policy developments in regions, and the everyday activities of professionals and young people themselves. As outlined by the Commission on the Social Sciences (2003), local and regional engagement is a critical area where the social sciences need to be more active. As our previous discussions have shown, the importance of the locality in shaping the many diverse areas of young people's lives, and their opportunities, supports this view, suggesting this should be a major site of our active engagement with both policy and practice.

Communicative action in evidence-based practice

Such an approach requires new forms of partnerships to be constructed that create a dialogue (Sanderson 2004) and that recognise the contribution of a wide range of partners (Randall 2002). This takes us, as social researchers, into the realms of evidence-based practice and the active involvement in helping instigate change at the micro levels of social life (Sanderson 2004; Byrne 2005). Active engagement is not simple and straightforward, but in these processes we need to go beyond the simple production of 'findings'. There is a greater need for 'communicative dialogue' (Sanderson 2004) in a localised policy discourse (Percy-Smith and Weil 2003). Two good examples of how this approach can operate can be seen in the work of Loader (1996) and Percy-Smith and Weil (2003).

Loader (1996) researches youth–police relationships and argues that the new managerialism of policing has had a detrimental impact. In this, we are seeing a shift away from the notion of 'policing by consent' to one more concerned with financial accountability, performance targets and customer satisfaction. In his research he shows how this new managerialism has little to offer the young. Their experiences as service users or customers are generally ignored within discourses about policing of communities. But by drawing upon Habermas's (1984) notions of 'communicative action', Loader argues that a more democratic, inclusive and viable alternative to the new managerialism can exist, which will increase the opportunities for a democratic form of policing at the local level. By creating new institutional arrangements that increase the opportunities for dialogue between marginalised young people and the police, a new form of democratic accountability can be created that ensures the needs and concerns of the young are brought into a localised strategy to combat social problems.

Percy-Smith and Weil (2003) take a similar position, and show that social policy interventions with the young have had little impact mainly because of the failure of policy implementation to recognise the complexity of young people's lives and to recognise their needs. The professional focus and the need to reach policy targets limit their ability to address complex lives and circumstances. Such structures have no 'communicative action space' for dialogue between practitioners and young people to identify workable solutions. An alternative approach requires a practice of 'critical reflexive action research'. This involves the development of mechanisms that are collaborative, bringing together a range of perspectives, aided by research, that help understand the complexities of young people's lives. It aims to bring together the young person and practitioner in a 'communicative dialogue' that helps identify the extent of the problem and possible solutions that can then inform not only organisational structures and practice, but also future policy development. Research can have a critical role to play in helping identify practice that works, creating space and opportunity for a more empowering form of practice. In both these examples, social research works in partnership with both young people and professionals to ensure that their voices are included in shaping practice and policy responses. Within these dialogues, opportunities exist to contribute to introducing new knowledges about youth, and to opening up spaces to construct more diverse understanding of the young in late modernity.

The youth question and a 'new' public social science?

In this final section I want to explore the important role youth researchers can play in bringing to bear our new knowledges of the youth question to wider public debates. Social science has a critical role to play in contributing and shaping these (Wright Mills 1959; Lauder *et al.* 2004; Burawoy 2005). Our relationship to the public should go beyond the simple engagement with policy and practice (Lauder *et al.* 2004; Burawoy 2005) into the realms of public discourse. Historically, a wide range of social scientists from across the disciplines have taken an active role in contributing to such debates, adding weight and insight to major social phenomena of the times (Eldridge 2000).

While policy-focused social science has been recognised as important (Commission on the Social Sciences 2003), it has also been suggested that disciplines such as sociology need to make a broader contribution (Burawoy 2005; Lauder *et al.* 2004). My own discipline of sociology, for example, needs to be concerned with creating a series of constructive dialogues with wider audiences than just policy-makers and politicians. It needs to engage more with other audiences in important debates of the day. Social science can make a range of contributions to such debates by constructing 'democratic conversations' (Lauder *et al.* 2004). For example, it can not only scrutinise government actions, bringing them to account, but also examine underlying assumptions and claims, making 'visible the invisible' and the 'private public' (Burawoy 2005: 267). It can challenge the orthodoxy, the assumed, and the 'given', offering alternative approaches and different interpretations (Lauder *et al.* 2004). Social science can also help create a more informed citizenry, by influencing public opinion through providing new information and evidence of preconceived social problems and solutions, helping us think reflexively about the type of society we want to live in (Burawoy 2005). It is within this context that the new orthodoxies of youth research need to be more proactive, bringing new knowledges and conclusions to wider public notice. Youth researchers have a critical role and responsibility to challenge some of the more entrenched and outdated assumptions about young people that infiltrate not only political discourses, but also public opinion and 'common sense'. Such a process is not without its difficulties. For example, entering into dialogue with the media, finding interest amongst the public, and entering into constructive debate over volatile and sensitive subjects, such as youth crime and social (dis)order, can be challenging. But if we, as social scientists, are to contribute to challenging some of the misunderstandings and assumptions of what youth means in late modernity, then we need to actively engage in bringing our new knowledges of the youth question to a wider audience.

Notes

Chapter 1

1 The apprenticeships would last until they were approximately 24 years old (Griffiths 1996).
2 According to Springhall (1986: 101), this term describes the large number of adolescents who migrated between jobs and were seen as being unemployable and having no real direction or stability.

Chapter 2

1 Giddens (1991: 38) calls this the 'reflexive monitoring of action'.
2 See Hendrick (1990: 101–18) for a detailed discussion on how Hall's work and ideas infiltrated Victorian ideology.
3 See Garland (2002) for a detailed history of criminology.
4 See Farrington (1996, 2002) for more details of the evidence underpinning this argument.
5 See Chapter 3 of Downes and Rock (2003) for a good reflective review of its influence and approach.

Chapter 3

1 For a good detailed discussion, see McGuigan (1992), Muncie (2004) and McRobbie (1980).
2 See Hoikkala and Suurpää (2005) for its impact on Finnish youth research, Maira and Soep (2004) for its impact on US youth research and Wyn and Harris (2004) for its impact in Australia and New Zealand.
3 See Finn (1987) as a good example of work that explored the social reproduction of training programmes.
4 As we saw, this approach was more successful in the CCCS, as discussed earlier.
5 A small number of exceptions exist, among them Willis (1977).
6 Unlike Paul Willis, McRobbie asked the girls about these kind of issues.

Chapter 4

1 This was reduced to £1.5 billion when it was realised the target group was smaller than assumed.
2 See Tomlinson (2005a) for a good review.
3 See Crompton (1998) for a good review.
4 For example, see Willis (1977).

Chapter 5

1 Section 11 grants were set up in 1966 and were used to fund special initiatives for work with ethnic minorities.
2 For a good detailed overview of the policies that shaped this development, and the objectives and funding base for each type of school, see Tomlinson (2005a).

Chapter 6

1 This happened because of encouragement by the Home Office for the legislation to be used.
2 See Norris and Armstrong (1999) for a review.

Chapter 7

1 S and Fg represent young people who were interviewed in the research.
2 Livingstone *et al.* (2005), for example.

Chapter 8

1 See Redhead (1990) and Bennett (1999), for example.

Chapter 9

1 One exception is the work of Mitchell *et al.* (2004).
2 See Nutley and Webb (2000) for a good of review.
3 Young people, offending, and life chances: Workshop on exploring the evidence, HM Treasury 31 January 2006.

References

Aapola, S., Gonick, M. and Harris, A. (2005) *Young Femininity: Girlhood, Power and Social Change*. London: Palgrave.

Abbot, P., Wallace, C. and Taylor, M. (2005) *An Introduction to Sociology: Feminist Perspectives*, 3rd edn. London: Routledge.

Abrams, M. (1959) *The Teenage Consumer*, LPE Paper 5. London: Press Exchange.

Abrams, P. (1982) *Historical Sociology*. Shepton Mallet: Open Books Publishing.

Abrams, P. and Little, A. (1965) The young activist in British politics, *British Journal of Sociology*, 16: 315–33.

Adams, B., Beck, U. and Van Loon, J. (2000) *The Risk Society and Beyond: Critical Issues for Social Theory*. London: Sage.

Adorno, T. and Horkheimer, M. (1979) *Dialectic of Enlightenment*. London: Verso.

Advisory Group on Citizenship (1998) *Education for Citizenship and the Teaching of Democracy in Schools*. London: Qualification and Curriculum Authority.

Alcohol Concern (2004) *Fact Sheet 20: Binge Drinking*. London: Alcohol Concern.

Alexander, C. (2000) *The Asian Gang*. Oxford: Berg.

Alexander, C. (2004) Imagining the Asian gang: Ethnicity, masculinity and youth after the 'riots', *Critical Social Policy*, 24(4): 526–49.

Alexander, S. (1982) Women's work in nineteenth-century London: A study of the years 1820–50, in E. Whitelegg, M. Arnot, V. Beechey, L. Birke, S. Himmelweit, D. Leonard, S. Ruehl and A. Speakman, *The Changing Experience of Women*. Oxford: Martin Robertson.

Alexiadou, N. (2002) Social inclusion and social exclusion in England: Tensions in education policy, *Journal of Education Policy*, 17(1): 71–86.

Allen, J. and Massey, D. (1989) *The Economy in Question*. Milton Keyes: Open University.

Allen, S. (1968) Some theoretical problems in the study of youth, *Sociological Review*, 16: 319–31.

Althusser, L. (1969) *For Marx*. London: Penguin.

Anderson, B., Beinart, S., Farrington, D., Langman, J., Sturgis, P. and Utting, D. (2001) *Risk and Protective Factors Associated with Youth Crime and Effective Interventions to Prevent It*, Research Note No. 5. London: Youth Justice Board.

Anderson, S., Kinsey, R., Loader, I. and Smith, C. (1994) *Cautionary Tales: Young People, Crime and Policing in Edinburgh*. Aldershot: Avebury.

Archer, L. (2003) *Race, Masculinity and Schooling: Muslim Boys and Education*. Maidenhead: Open University Press.

Archer, L. and Yamashita, H. (2003) 'Knowing their limits?' Identities, inequalities and inner city school leavers' post-16 aspirations, *Journal of Education Policy*, 18(1): 53–69.

Archer, L., Hutchings, M., Ross, A., Leathwood, C., Gilchrist, R. and Phillips, D. (2003) *Higher Education and Social Class: Issues of Exclusion and Inclusion*. London: RoutledgeFalmer.

Ariés, P. (1960) *Centuries of Childhood*. London: Cape.

Armstrong, D. (2004) A risky business? Research, policy, governmentality and youth offending, *Youth Justice*, 4(2): 100–16.

Armstrong, D. (2005) Reinventing 'inclusion': New Labour and the cultural politics of special education, *Oxford Review of Education*, 31(1): 135–51.

Armstrong, D., France, A. and Hine, J. (2006) *Pathways into and out of Crime. Final Report*. London: ESRC.

Arnot, M. and Miles, P. (2005) A reconstruction of the gender agenda: The contradictory gender dimensions in New Labour's educational and economic policy, *Oxford Review of Education*, 31(1): 173–89.

Ashton, D., Maguire, M. and Spilsbury, M. (1990) *Restructuring the Labour Market: Implications for Youth*. Basingstoke: Macmillan Press.

Back, L. (1996) *New Ethnicities and Urban Culture*. London: UCL Press.

Ball, S.J. (1999) Labour, learning and the economy: A policy sociology perspective, *Cambridge Journal of Education*, 29(2): 195–206.

Ball, S.J. (2003) *Class Strategies and the Education Market: Middle Classes and Social Advantage*. London: RoutledgeFalmer.

Ball, S., Maguire, M. and Macrae, S. (2000) *Choice, Pathways and Transitions post 16*. London: RoutledgeFalmer.

Bassett, C. (1991) Virtually gendered: Life in an on-line world, in K. Gelder and S. Thornton (eds) *The Subcultures Reader*. London: Routledge.

Bates, I. (1992) 'When I have my own studio . . .', in I. Bates and G. Riseborough, *Youth Inequality*. Milton Keyes: Open University Press.

Beck, U. (1992) *The Risk Society*. London: Sage.

Beck, U. and Beck-Gernsheim, E. (2002) *Individualization*. London: Sage.

Becker, H. (1963) *Outsiders*. New York: Free Press.

Beinart, S., Anderson, B., Lee, S. and Utting, D. (2002) *Youth At Risk? A National Survey of Risk Factors, Protective Factors and Problem Behaviour among Young People in England, Scotland and Wales*. London: Communities That Care.

Bell, R. (2001) 'Finding and managing' part-time work: Young people, social networks and family support, *ESRC Youth, Citizenship and Social Change Newsletter*, Autumn.

Bennett, A. (1999) Subcultures or neo-tribes? Rethinking the relationship between youth, style and musical taste, *Sociology*, 33(3): 599–617.

Bennett, A. (2000) *Popular Music and Youth Culture: Music, Identity and Place*. Basingstoke: Macmillan.

Bennett, A. (2005) *Culture and Everyday Life*. London: Sage.

Bessant, J., Hil, R. and Watts, R. (2002) *'Discovering' Risk*. Oxford: Peter Lang.

Birkland, T.A. (1997) *After Disaster: Agenda Setting, Public Policy, and Focusing Events*. Washington, DC: Georgetown University Press.

Blackman, S.J. (1996) Has drug culture become an inevitable part of youth culture? A critical assessment of drug education, *Educational Review*, 48(2): 131–42.

Blackman, S.J. (2004) *Chilling Out: The Cultural Politics of Substance Consumption, Youth and Drug Policy*. Maidenhead: Open University Press.

Blackman, S.J. (2005) Youth cultural theory: A critical engagement with the concept, its origins and politics, from the Chicago School to postmodernism, *Journal of Youth Studies*, 8(1).

Blake, L. (2002) 'Ain't misbehavin', *Estates Gazette*, 23: 140–1.

Bloom, A. (2004) Gifted club eases path to universities, *Times Educational Supplement*, 3 December.

Board of Education (1923) *Consultative Committee on the Differentiation of the Curriculum for Boys and Girls Respectively in Secondary Schools*. London: HMSO.

Bottoms, A. and Pratt, J. (1989) Intermediate treatment for girls in England and Wales, in M. Cain, *Growing Up Good: Policing Behaviour of Girls in Europe*. London: Sage.

Bourdieu, P. (1990) *Reproduction in Education, Society and Culture*, 2nd edn. London: Sage.

Bourdieu, P. (1991) *The Logic of Practice*. Cambridge: Polity.

Bowles, S. and Gintis, H. (1976) *Schooling in Capitalist America: Educational Reform and Contradictions of Economic Life*. London: Routledge & Kegan Paul.

Bowling, B. and Phillips, C. (2002) *Racism, Crime and Justice*. London: Longman.

Brain, K. (1998) Youth alcohol, and the emergence of the post-modern alcohol order. Paper presented to the 11th International Conference on Alcohol, Liverpool, UK.

Brain, K., Parker, H. and Carnworth, T. (2000) Drinking with design: Young drinkers as psychoactive consumers, *Drugs Education and Prevention Policy*, 7(1): 5–20.

Brake, M. (1985) *Comparative Youth Culture*. London: Routledge & Kegan Paul.

Brown, A. (2004) Anti-social behaviour, crime control and social control, *Howard Journal*, 43(2): 203–11.

Brown, P. (1987) *Schooling Ordinary Kids*. London: Tavistock Publications.

Brown, P. (1997) Cultural capital and social exclusion: Some observations on recent trends in education, employment and the labour market, in A.H. Halsey, H. Lauder, P. Brown and A.S. Wells, *Education, Culture, Economy and Society*. Oxford: Oxford University Press.

Brown, S. (2005) *Understanding Youth and Crime*. Maidenhead: Open University Press.

Buckingham, D. (2002) The electronic generation? Children and new media, in L. Lievrouw and S. Livingstone (eds) *Handbook of New Media*. London: Sage.

Bulmer, M. (ed.) (1987) *Social Science Research and Government: Comparative Essays on Britain and the United States*. Cambridge: Cambridge University Press.

Bunton, R., Crawshaw, P. and Green, E. (2004) Risk, gender and youthful bodies, in W. Mitchell, R. Bunton and E. Green, *Young People, Risk and Leisure*. London: Palgrave.

Burawoy, M. (2005) 2004 American Sociological Association Presidential address: For public sociology, *British Journal of Sociology*, 56(2): 259–94.

Burstyn, J. (1980) *Victorian Education and the Ideal of Womanhood*. London: Croom Helm.

Burt, C. (1925) *The Young Delinquent*. London: University of London Press.

Bynner, J. (2001) British youth transitions in comparative perspective, *Journal of Youth Studies*, 4(1): 5–24.

Bynner, J., Chisholm, L. and Furlong, A. (1997) *Youth, Citizenship and Social Change in a European Context*. London: Ashgate.

Byrne, D. (2005) *Social Exclusion*, 2nd edn. Maidenhead: Open University Press.

Cabinet Office (1999) *Modernising Government*, Cm. 4320. London: HMSO.

Cabinet Office Strategy Unit (2004) *Alcohol Harm Reduction Strategy for England*. *www.strategy.gov.uk/downloads/su/alcohol/pdf/CabOffc%20AlcoholHar.pdf* (accessed 26 October 2006).

Campbell, B. (1993) *Goliath: Britain's Dangerous Places*. London: Methuen.

Carabine, J. (1996) Heterosexuality and social policy, in D. Richardson, *Theorising Heterosexuality*. Buckingham: Open University Press.

Carter, M. (1966) *Into Work*. London: Pelican.

Chaney, D. (2004) Fragmented culture and subcultures, in A. Bennett and K. Kahn-Harris, *After Subculture*. Basingstoke: Palgrave.

Chisholm, L. (1997) Initial transitions between education, training and employment in the learning society, *International Bulletin of Youth Research*, 15: 6–16.

Clarke, J. (1973) The three R's – repression, rescue and rehabilitation: Ideologies of control of working class youth. CCCS Occasional Paper No. 41, University of Birmingham.

Clarke, J. (1975) The skinheads and the magical recovery of community, in S. Hall and T. Jefferson (eds) *Resistance through Rituals: Youth Subcultures in Post-War Britain*. Birmingham: Centre for Contemporary Cultural Studies, University of Birmingham.

Clarke, J., Hall, S., Jefferson, T. and Roberts, B. (1975) Subcultures, cultures and class: a theoretical overview, in S. Hall and T. Jefferson (eds) *Resistance through Rituals: Youth Subcultures in Post-War Britain*. London: Routledge & Kegan Paul.

Clarke, J., Gewirtz, S. and McLaughlin, E. (2000) *New Managerialism New Welfare?* London: Sage.

Clarke, T., Lipset, S.M. and Rempel, M. (1993) The declining political significance of class, *International Sociology*, 8: 293–316.

Cloward, R. and Ohlin, L. (1961) *Delinquency and Opportunity: A Theory of Delinquent Gangs*. London: Routledge & Kegan Paul.

Cockburn, C. (1987) *Two-Track Training: Sex Inequalities and the YTS*. Basingstoke: Macmillan Education Press.

Coffield, F. (1997) 'Introduction and overview: Attempts to reclaim the concept of the learning society', *Journal of Education Policy*, 12(6): 449–55.

Coffield, F., Borrill, C. and Marshall, S. (1986) *Growing Up on the Margins*. Milton Keynes: Open University Press.

Cohen, A. (1955) *Delinquent Boys: The Culture of the Gang*. Chicago: Chicago Free Press.

Cohen, P. (1997) *Rethinking the Youth Question*. London: Macmillan Press.

Cohen, P. (2003) Mods and Shockers: Youth cultural studies in Britain, in A. Bennett, M. Cieslik and S. Miles, *Researching Youth*. London: Palgrave.

Cohen, P. and Ainley, P. (2000) In the country of the Blind? *Journal of Youth Studies*, 3(1): 79–96.

Cohen, S. (1980) *Folk Devils and Moral Panics: The Creation of Mods and Rockers*, 3rd edn. London: Paladin.

Cohen, S. (1985) *Visions of Social Control*. Cambridge: Polity Press.

Coleman, J. (1961) *The Adolescent Society*. New York: Free Press.

Coles, B. (1995) *Youth and Social Policy: Youth Citizenship and Young Careers*. London: UCL Press.

Coles, B. (2000) *Joined-Up Youth Research, Policy and Practice*. Leicester: Youth Work Press.

Colley, H. and Hodkinson, P. (2001) Problems with bridging the gap: The reversal of structure and agency in addressing social exclusion, *Critical Social Policy*, 21(3): 335–59.

Collier, R. (1998) *Masculinities, Crime and Criminology*. London: Sage.

Collin, M. and Godfrey, J. (1997) *Altered State: The Story of Ecstasy Culture and Acid House*. London: Serpent's Tail.

Commission on the Social Sciences (2003) *Great Expectations: The Social Sciences in Britain*. London: Commission on the Social Sciences.

Committee on Higher Education (1963) *Report on Higher Education*, Cmnd. 2154 (Robbins Report). London: HMSO.

Connell, R. (2002) *The Men and the Boys*. Cambridge: Polity.

Connolly, P. (1998) *Racism, Gender Identities and Young Children: Social Relations in a Multi-ethnic Inner-City Primary School*. London: Routledge.

Connolly, P. and Neill, J. (2001) Constructions of locality and gender and their impact on the educational aspirations of working class children, *International Studies in Sociology of Education*, 11(2): 107–29.

Cornwell, J. (1984) *Hard Earned Lives: Accounts of Health and Illness from East London*. London: Taverstock.

Cowie, J., Cowie, V. and Slater, E. (1968) *Delinquency in Girls*. London: Heinemann.

Crawford, A. (1998) *Crime Prevention and Community Safety*. Harlow: Longman.

Crawford, A. (2002) Joined-up but fragmented: Contradiction, ambiguity and ambivalence at the heart of New Labour's 'Third Way', in R. Matthews and J. Pitts, *Crime, Disorder and Community Safety*. London: Routledge.

Crawford, G. and Gosling, V. (2005) Toys for boys? Women's marginalization and participation as digital gamers, *Sociological Research Online*, 10(1). *www.socresonline.org.uk/10/1/crawford.html*.

Critcher, C. (2000) 'Still raving': Social reaction to Ecstasy, *Leisure Studies*, 19: 145–62.

Critcher, C. (2003) *Moral Panics and the Media*. Buckingham: Open University Press.

Crompton, R. (1998) *Class and Stratification: An Introduction to Current Debates*. Oxford: Polity Press.

Crompton, R. and Scott, J. (2005) Class analysis: Beyond the cultural turn, in F. Devine, M. Savage, J. Scott and R. Crompton (eds) *Rethinking Class: Culture, Identities and Lifestyle*. London: Palgrave.

Cuff, E.C. and Payne, G. (eds) (1979) *Perspectives in Sociology*. London: George Allen & Unwin.

Davies, B. (1986) *Threatening Youth: Towards a National Youth Policy*. Milton Keynes: Open University Press.

Davies, B. (2003) Death to critique and dissent? The politics and practices of new managerialism and of 'evidence-based practice', *Gender and Education*, 15(1): 91–103.

Davies, L. (1984) *Pupil Power: Deviance and Gender in Schools*. London: Falmer Press.

Davis, J. (1990) *Youth and the Condition of Britain*. London: Athlone.

Davis, J. (2004) Negotiating femininities online, *Gender and Education*, 16(1): 35–49.

Davis, N. (1971) The reasons for misrule: Youth groups and charivaris in sixteenth-century France, *Past and Present*, 50(1): 41–75.

Delanty, G. (1999) *Social Theory in a Changing World*. Cambridge: Polity Press.

Department for Education and Employment (1997a) *Excellence in Education*. London: DfEE.

Department for Education and Employment (1997b) *Excellence for All Children: Meeting Special Educational Needs*. London: DfEE.

Department for Education and Employment (2000) *Influence or Irrelevance: Can Social Science Improve Government?* London: DfEE.

Department for Education and Science (1985) *Excellence for All*, Cmnd. 9453 (Swann Report). London: HMSO.

Department for Education and Skills (2004a) *Removing Barriers to Achievement: The Government's Strategy for SEN*. London: DfES.

Department for Education and Skills (2004b) *The Highest Qualification Held by Young People and Adults: England 2003*. London: DfES.

Department for Education and Skills (2005) *Youth Matters*, Cm. 6629. London: DfES.

Devine, F. (2004) *Class Practices: How Parents Help Their Children to Get Good Jobs*. Cambridge: Cambridge University Press.

Devine, F. and Savage, M. (2005) The cultural turn, sociology and class analysis, in F. Devine, M. Savage, J. Scott and R. Crompton (eds) *Rethinking Class: Culture, Identities and Lifestyle*. London: Palgrave.

Devine, F., Savage, M., Scott, J. and Crompton, R. (eds) (2005) *Rethinking Class: Culture, Identities and Lifestyle*. London: Palgrave.

Doolittle, M. (2004) Sexuality, parenthood and population: Explaining fertility decline in Britain from the 1980s to 1920s, in J. Carabine (ed.) *Sexualities: Personal Lives and Social Policy*. Bristol: Policy Press.

Downes, D. (1966) *The Delinquent Solution*. London: Routledge & Kegan Paul.

Downes, D. and Rock, P. (2003) *Understanding Deviance*. Oxford: Oxford University Press.

Driscoll, C. (1999) Girl culture, revenge and global capitalism: Cybergirls, Riot Grrls, Spice Girls, *Australian Feminist Studies*, 14(29): 173–93.

Driver, S. and Martell, L. (2000) Left, Right and the third way, *Policy and Politics*, 28(2): 147–61.

Drotner, K. (1992) Modernity and moral panics, in M. Skovmand and K. Schroder (eds) *Media Cultures: Reappraising Transnational Media*. London: Routledge.

Dwyer, C. (1998) Contested identities: Challenging dominant representations of young British Muslim women, in T. Skelton and G. Valentine (eds) *Cool Places*. London: Routledge.

Dyhouse, C. (1981) *Girls Growing Up in Late Victorian and Edwardian England*. London: Routledge & Kegan Paul.

Eisenstadt, S.N. (1956) *From Generation to Generation*. New York: Free Press.

Eldridge, J. (2000) Sociology and the third way, in J. Eldridge, J. MacInnes, S. Scott, C. Warhurst and A. Witz, *For Sociology: Legacies and Prospects*. Durham: Sociology Press.

Entertainment Software Association (2006) *Essential Facts about Computer and Video Games*. Washington, DC: Entertainment Software Association.

Epstein, D. and Johnson, R. (1998) *Schooling Sexualities*. Buckingham: Open University Press.

Epstein, D., Elwood, J., Hey, V. and Mew, J. (eds) (1998) *Failing Boys: Issues in Gender and Achievement*. Buckingham: Open University Press.

Etzioni, A. (1995) *New Communitarian Thinking*. Charlottesville: University of Virginia.

Farrington, D. (1994) Human development and criminal careers, in M. Maguire, R. Morgan and R. Reiner (eds) *The Oxford Handbook of Criminology*. Oxford: Oxford University Press.

Farrington, D. (1996) *Understanding and Preventing Youth Crime*. York: Joseph Rowntree Foundation.

Farrington, D. (2000) Explaining and preventing crime: The globalisation of knowledge. Keynote Address to the American Society for Criminology, 1999, *Criminology*, 38(1): 1–24.

Farrington, D. (2002) Developmental criminology and risk focused prevention, in M. Maguire, R. Morgan and R. Reiner (eds) *The Oxford Handbook of Criminology*. Oxford: Oxford University Press.

Featherstone, M. (1992) *Consumer Culture and Postmodernism*. London: Sage.

Featherstone, M. (1995) *Undoing Culture: Globalization, Postmoderism and Identity*. London: Sage.

Finn, D. (1987) *Training without Jobs*. Basingstoke: Macmillan.

Finn, D. (2003) The 'employment-first' welfare state: Lessons from New Deal for young people, *Social Policy and Administration*, 37(7): 709–24.

Finney, A. and Toofail, J. (2004) Levels and trends, in T. Dodd, S. Nicholas, D. Povey and A. Walker (eds) *Crime in England and Wales 2003/2004*. London: Home Office.

Flood-Page, C., Campbell, S., Harrington, V. and Miller, J. (2000) *Youth Crime: Findings from the 1998/99 Youth Lifestyles Survey*, Home Office Research Study 209. London: Home Office.

France, A. (1996) Youth and citizenship in the 1990s, *Youth and Policy*, 43: 28–43.

France, A. (1998) 'Why should we care?' Young people, citizenship and questions of social responsibility, *Journal of Youth Studies*, 1(1): 97–112.

France, A. (2000) Towards a sociological understanding of youth and their risk taking, *Journal of Youth Studies*, 3: 317–31.

France, A. and Homel, R. (2006) Societal access routes and developmental pathways: Putting social structure and young people's voice into the analysis of pathways into and out of crime. *Australian and New Zealand Journal of Criminology*, 39: No 3 295–309.

France, A. and Utting, D. (2005) The paradigm of 'risk and protection-focused prevention' and its impact on services for children and families, *Children and Society*, 19(2): 77–90.

France, A., Hine, J., Armstrong, D. and Camina, M. (2004) *The On Track Early Intervention and Prevention Programme: From Theory to Action*, Home Office Report 10/04. London: Home Office.

Fraser, D. (1973) *The Evolution of the British Welfare State*. London: Macmillan Press.

Frith, S. (1984) *The Sociology of Youth*. Ormskirk: Causeway Press.

Frith, S. (2004) Afterword, in A. Bennett and K. Kahn-Harris (eds) *After Subculture*. Basingstoke: Palgrave.

Frosh, S., Phoenix, A. and Pattman, R. (2002) *Young Masculinities*. London: Palgrave.

Frost, L. (2001) *Young Women and the Body*. London: Palgrave.

Fuller, E. (ed.) (2004) *Smoking, Drinking and Drug Use amongst Young People in England*. London: Health and Social Care Information Centre.

Furlong, A. (1997) Education and the reproduction of class-based inequalities, in H. Jones (ed.) *Towards a Classless Society?* London: Routledge.

Furlong, A. (2005) Maintaining middle class advantage, *British Journal of Sociology of Education*, 26(5): 683–5.

Furlong, A. and Cartmel, F. (1997) *Young People and Social Change: Individualization and Risk in Late Modernity*. Buckingham: Open University Press.

Fyfe, A. (1989) *Child Labour*. Cambridge: Polity Press.

Garland, D. (1994) Of crimes and criminals: The development of contemporary criminology, in M. Maguire, R. Morgan, and R. Reiner (eds) *The Oxford Handbook of Criminology*. Oxford: Oxford University Press.

Garland, D. (2000) *The Culture of Control: Crime and Social Order in Contemporary Society*. Oxford: Oxford University Press.

Garland, D. (2002) Of crimes and criminals: The development of criminology in Britain, in M. Maguire, R. Morgan and R. Reiner, *The Oxford Handbook of Criminology*. Oxford: Oxford University Press.

Geraci, J. and Nagy, J. (2004) Millennials – the new media generation, *Advertising and Marketing to Children*, 5(1): 1–8.

Geraci, J., Silsbee, P., Fauth, S. and Campbell, J. (2000) Understanding youth: What works and doesn't work when researching and marketing to young audiences. Paper presented to Reinventing Advertising – The Worldwide Advertising Conference (European Society for Opinion and Marketing Research/Advertising Research Foundation).

Gewirtz, S. (1998) Post-welfarist schooling: A social justice audit, *Education and Social Justice*, 1(1): 52–64.

Gewirtz, S. (2000) Social justice, New Labour and school reform, in G. Lewis, S. Gewirtz and J. Clarke (eds) *Rethinking Social Policy*. London: Sage.

Gewirtz, S. and Cribb, A. (2003) Recent readings of social reproduction: 'Four fundamental problematics', *International Studies in Sociology of Education*, 13(3): 243–60.

Giddens, A. (1991) *Modernity and Self-Identity*. Cambridge: Polity Press.

Giddens, A. (1994) Living in a post traditional society, in U. Beck, A. Giddens and S. Lash, *Reflexive Modernization*. Cambridge: Polity Press.

Gillies, V. (2005) Raising the 'meritocracy': Parenting and the individualization of social class, *Sociology*, 39(5): 834–53.

Gillis, J.R. (1974) *Youth and History*. London: Academic Press.

Gilroy, P. (1987) *There Ain't No Black in the Union Jack*. London: Routledge.

Glueck, S. and Glueck, E. (1950) *Unravelling Juvenile Delinquency*. New York: Harper & Row.

Goldson, B. (2000) *The New Youth Justice*. Lyme Regis: Russell House Publishing.

Goldthorpe, J. (1996) Class analysis and the reorientation of class theory: The case of persisting differentials in educational attainment, *Sociology*, 47: 481–506.

Goldthorpe, J.H., Lockwood, D., Bechhoffer, F. and Platt, J. (1968) *The Affluent Worker: Industrial Attitudes and Behaviour*. Cambridge: Cambridge University Press.

Goodey, J. (2001) 'The criminalization of British Asian youth': Research from Bradford and Sheffield, *Journal of Youth Studies*, 4(4): 429–50.

Goodnow, J. (2006) Adding social context to analysis of pathways and crime prevention, *Australian and New Zealand Journal of Criminology*, 39: No 3 327–338.

Gouldner, A.W. (1971) *The Coming Crisis of Western Sociology*. London: Heinemann.

Graham, K. and Wells, S. (2003) 'Somebody's gonna get their head kicked in tonight!' Aggression among young males in bars – a question of values? *British Journal of Criminology*, 43: 546–66.

Gray, P. (2005) The politics of risk and young offenders' experiences of social exclusion and restorative justice, *British Journal of Criminology*, 45: 938–57.

Greer, G. (2000) *The Whole Woman*. London: Anchor.

Griffin, C. (1985) *Typical Girls? Young Women from School to the Job Market*. London: Routledge & Kegan Paul.

Griffin, C. (1993) *Representations of Youth*. Cambridge: Polity Press.

Griffin, C. (2000) Discourses of crisis and loss: Analysing the 'boys' underachievement' debate, *Journal of Youth Studies*, 3(2): 167–88.

Griffin, C. (2001) Imagining new narratives of youth: Youth research, the 'new Europe' and global youth culture, *Childhood*, 8(2): 147–66.

Griffiths, P. (1996) *Youth and Authority*. Oxford: Oxford University Press.

Gunter, B. and Furnham, A. (1998) *Children as Consumers: A Psychological Analysis of the Young People's Market*. London: Routledge.

Habermas, J. (1984) *The Theory of Communicative Action: Vol. 1, Reason and the Rationalization of Society*. London: Heinemann Educational Books.

Hall, C. (1982) 'The butcher, the baker, the candlestick maker': The shop and the family in the industrial revolution, in E. Whitelegg, M. Arnot, V. Beechey, L. Birke, S. Himmelweit, D. Leonard, S. Ruehl and A. Speakman, *The Changing Experience of Women*. Oxford: Martin Robertson.

Hall, G.S. (1903) *Adolescence, Its Psychology and Its Relations to Physiology, Anthropology, Sociology, Sex, Crime, Religion and Education*. New York: Appleton.

Hall, S. (1988) *The Hard Road to Renewal*. London: Verso.

Hall, S. (1992) What is 'black' in black popular culture?, in M. Wallace and G. Dent (eds) *Black Popular Culture*. Settle: Bay Press.

Hall, S. and Jefferson, T. (eds) (1975) *Resistance through Rituals*. Birmingham: Centre for Contemporary Cultural Studies, University of Birmingham.

Hall, S., Critcher, C., Jefferson, T., Clarke, J. and Roberts, B. (1978) *Policing the Crisis*. London: Macmillan.

Halsey, A.H., Lauder, H., Brown, P. and Wells, A.S. (1997) *Education, Culture, Economy and Society*. Oxford: Oxford University Press.

Hannigan, J. (1998) *Fantasy City. Pleasure and Profit in the Post-modern Metropolis*. London: Routledge.

Hargreaves, D.H. (1972) *Interpersonal Relations and Education*. London: Routledge & Kegan Paul.

Harris, A. (2003) 'gURL scenes and grrrl zines: The regulation and resistance of girls in late modernity', *Feminist Review*, 75: 38–56.

Harvey, D. (1989) *The Condition of Post-modernity*. Oxford: Blackwell.

Haywood, C. and Mac an Ghaill, M. (2005) *Young Bangladeshi People's Experience of Transitions to Adulthood*. York: Joseph Rowntree Foundation.

Heath, S. (2002) Domestic and housing transitions and the negotiation of intimacy, in M. Cieslik and G. Pollock, *Young People in Risk Society*. Aldershot: Ashgate.

Hebdige, D. (1979) *Subculture: The Meaning of Style*. London: Methuen.
Hebdige, D. (1988) *Hiding in the Light: On Images and Things*. London: Routledge.
Heidensohn, F. (1985) *Women and Crime*. London: Macmillan.
Heim, M. (1998) *Virtual Realism*. Oxford: Oxford University Press.
Henderson, S. (1997) *Ecstasy: Case Unsolved*. London: HarperCollins.
Hendrick, H. (1990) *Images of Youth. Age, Class and the Male Youth Problem*. Oxford: Clarendon Press.
Hetherington, K. (1998) Vanloads of uproarious humanity: New Age travellers and the utopics of the countryside, in T. Skelton and G. Valentine (eds) *Cool Places: Geographies of Youth Cultures*. London: Routledge.
Higher Education Funding Council for England (2004) *Entry to Higher Education by Post Code*. Bristol: HEFC.
Hill, A. (2002) Acid House and Thatcherism: Noise, the mob, and the English countryside, *British Journal of Sociology*, 53(1): 89–105.
Hine, J. (2005) Early multiple intervention: A view from On Track, *Children and Society*, 19(2): 117–30.
HMSO (2001) *Special Educational Needs and Disability Act*. London: HMSO.
Hobbs, D., Lister, S., Hadfield, P. and Hall, S. (2000) Receiving shadows: Governance, liminality in the night-time economy, *British Journal of Sociology*, 51(4): 701–17.
Hobsbawm, E.J. (1968) *Industry and Empire*. London: Weidenfeld and Nicolson.
Hobsbawm, E.J. (1987) *The Age of Empire*. London: Weidenfeld and Nicolson.
Hodkinson, P. (2002) *Goth: Identity, Style and Subculture*. Oxford: Berg.
Hoikkala, T. and Suurpää, L. (2005) Finnish youth cultural research and its relevance to youth policy, *Young*, 13(3): 285–312.
Holdaway, S. (1983) *Inside the British Police*. Oxford: Blackwell.
Hollands, R. (2002) Divisions in the dark: Youth cultures, transitions and segmented consumption spaces in the night-time economy, *Journal of Youth Studies*, 5(2): 153–71.
Hollands, R. and Chatterton, P. (2003) Producing nightlife in the new urban entertainment economy: Corporatization, branding and market segmentation, *International Journal of Urban and Regional Research*, 27(2): 361–85.
Hollin, C. (2002) Criminological psychology, in M. Maguire, R. Morgan and R. Reiner (eds) *The Oxford Handbook of Criminology*. Oxford: Oxford University Press.
Holloway, L. S. and Valentine, G. (2003) *Cyber Kids: Children in the Information Age*. London: RoutledgeFalmer.
Home Office (2005) *Drinking Responsibly*. London: Home Office.
Hooton, E. (1939) *Crime and Man*. Cambridge, MA: Harvard University Press.
Huddleston, P. and Oh, S. (2004) 'The magic roundabout': Work related learning within the 14–19 curriculum. *Oxford Review of Education*, 30(1): 83–103.
Hudson, A. (1989) Troublesome Girls, in M. Cain, (ed.) *Growing Up Good: Policing the Behaviour of Girls in Europe*. London: Sage.

Hudson, B. (1982) 'All things nice?', *Social Work Today*, Vol.13 No 41, pp13–14.

Hudson, B. (1989) Justice or welfare? in M. Cain, *Growing Up Good: Policing Behaviour of Girls in Europe*. London: Sage.

Humphery, S. (ed.) (1998) *Shelf Life: Supermarkets and the Changing Cultures of Consumption*. Cambridge: Cambridge University Press.

Hurd, D. (1989) God versus Caesar?, *The Church Times*, 9 September: 1–2.

Hutson, S. and Jenkins, R. (1989) *Taking the Strain*. Milton Keynes: Open University.

Institute of Alcohol Studies (2005) *Binge Drinking: Nature, Prevalence and Causes: Fact Sheet on Binge Drinking*. St Ives: Institute of Alcohol Studies.

Irwin, S. (2003) Interdependencies, values and the shaping of difference: Gender and generation at the birth of the twentieth-century modernity, *British Journal of Sociology*, 54(4): 565–84.

James, A. and James, A.L. (2004) *Constructing Childhood. Theory, Policy and Social Practice*. Basingstoke: Palgrave.

James, A.L. and James, A. (2001) Tightening the net: Children, community, and control, *British Journal of Sociology*, 52(2): 211–28.

Jeffery, C. and McDowell, L. (2004) Youth in comparative perspective: Global change, local lives, *Youth and Society*, 36(2): 131–42.

Jenkins, R. (1983) *Lads, Citizens and Ordinary Kids: Working Class Youth Lifestyles in Belfast*. London: Routledge & Kegan Paul.

Jephcott, P. (1954) *Some Young People*. London: Allen & Unwin.

Jewkes, Y. (2004) *Media and Crime*. London: Sage.

Jones, G. (2002) *The Youth Divide*. York: Joseph Rowntree Foundation, York Publishing Service.

Jones, G. and Wallace, C. (1992) *Youth, Family and Citizenship*. Buckingham: Open University Press.

Jones, S. (1997) *Virtual Culture: Identity and Communication in Cyberspace*. London: Sage.

Kemshall, H., Marsland, L., Boeck, T. and Dunkerton, L. (2006) Young people and pathways: Beyond risk factors, *Australian and New Zealand Journal of Criminology*, 39: No 3 354–370.

Kenway, J. and Bullen, E. (2003) *Consuming Children*. Maidenhead: Open University Press.

Kidd-Hewitt, D. and Osborne, R. (eds) (1995) *Crime and the Media: The Post Modern Spectacle*. London: Pluto.

Klein, R. (2000) From evidence-based medicine to evidence-based policy, *Journal of Health Services Research and Policy*, 5(2): 65–6.

Kline, S. (1993) *Out of the Garden: Toys, TV and Children's Culture in the Age of Marketing*. London: Verso.

Krotoski, A. (2004) Chicks and joysticks: An exploration of women and gaming, ELSPA White Paper. www.elspa.com/assets/files/c/chicksandjoysticksanexplorationofwomenandgaming_176.pdf.

Kumar, K. (1995) *From Post-industrial to Post-modern Society*. Cambridge: Blackwell.

Laidler, K. and Hunt, G. (2001) Accomplishing femininity among the girls in the gang, *British Journal of Criminology*, 41: 656–78.

Lanuza, G. (2004) The theoretical state of Philippine youth studies, *Young*, 12(4): 357–76.

Lather, P. (2004) Scientific research in education: A critical perspective, *British Educational Research Journal*, 30(6): 759–72.

Laub, J. and Sampson, R. (2005) *Shared Beginnings, Divergent Lives: Delinquent Boys to Age 70*. Cambridge, MA: Harvard University Press.

Lauder, H., Brown, P. and Halsey, A.H. (2004) Sociology and political arithmetic: Some principles of a new policy science, *British Journal of Sociology*, 55(1): 3–22.

Lawson, N. (2005) *Dare More Democracy*. London: Compass Publications.

Lee, D. and Newby, H. (1986) *The Problem of Sociology*. London: Hutchinson.

Lee, L. (2005) 'Young people and the Internet', *Young*, 13(4): 315–26.

Lee, M. (1993) *Consumer Culture Reborn: The Cultural Politics of Consumption*. London: Routledge.

Lees, S. (1986) *Losing Out*. London: Hutchinson.

Leiss, W., Kline, S. and Jhally, S. (2000) The bonding of media and advertising, in M. Lee (ed.) *The Consumer Society Reader*. Malden, MA: Blackwell.

Liazos, A. (1972) The poverty of sociology of deviance: Nuts, sluts and perverts, *Social Problems*, 20: 103–20.

Lincoln, Y. and Guba, E. (1985) *Naturalistic Inquiry*. London: Sage.

Lingard, B. (2003) Where to in gender policy in education after recuperative masculinity politics?, *International Journal of Inclusive Education*, 7: 33–56.

Lister, R. (2001) New Labour: A study in ambiguity from a position of ambivalence, *Critical Social Policy*, 21(4): 425–47.

Livingstone, S. (2002) *Young People and New Media*. London: Sage.

Livingstone, S. and Bovill, M. (2001) *Children and Their Changing Media Environment*. Mahwah, NJ: Lawrence Erlbaum.

Livingstone, S., Bober, M. and Helsper, E. (2005) *Inequalities and the Digital Divide in Children and Young People's Internet Use*. London: Children Go On-line Project. *www.children-go-online.net* (accessed 5 December 2005).

Loader, I. (1996) *Youth Policing and Democracy*. London: Macmillan Press.

Lombroso, C. (1876) *L'Uomo Delinquente*. Milan: Hoepli.

Looker, E. and Dwyer, P. (1998) 'Education and negotiated reality': Complexities facing rural youth in the 1990s, *Journal of Youth Studies*, 1(1): 5–22.

Lucey, H. and Walkerdine, V. (1999) 'Boys' underachievement: Social class and changing masculinities', in T. Cox (ed.) *Combating Educational Disadvantage*. London: Falmer Press.

Lupton, D. (1999) *Risk*. London: Routledge.

Lydon, N. (1996) Man trouble, *Guardian*, 14 May.

Lyng, S. (1990) Edgework: A social psychology analysis of voluntary risk taking, *American Journal of Sociology*, 95(4): 851–86.

Lyon, J., Dennison, C. and Wilson, A. (2000) *'Tell Them So They Listen': Messages from Young People in Custody*, Home Office Research Study 201. London: Home Office.

Mac an Ghaill, M. (1994) *The Making of Men: Masculinities, Sexualities and Schooling*. Buckingham: Open University Press.

Mac an Ghaill, M. (ed.) (1996) *Understanding Masculinities*. Buckingham: Open University Press.

MacDonald, R. (ed.) (1997) *Youth, the 'Underclass' and Social Exclusion*. London: Routledge.

MacDonald, R. and Marsh, J. (2004) Missing school: Educational engagement, youth transitions, and social exclusion, *Youth and Society*, 36(2): 143–62.

MacDonald, R. and Marsh, J. (2005) *Disconnected Youth? Growing Up in Poor Britain*. Basingstoke: Palgrave.

Maczewski, M. (2002) Exploring identities through the Internet: Youth experiences online, *Child and Youth Care Forum*, 31(2): 111–29.

Maffesoli, M. (1996) *The Time of the Tribes: The Decline of Individualism in Mass Society*. London: Sage.

Maira, S. and Soep, E. (2004) United States of Adolescence? Reconsidering US youth culture studies, *Youth*, 12(3): 245–69.

Malbon, B. (1999) *Clubbing: Dancing, Ecstasy and Vitality*. London: Routledge.

Malone, K. (1999) Growing up in cities as a model of participative planning and 'place making' with young people, *Youth Studies Australia*, June: 17–23.

Mamon, S. (2004) Mapping the attainment of Black children in Britain, *Race and Class*, 46(2): 78–91.

Mannheim, K. (1952) The problem of generations, in K. Mannheim, *Essays on the Sociology of Knowledge*. London: Routledge & Kegan Paul.

Mansell, R. (2004) Political economy, power and the new media, *New Media and Society*, 6(1): 96–105.

Marshall, G. (1997) *Repositioning Class*. Cambridge: Polity Press.

Martin, G. (1998) Generational differences amongst New Age travellers, *Sociological Review*, 46(4): 735–56.

Mawby, B.I. and Batta, I.D. (1980) *Asians and Crime: The Bradford Experience*. London: Scope.

McCahill, M. (2002) *The Surveillance Web*. London: Willan Publishing.

McClelland, K. (2000) England's greatness, the working man, in C. Hall, K. McClelland and J. Randal, *Defining the Victorian Nation: Class, Race, Gender and the British Reform Act of 1867*. Cambridge: Cambridge University Press.

McDowell, L. (2000) Learning to serve? Employment aspirations and attitudes of working class men in an era of labour market restructuring, *Gender, Place and Culture*, 7(4): 389–416.

McDowell, L. (2002) Transitions to work: Masculine identities, youth inequality and labour market change, *Gender, Place and Culture*, 9(1): 39–59.

McDowell, L. (2004) Masculinity, identity and labour market change: Some reflections on the implications of thinking rationally about difference and the politics of inclusion, *Geografiska Annaler: Series B*, 86(1): 45–56.

McGuigan, J. (1992) *Cultural Populism*. London: Routledge.

McRobbie, A. (1978) Working class girls and the culture of femininity, in Women's Studies Group, Centre for Contemporary Cultural Studies, *Women Take Issue: Aspects of Women's Subordination*. London: Hutchinson.

McRobbie, A. (1980) 'Settling accounts with subculture': A feminist critique, *Screen Education*, 34: 37–50.

McRobbie, A. (1994) *Post Modernism and Popular Culture*. London: Routledge.

Messerschmidt, J. (1994) Schooling, masculinities and youth crime by white boys, in T. Newburn and E. Stanko (eds) *Just Boys Doing the Business*. London: Routledge.

Messerschmidt, J. (1995) From patriarchy to gender: feminist theory, criminology and the challenge of diversity, in N. Hahn Rafter and F. Heidensohn (eds) *International Feminist Perspectives in Criminology: Engendering a Discipline*. Buckingham: Open University Press.

Messerschmidt, J. (1997) *Crime as Structured Action*. Thousand Oaks, CA: Sage.

Miles, S. (2000) *Youth Lifestyles in a Changing World*. Buckingham: Open University Press.

Miller, J. (2002) The strengths and limits of 'doing gender' for understanding street crime, *Theoretical Criminology*, 6(4): 433–60.

Millie, A., Jacobson, J., McDonald, E. and Hough, M. (2005) *Anti Social Behaviour Strategies: Finding a Balance*. York: Joseph Rowntree Foundation.

Ministry of Education (1960) *The Youth Service in England and Wales*, Cmnd. 929. London: HMSO.

Mintel (1996) *Nightclubs and Discotheque*. London: Mintel.

Mintel (2003) *Teenage Shopping Habits*. *www.reports.mintel.com/sinatra/reports* (accessed 5 December 2005).

Mitchell, W., Bunton, R. and Green, E. (2004) *Young People, Risk and Leisure*. London: Palgrave.

Mitterauer, M. (1992) *A History of Youth*. Oxford: Blackwell.

Mizen, P. (1995) *The State, Young People and Youth Training: In and Against the Training State*. London: Mansell.

Mizen, P. (2003) 'The best days of your life?' Youth, policy and Blair's New Labour, *Critical Social Policy*, 23(4): 453–76.

Mizen, P. (2004) *The Changing State of Youth*. London: Palgrave.

Moffitt, T. (1993) Adolescence-limited and life-course-persistent antisocial behavior: A developmental taxonomy, *Psychological Review*, 100: 674–701.

Muggleton, D. (2000) *Inside Subculture: The Post-modern Meaning of Style*. Oxford: Berg.

Muncie, J. (2004) *Youth and Crime*. London: Sage.

Muncie, J. (2005) The globalization of crime control – the case of youth and juvenile justice, *Theoretical Criminology*, 19(1): 35–64.

Musgrove, F. (1964) *Youth and the Social Order*. London: Routledge & Kegan Paul.

Naughton, M. (2005) Evidence-based policy and the government of the criminal justice system – only if the evidence fits!, *Critical Social Policy*, 25(1): 47–69.

Nava, M. and Nava, O. (1992) Discriminating or duped? Young people as consumers of advertising, in M. Nava, *Changing Cultures: Feminism, Youth and Consumption*. London: Sage.

Nayak, A. (2003) 'Boyz to men': Masculinities, schooling and labour market transitions in de-industrial times, *Educational Review*, 55(2): 147–59.

Nesbet, R.A. (1967) *The Sociological Tradition*. London: Heinemann.

Neustatter, A. (1998) Kids – what the papers say, *Guardian*, 8 April: 8–9.

Newburn, T. (2002) Young people and youth justice, in M. Maguire, R. Morgan and R. Reiner (eds) *The Oxford Handbook of Criminology*. Oxford: Oxford University Press.

Newburn, T. and Shiner, M. (2001) *'Teenage Kicks?' Young People and Alcohol: A Review of the Literature*. York: John Rowntree Foundation.

Newburn, T. and Shiner, M. (2005) *Dealing with Disaffection*. Cullompton: Willan Publishing.

Newburn, T. and Stanko, E. (eds) (1994) *Just Boys Doing the Business*. London: Routledge.

Nichols, G. (2002) Young offenders, risk and personal development programmes, in M. Cieslik and G. Pollock, *Young People in Risk Society*. Aldershot: Ashgate.

Noden, P., West, A., David, M. and Edge, A. (1998) Choices and destinations of transfer to secondary schools in London, *Journal of Education Policy*, 13: 221–36.

Norris, C. and Armstrong, G. (1999) *The Maximum Surveillance Society*. Oxford: Berg.

Novak, T. (1998) Young people, class and poverty, in H. Jones (ed.) *Towards a Classless Society?* London: Routledge.

Nutley, S. and Webb, J. (2000) Evidence and the policy process, in H.T.O. Davies, S. Nutley, and P. Smith, *What Works? Evidence-Based Policy and Practice in Public Services*. Bristol: Policy Press.

Oakley, A. (1972) *Sex, Gender and Society*. London: Temple Smith.

Office for National Statistics (2004) *Health Survey of UK*. London: ONS.

Ofsted (1993) *Access and Achievement in Urban Education. A Report from HMI*. London: Ofsted.

Ong, A. (2004) Higher learning: Educational availability and flexible citizenship in global space, in J.A. Banks (ed.) *Diversity and Citizenship Education*. San Francisco: Jossey-Bass.

Osgerby, B. (1998) *Youth in Britain since 1945*. London: Blackwell.

Osler, A. and Starkey, H. (2003) Learning for cosmopolitan citizenship: Theoretical debates and young people's experience, *Education Review*, 55(3): 243–54.

Osler, A. and Starkey, H. (2005) Violence in schools and representation of young people: A critique of government policies in France and England, *Oxford Review of Education*, 31(2): 195–215.

Osler, A. and Vincent, K. (2003) *Girls and Exclusion*. London: RoutledgeFalmer.

Park, A., Phillips, M. and Johnson, M. (2004) *Young People in Britain: The Attitudes and Experiences of 12 to 19 Year Olds*, Research Report RR564. London: DfES.

Parker, H. (1974) *View from the Boys*. Newton Abbot: David and Charles.

Parker, H., Casburn, M. and Turnbull, D. (1981) *Receiving Juvenile Justice*. London: Basil Blackwell.

Parker, H., Aldridge, J. and Measham, F. (1998) *Illegal Leisure: The Normalization of Adolescent Recreational Drug Use*. London: Routledge.

Parker, H., Williams, L. and Aldridge, J. (2002) The normalization of 'sensible' recreational drug use: Further evidence from the North West England Longitudinal Study, *Sociology*, 36(4): 941–64.

Parsons, C. (2005) School exclusion: The will to punish, *British Journal of Educational Studies*, 53(2): 187–211.

Parsons, T. (1942) Age and sex in the social structure of the United States, *American Sociological Review*, 7(5): 604–616.

Parsons, T. (1964) *Essays in Sociological Theory*. Chicago: Free Press.

Paterson, M. (2005) *Consumption and Everyday*. London: Routledge.

Payne, G. and Williams, M. (2005) Generalization in qualitative research, *Sociology*, 39(2): 295–314.

Pearson, G. (1983) *Hooligan: A History of Respectable Fears*. London: Macmillan Press.

Pearson, G. (1994) Youth, crime and society, in M. Maguire, R. Morgan and R. Reiner (eds) *The Oxford Handbook of Criminology*. Oxford: Oxford University Press.

Percy-Smith, B. and Weil, S. (2003) Practice-based research as development: Innovation and empowerment in youth intervention initiatives using collaborative action inquiry!, in A. Bennett, M. Cieslik and S. Miles, *Researching Youth*. London: Palgrave.

Phipps, L. (2000) New communications technologies: A conduit for social inclusion, *Information, Communication and Society*, 3(1): 39–68.

Pilcher, J. (1994) *Age and Generation in Modern Britain*. Oxford: Oxford University Press.

Pilkington, H. (2004) Youth strategies for glocal living: Space, power and communication in everyday cultural practice, in A. Bennett and K. Kahn-Harris, *After Subculture*. Basingstoke: Palgrave.

Pitts, J. (2001) *The New Politics of Youth Crime: Discipline or Solidarity?* Lyme Regis: Russell House Publishing.

Plant, M. and Plant, M. (1992) *Risk-Takers: Alcohol, Drugs, Sex and Youth*. London: Routledge.

Plummer, G. (2000) *Failing Working Class Girls*. London: Trentham Books.

Prime, D., Zimmeck, M. and Zurawan, A. (2002) *Active Communities: Initial Findings from 2001 Home Office Citizenship Survey*. London: Home Office.

Projansky, S. and Vande Berg, L. (2000) Sabrina, the teenage witch: Girls, witches, mortals and the limitations of prime time feminism, in E.R. Helford (ed.)

Fantasy Girls: Gender in the New Universe of Science Fiction and Fantasy Television. Lanham, MD: Rowman & Littlefield.

Putman, R. D. (2000) *Bowling Alone: The Collapse and Revival of American Community*. New York: Simon and Schuster.

Raby, R. (2005) What is resistance?, *Journal of Youth Studies*, 8(2): 151–72.

Raffe, D. (2003) Pathways linking education and work: A review of concepts, research and policy debates, *Journal of Youth Studies*, 6(1): 3–20.

Randall, J. (2002) The practice–research relationship: A case of ambivalent attachment, *Journal of Social Work*, 2(1): 105–22.

Raphael Reed, L. (1999) Troubling boys and disturbing discourses on masculinity and schooling: A feminist exploration of current debates and interventions concerning boys in school, *Gender and Education*, 11(1): 93–110.

Rattansi, A. (1992) Changing the subject? Racism, culture and education, in J. Donald and A. Rattansi, *Race, Culture and Difference*. London: Sage.

Reay, D. (2000) Children's urban landscapes: Configurations of class and place, in S. Munt (ed.) *Cultural Studies and the Working Class*. London: Cassell.

Redhead, S. (1990) *The End of the Century Party: Youth and Pop towards 2000*. Manchester: Manchester University Press.

Redhead, S. (1993) *Rave Off: Politics and Deviance in Contemporary Youth Culture*. Aldershot: Avebury.

Reeve, A. (1996) The private realm of the managed town centre, *Urban Design International*, 1(1): 61–80.

Release (1997) *Release Drugs and Dance Survey: An Insight into the Culture*. London: Release.

Richardson, A. and Budd, T. (2003) *Alcohol, Crime and Disorder: A Study of Young Adults*, Home Office Research Study 263. London: Home Office.

Riley, R. and Young, G. (2001) *The Macroeconomic Impact of the New Deal for Young People*, NIESR Discussion Paper 184. London: National Institute for Economic and Social Research.

Roberts, K. (1975) The developmental theory of occupational choice: A critique and an alternative, in G. Esland, G. Salaman and M.-A. Speakman (eds) *People and Work*. Edinburgh: Holmes-McDougal.

Roberts, K. (1995) *Employment in Modern Britain*. Oxford: Oxford University Press.

Roberts, K. (1997) Is there an emerging British 'underclass'? The evidence from youth research, in R. MacDonald, *Youth, the 'Underclass' and Social Exclusion*. London: Routledge.

Roberts, K. (2003) Change and continuity in transitions in Eastern Europe: Lessons for Western sociology, *Sociological Review*, 51(4): 484–505.

Robins, D. and Cohen, P. (1978) *Knuckle Sandwich*. London: Pelican.

Rose, D. and Pevalin, D. (2003) *A Researchers Guide to the National Statistics Socio-economic Classification*. London: Sage.

Rose, N. (1999) *Powers of Freedom: Reframing Political Thought*. Cambridge: Cambridge University Press.

Rugg, J., Ford, J. and Burrows, R. (2004) Housing advantage? The role of student renting in the constitution of housing biographies in the United Kingdom, *Journal of Youth Studies*, 7(1): 19–34.

Russell, R. and Tyler, M. (2002) 'Thank Heaven for Little Girls: "Girl Heaven" and the Commercial Context of Feminine Childhood', in *Sociology*, 36(3): 619–37.

Rutherford, A. (1986) *Growing Out of Crime: Society and Young People in Trouble*. Harmondsworth: Penguin.

Rutter, M. (1980) *Changing youth in a changing society*. Cambridge, Massachusetts: Harvard University Press.

Rutter, M., Giller, H. and Hagell, A. (1998) *Anti Social Behaviour by Young People*. Cambridge: Cambridge University Press.

Rutter, M., Maughn, B., Mortimore, P., Ouston, J. and Smith, A. (1979) *Fifteen thousand hours: secondary schools and their effects on pupils*. London: Open Books.

Sanderson, I. (2002) Evaluation, policy learning and evidence based policy making, *Public Administration*, 80(1): 1–22.

Sanderson, I. (2004) Getting evidence into practice: Perspectives on rationality, *Evaluation*, 10(3): 366–79.

Saunders, N. (1995) *Ecstasy and the Dance Culture*. London: N. Saunders.

Savage, M. (2003) A new class paradigm?, *British Journal of Sociology of Education*, 24(4): 535–41.

Savage, S. and Robins, L. (1990) *Public Policy under Thatcher*. Basingstoke: Macmillan.

Scarman, L.G. (1981) *The Brixton Disorders 10–12 April 1981: Report of an Inquiry*, Cmnd. 8427. London: HMSO.

Scraton, P. (2002) The demonisation, exclusion and regulation of children: From moral panic to moral renewal, in A. Boran (ed.) *Crime: Fear or Fascination?* Chester: Chester Academic Press.

Seabrook, T. and Green, E. (2004) Streetwise or safe? Girls negotiating time and space, in W. Mitchell, R. Bunton and E. Green, *Young People, Risk and Leisure*. London: Palgrave.

Selwyn, N. (2002) 'E-stablishing' an inclusive society? Technology, social exclusion and UK policy making, *Journal of Social Policy*, 31(1): 1–20.

Selwyn, N. (2004) Reconsidering political and popular understandings of the digital divide, *New Media and Society*, 6(3): 341–62.

Servon, L. and Nelson, M. (2001) Community technology centres: Narrowing the digital divide in low income, urban communities, *Journal of Urban Affairs*, 23(3–4): 279–90.

Sewell, T. (1998a) *Black Masculinities and Schooling: How Black Boys Survive Modern Schooling*. Stoke: Trentham Books.

Sewell, T. (1998b) Loose canons: exploding the myth of the black macho lad, in D. Epstein, J. Elwood, V. Hey and J. Mew (eds) *Failing Boys: Issues in Gender and Achievement*. Buckingham: Open University Press.

Shain, F. (2003) *The Schooling and Identities of Asian Girls*. Stoke: Trentham Books.
Sharpe, S. (1981) *Just Like a Girl: How Girls Learn to Be Women*. London: Penguin.
Shaw, C.R. (1929) *Delinquency Areas*. Chicago: Chicago Press.
Shaw, C.R. and MacKay, H.D. (1942) *Juvenile Delinquency and Urban Areas*. Chicago: Chicago University Press.
Shaw, I. (1999) *Qualitative Evaluation*. London: Sage.
Shearing, C. (1981) Subterranean processes in the maintenance of power, *Canadian Review of Sociology and Anthropology*, 18(3): 283–98.
Sheldon, W. (1949) *Varieties of Delinquent Youth*. New York: Harper.
Shildrick, T. (2002) Young people and illicit drug use in postmodern times?, in M. Cieslik and G. Pollock, *Young People in Risk Society*. Aldershot: Ashgate.
Shiner, M. (2003) Out of harm's way? Illicit drug use, medicalization and the law, *British Journal of Criminology*, 43: 772–96.
Shiner, M. and Newburn, T. (1997) Definitely, maybe not? The normalisation of recreational drug use amongst young people, *Sociology*, 31(3): 511–31.
Sibley, D. (1995) *Geographies of Exclusion: Society and Difference in the West*. London: Routledge.
Skeggs, B. (1997) *Formations of Class and Gender*. London: Sage.
Skelton, C. (1998) Feminism and research into masculinities and schooling, *Gender and Education*, 11(2): 227–8.
Skelton, T. (2002) Research on youth transitions: some ethical interventions, in M. Cieslik and G. Pollock, *Young People in Risk Society*. Aldershot: Ashgate.
Skogan, W. and Hartnett, S. (1997) *Community Policing, Chicago Style*. New York: Oxford University Press.
Slee, R. and Allen, J. (2001) Excluding the included: A reconsideration of inclusive education, *International Studies in Sociology of Education*, 11(2): 173–92.
Smart, C. (1977) *Women, Crime and Criminology*. London: Routledge & Kegan Paul.
Smith, A. (1973) *The Concept of Social Change*. London: Routledge & Kegan Paul.
Smith, D. (2003) New Labour and youth justice, *Children and Society*, 17(3): 226–35.
Smith, D. and Gray, J. (1983) *The Police in Action*. London: Policy Studies Institute.
Smith, N., Lister, R., Middleton, S. and Cox, L. (2005) Young people as real citizens: Towards an inclusionary understanding of citizenship, *Journal of Youth Studies*, 8(4): 425–43.
Smith, T. and Noble, M. (1995) *Education Divides. Poverty and Schooling in the 1990s*. London: Child Poverty Action Group.
Social Exclusion Unit (1998a) *Bridging the Gap: New Opportunities for 16–18 Year Olds Not in Education, Employment or Training*, Cm. 4405. London: HMSO.
Social Exclusion Unit (1998b) *Truancy and Exclusion from School*. London: HMSO.
Social Exclusion Unit (1999) *Teenage Pregnancy Report*. London: HMSO.
Social Exclusion Unit (2000) *National Strategy for Neighbourhood Renewal: Report of Policy Action Team 12 – Young People*. London: HMSO.
Social Exclusion Unit (2002) *Young Runaways*. London: HMSO.
Social Exclusion Unit (2003) *A Better Education for Children in Care*. London: HMSO.

Solomos, J. (1988) *Black Youth, Racism and The State*. Cambridge: Cambridge University Press.

Solomos, J. (1993) *Race and Racism in Britain*, 2nd edn. Basingstoke: Macmillan.

Springhall, J. (1986) *Coming of Age: Adolescence in Britain 1860–1960*. London: Gill and Macmillan.

Squires, P. and Stephen, D. (2005) *Rougher Justice: Anti-social Behaviour and Young People*. Cullompton: Willan Publishing.

Stewart, F. (1992) The adolescent as consumer, in J. Coleman and C. Warren-Anderson (eds) *Youth Policy in the 1990s: The Ways Forward*. London: Routledge.

Sutherland, E. (1939) *Principles of Criminology*. Philadelphia: Lippincott.

Sweeting, H. and West, P. (2003) Young people's leisure and risk-taking behaviours: Changes in gender patterning in the West of Scotland during the 1990s, *Journal of Youth Studies*, 6(4): 391–412.

Taft, J. (2001) Defining girl power: The culture machine vs. the girl activist. Unpublished presentation at A New Girl Order? Young Women and the Future of Feminist Inquiry Conference, London, 12–14 November.

Tapscott, D. (1998) *Growing Up Digital: The Rise of the Net Generation*. New York: McGraw-Hill.

Taylor, D. (2000) The word on the street: Advertising, youth culture and legitimate speech in drug education, *Journal of Youth Studies*, 3(3): 333–53.

Taylor, I. and Jamieson, R. (1997) Proper little mesters: Nostalgia and protest masculinity in de-industrialised Sheffield, in S. Westwood and J. Williams (eds) *Imaging Cities*. London: Routledge.

Taylor, I., Walton, P. and Young, J. (1973) *The New Criminology: For a Social Theory of Deviance*. London: Routledge & Kegan Paul.

Taylor, R. (2005) Lifelong learning and the Labour governments 1997–2004, *Oxford Review of Education*, 31(1): 101–18.

Thompson, R. (1994) Moral rhetoric and public health pragmatism: The contemporary politics of sex education, *Feminist Review*, 48: 40–60.

Thompson, R. (2004) 'Sexuality and young people': Polices, practices and identities, in J. Carabine, *Sexualities: Personal Lives and Social Policy*. Bristol: Policy Press.

Thomson, R. and Holland, J. (2004) *Youth Values and Transitions to Adulthood: An Empirical Investigation*, Families & Social Capital ESRC Research Group, Paper 4. London: London South Bank University.

Thomson, R., Bell, R., Henderson, S., Holland, S., McGrellis, S. and Sharpe, S. (2002) 'Critical moments': Choice, chance and opportunity in young people's narratives of transition to adulthood, *Sociology*, 36(2): 335–54.

Thomson, R., Holland, J., McGrellis, S., Bell, R., Henderson, S. and Sharpe, S. (2004) Inventing adulthood: A biographical approach to understanding youth and citizenship, *Sociological Review*, 52(2): 218–39.

Thornton, D., Curran, C., Grayson, D. and Holloway, V. (1984) *Tougher Regimes in Detention Centres*. London: HMSO.

Thornton, S. (1995) *Club Cultures: Music, Media and Subcultural Capital*. Cambridge: Polity Press.

Thorpe, D., Smith, D., Green, C. and Paley, J. (1980) *Out of Care: Community Support of Juvenile Offenders*. London: George Allen & Unwin.

Thorpe, K. and Wood, M. (2004) Anti social behaviour, in S. Nicholas and A. Walker (eds) *Crime in England and Wales 2002/3: Supplementary Volume 2: Crime, Disorder and the Criminal Justice System – Public Attitudes and Perceptions*, Home Office Statistical Bulletin 02/04. London: Home Office.

Thrupp, M. (1999) *Schools Making a Difference: Let's Be Realistic*. Buckingham: Open University Press.

Tierney, J. (1996) *Criminology: Theory and Context*. London: Harvester Wheatsheaf.

Tilly, L. and Scott, J. (1989) *Women, Work and Family*. London: Routledge.

Tomlinson, S. (2003) 'New Labour and education', *Children and Society*, 17: 195–204.

Tomlinson, S. (2005a) *Education in a Post-welfare Society*, 2nd edn. Maidenhead: Open University Press.

Tomlinson, S. (2005b) Race, ethnicity and education under New Labour, *Oxford Review of Education*, 31(1): 153–71.

Walford, G. (1993) *The Private Schooling of Girls*. London: Woburn Press.

Walker, R. (2000) Welfare policy: Tendering for evidence, in H.T.O. Davies, S.M. Nutley and P. Smith, *What Works? Evidence-Based Policy and Practice in Public Services*. Bristol: Policy Press.

Walkerdine, V., Lucey, H. and Melody, J. (2001) *Growing Up Girl*. London: Palgrave.

Walklate, S. and Evans, K. (1999) *Zero Tolerance or Community Tolerance? Managing Crime in High Crime Areas*. Aldershot: Ashgate.

Wallace, C. (1987) *For Richer for Poorer*. London: Tavistock Publications.

Webster, C. (1997) The construction of British 'Asian' criminality, *International Journal of the Sociology of Law*, 25(1): 65–86.

Webster, C., Simpson, D., MacDonald, R., Abbas, A., Cieslik, M., Shildrick, T. and Simpson, M. (2004) *Poor Transitions*. Bristol: Policy Press.

West, D.J. and Farrington, D. (1977) *The Delinquent Way of Life*. London: Heinemann.

Whitty, G. (2001) Education, social class and social exclusion, *Journal of Education Policy*, 16(4): 287–95.

Wikström, P.-O.H. and Sampson, R.J. (2003) Social mechanisms of community influences on crime and pathways in criminality, in B. Lahey, T. Moffitt and A. Caspi (eds) *Causes of Conduct Disorder and Juvenile Delinquency*. New York: Guilford Press.

Wilber, S. (1997) An archaeology of cyberspaces: Virtuality, community, identity, in D. Porter (ed.) *Internet Culture*. London: Routledge.

Wiles, P. (2004) Policy and sociology, *British Journal of Sociology*, 55(1): 31–4.

Williams, M. and May, T. (1996) *Introduction to Philosophy of Social Research*. London: Routledge.

Williams, S., Bendelow, G. and France, A. (2003) *Beliefs of Young People in Relation to Health, Risk and Lifestyle* (MCH 18–03). London: Department of Health.

Williamson, H. (2004) *The Milltown Boys*. Oxford: Berg.

Willis, P. (1977) *Learning to Labour – How Working Class Kids Get Working Class Jobs*. Farnborough: Saxon House.

Willis, P. (1990) *Common Culture: Symbolic Work at Play in Everyday Cultures of the Young*. Milton Keynes: Open University Press.

Wilson, D. (2004) 'Keeping quiet' in 'going nuts': Stategies used by young black men in custody, *Howard Journal*, 43(3): 317–30.

Wilson, J.Q. and Kelling, G. (1982) Broken windows, *Atlantic Monthly*, March: 29–38.

Wood, M. (2004) *Perceptions and Experience of Antisocial Behaviour: Findings from the 2003/2004 British Crime Survey*, Home Office Online Report 49/04. London: Home Office.

Woods, P. (1983) *Sociology and the School*. London: Routledge & Kegan Paul.

Wright Mills, C. (1959) *The Sociological Imagination*. Oxford: Oxford University Press.

Wyn, J. and Dwyer, P. (1999) New directions on youth transitions, *Journal of Youth Studies*, 2(1): 5–22.

Wyn, J. and Harris, A. (2004) Youth research in Australia and New Zealand, *Young*, 12(3): 271–89.

Wyn, J. and White, R. (1997) *Rethinking Youth*. London: Sage.

Young, A. (1996) *Imagining Crime*. London: Sage.

Youth Justice Board (2005) *Anti-social Behaviour Report*. London: Youth Justice Board.

Index

Aapola, S., 128, 129
Abbott, P., 21, 22
Abrams, M., 16, 17, 117
Abrams, P., 42
Adams, B, 146
adolescence, 25–27
Adorno, T., 24
Advisory Group in Citizenship, 68
Ainley, P., 45, 74, 130, 131
Albermarle Commission, 16
Alcohol Concern, 137
Alexander, C., 95, 96, 101, 111, 112
Alexander, S., 9
Alexiadou, N., 84
Allen, J., 17, 85, 168
Allen, S., 38, 168
Althorp's Factory Act, 11
Althusser, Louis, 43
American Dream, 36
American Sociological Association, 27
American 'War on Poverty,' 39
Anderson, B., 101, 107
Anderson, S., 50
anti-social behaviour order (ASBO), 102
The Apprentice (TV), 149
Archer, L., 80, 88, 93, 94, 95, 96
Ariés, P., 6
Armstrong, D., 83, 84, 86, 103, 108, 109, 110
Arnot, M., 92, 93, 94
Ashton, D., 18

Babyz (computer programme), 126
Back, L., 127, 144
Ball, S.J., 68, 70, 73, 80, 86, 87, 88, 89, 159
Bassett, C., 125
Bates, I., 47
Batta, I.D., 111
Beccaria, C., 31
Beck, U., 61, 70, 87, 146
Beck-Gernsheim, E., 61, 87
Becker, H., 48, 109
Beinart, S., 137, 138
Bell, R., 70
Bennett, A., 124, 143, 144
Bentham, J., 31
Bessant, J., 108
Betts, Leah, 136
Birkland, T.A., 97
Blackman, S.J., 136, 139, 140, 144, 145, 147
Blair, Tony, 86, 139, 140
Blake, L., 102
Bloom, A., 89
Blunkett, David, 160
Board of Education (1923), 14
Bottoms, A., 55
Bourdieu, Pierre, 72, 73, 74, 90
Bovill, M., 119
Bowles, S., 46
Bowling, B., 20, 101
Brain, K., 137, 140, 147, 148, 149
Brake, M., 17, 31, 38, 39
Bridging the Gap (SEU), 65
British Crime Survey, 103
Brown, P., 45, 46, 47, 88
Brown, S., 32, 33, 34, 36, 39, 51, 101, 102, 104, 112, 122, 123, 135, 136, 154
Buckingham, D., 119, 120, 122
Budd, T., 137, 138, 139
Buffy the Vampire Slayer (TV), 128
Bulger, James, 97, 106
Bullen, E., 116, 117, 118, 119, 128
Bulmer, M., 3, 160
Bunton, R., 149
Burawoy, M., 164, 165
Burstyn, J., 10
Burt, Cyril, 29, 30
Bynner, J., 59, 60, 107
Byrne, D., 65, 152, 153, 159, 163

Cabinet Office, 137, 162
Campbell, B., 112
Carabine, J., 22
Carpenter, Mary, 13
Carter, M., 16

Cartmel, F., 18, 70, 71, 87
CCCTV *see* closed circuit television
Census (1911), 10
Centre for Contemporary Culture Studies (CCCS), Birmingham, 43, 53, 124
Chaney, D., 143
changing nature of youth, 151–165
'new' public social science, 164–165
'democratic conversations, 165
social science should be active in public discourse, 165
'political discourses' and the youth question, 152–153
concept of youth seen to reflect the current state of civilisation, 152
little evidence that anxiety about present youth is justifiable, 152
New Labour and responsible citizenship, 153
politics and the youth question, 153–154
Government has tried to transfer its problems to youth, 153
moralising agenda blames attitudes of working class youth, 154
social science and policy nexus, 160–164
communicative action in evidence-based practice, 163–164
need for communicative dialogue, 163
youth-police relationships, 163–164
evidence-based policy (EBP), 160
limits of EBP in youth policy, 161–162
new youth green paper, 161, 162
political discourse influenced by developmental models, 161–162
problem of evidence used by politicians, 162
relationship between political ideology and evidence, 161
limits of EBP in youth policy, 161–162
what is to be done, 162–163
engagement with policy and practice, 163
rethink relationships, 163
youth research and the youth question, 154–159
challenges to the 'youth as a social problem' paradigm, 155–156
importance of class, 158–159
need for research into class effect in transitions, 159
reproduction of class divisions in Britain, 159
social science research clarifies the youth question, 154–155
youth, subjectivity and identity, 156–158
'agency' and 'structure,' 158
defining young male identity, 156
effects of globalisation, 157
'generalisation' as a problem, 158
ideas of girlhood, 156
locality critically important for the young, 157–158
racial identities, 157
Charlie's Angels (film), 128
Chatterton, P., 148
Chicago Area Project, 39
Chicago School, 32, 36, 37, 39
Children and Young Persons Act (1969), 15, 19, 22, 55
Chisholm, L., 61
Clarke, J., 14, 43, 62, 63, 87
closed circuit television (CCTV), 103
Cloward, R., 36, 39
Cockburn, C., 47
Coffield, F., 46, 67
Cohen, A., 36
Cohen, P., 1, 27, 35, 45, 74, 106, 130, 131, 152
Cohen, S., 16, 48, 50, 51, 52, 105, 109
Coleman, J., 35
Coles, B., 60, 160
Colley, H., 65
Collier, R., 112
Collin, M., 134, 135, 136
Commission on the Social Sciences (2003), 2, 158, 163, 165
Committee on Higher Education, 16
Common Culture (Willis), 124
Community Development Programme, 39
Connell, R., 112
Connolly, P, 90, 91, 96
Conservative Party:
and education, 78–79, 82, 87
Jobseekers Allowance, 64

and racial inequality, 80
tough on crime, 97
Cornwell, J., 140
counterculture movement, 4, 17, 21, 57, 133
Cowie, J., 30
Crawford, A., 99, 120, 202
Cribb, A., 72
Crime and Disorder Act (1998), 98, 99, 102
crime and youth, 97–114
politics of youth crime, 103–104
data do not support a 'youth crime wave,' 103
problem of anti-social behaviour, 104
'popular punitiveness' in youth policy, 104
youth crime used for political purposes, 104
role of the media, 105–106
example of Bulger case, 106
image of 'dangerous youth,' 106
problem of 'moral panics,' 105
youth crime exaggerated, 105–106
social science and youth crime, 106–113
criminalisation of Asian masculinity, 110–112
cultural dysfunction blamed, 111
myths about Asian gangs, 111
response of young Asian men to being labelled, 110–111
youths 'fighting back,' 111
criminalising process, 110
labelling process, 110
criminology and policy evaluation, 106
delinquent or criminal career, 107
Cambridge study, 107
life history perspective, 107
risk and protective factor paradigm, 107
gender and crime, 112–113
girls and crime, 112–113
involvement in gangs, 113
'masculinity turn' relationship between masculinity and crime, 112
limitations of criminal career research, 108–109
assumption that delinquency can be measured by number of offences, 108
lack of input from the justice system, 109
linkage to biological or psychological dysfunctioning, 108
new directions in criminal career research, 109–110
retrospective analysis of pathways, 109
youth attitude to crime, 109–110
youth justice policy in late modernity, 97–100
'collective agony' of James Bulger murder, 97
Conservative Party tough on crime, 97
crime prevention policy under New Labour, 99
Criminal Justice and Public Order Act (1994), 97–98
custody for young offenders, 100
expansion of penal sentences, 99
new form of youth justice, 98
principle of *doli incapax,* 98
responsibilities, 99
United Nations and age of criminal responsibility, 98
youth policy and policing of space, 100–103
legislation for anti-social behaviour orders (ASBO), 102
New Labour and 'anti-social behaviour,' 101–102
recent changes in policing of the young, 101
'respectables' and 'roughs,' 100
use of closed-circuit television (CCTV), 103
youth seen as dangerous age, 100
Criminal Justice Act (2003), 102
Criminal Justice and Public Order Act (1994), 97, 134, 136
Critcher, C., 105, 134, 135, 137
Crompton, R., 71, 74, 87
Crouching Tiger, Hidden Dragon (film), 128
Cuff, E.C., 36
culture of youth and risk-taking, 133–150
E generation, 133–137
anxiety about drug use, 136

death of young girls, 136
problem in controlling use of ecstasy, 136
New Age travellers and eco-warriors, 133–134
based in counterculture movement, 133–134
challenge to rural life, 134
rave culture, 134–135
ecstasy as recreational drug, 134
popular activity for young, 134–135
rise of clubbing, 135
use of drugs, 135
venues catering for rave culture, 135
risk-taking in late modernity, 137–141
binge drinking, 137–138
acts as catalyst for other risks, 138
evidence not clear, 137–138
normalisation of drug usage, 138
access to drugs is increasing, 138
growing acceptance of drug use, 138
socially more acceptable, 138
survey indicated 20-30% usage, 138
trying drugs by young people increasing, 138
risk-taking, moral panics and governance, 139–141
drug normalisation, 141
drug-taking not the norm, 139
drug users as 'delinquents,' 141
exaggeration of binge drinking by the media, 139
government policy to create 'responsible drinking,' 140
importance of cultural factors and social context, 140
'respect agenda' of New Labour, 139–140
website about risks of drug-taking, 140
'risk-taking generation,' 137
youth culture and social research, 141–149
in defence of subcultural theory, 144–145
British Goth subculture, 145
structural contradicitions of the young, 145
influence of post-structuralist and post-modernist thinking, 141
'neo-tribalism' and 'hybrid cultures,' 143–144
construction of new ethnicities, 144
neo-tribes described, 143–144
relation between structure and agency, 143
relevance of subcultural theory, 142–143
advent of rave culture, 142
views of club cultures, 142–143
understanding 'risk-taking,' 146–149
development of leisure industry, 148
drug use varies with local fashions, 147
importance of local context, 146
increase in risk-taking not explained, 146
realist position on youth, 146
relationship between advertising industry and drug use, 147
risk-taking as positive part of normal life, 148–149

Davies, B., 15, 16, 18, 21, 93, 126
Davies, L., 56
Davis, J., 6, 7, 8, 11, 13, 14, 16, 25, 26, 35, 42
Delanty, G., 24
Department for Education and Employment (DfEE), 85, 86, 160
Department for Education and Skills (DfES), 66, 68, 84, 85, 100, 161, 162
Department of Education and Science, 94
Devine, F., 71, 88, 89
Devine, F, 73
Downes, D., 33, 38, 39, 40, 52, 106, 110
Driscoll, C., 128, 129
Driver, S., 62
Drotner, K., 122
Durkheim, E., 34, 36, 108
Dwyer, C., 59, 61, 127, 130
Dyhouse, C., 7, 10, 14, 27

Economic and Social Research Council (ESRC), 160
Education Act (1986), 22
Education Action Zones, 81
education and politics, 78–96

Conservative government and education, 78–80
control moved from local to national government, 79
curriculum changes, 79
expansion of choice, 78
importance of market forces, 78
increased inequality, 79
parents and teachers blamed for school failures, 80
New Labour and inclusive education, 80–82
diversity within the education system, 81–82
improving standards, 81
Labour promise to tackle social exclusion, 81
selection within the comprehensive system, 82
problem of social exclusion, 84–87
achievement of social mobility, 86
'culture of poverty' holds back individual effort, 86
Labour Party policy designed to appeal to middle classes, 86–87
parenting orders, 85
pathologising the problem, 84
responsibilising agenda by New Labour, 85–86
'social acts of discrimination,' 84
social class effect on achievement, 86
social reproduction of inequality, 87–96
boys and underachievement, 92–94
'boys will be boys,' 93
comparison with girls, 94
crisis in masculinity, 92
mainly working class and Asian, 93
remasculination of education, 93–94
schools being feminised and failing, 92–93
class and education, 87–88
classification of class, 87
importance of class in education, 87–88
new paradigm of class theory, 88
gender and education, 92
masculinity studies, 92
middle class and education, 88–90
advantage of 'choice' policies, 88
evidence how parents benefit their childs' education, 88–89
involvement with schools, 90
use of private education, 89
race and education, 94–96
Asian girls, 95–96
multiculturalism, 94
New Labour policy, 95
problem of islamophobia, 96
working class and education, 90–92
cultural norms and values, 90
education not valued, 91
local and parental attitudes against education, 91–92
pupil culture within schools, 90
tackling social exclusion, 83
government programme, 83
increase in exclusions from school, 83
Eisenstadt, S.N., 34, 35
Eldridge, J., 165
Entertainment Act (1990), 136
Entertainment Software Association, 118
Epstein, D., 22, 93
Equal Opportunities Act, 21
Ethnic Minority and Traveller Achievement Group, 81
Etzioni, A., 62, 68
Evans, K., 40
evidence-based policy (EBP), 160

Factory Acts, 11, 13
Farrington, D., 30, 99, 107, 109
Featherstone, M., 115, 116, 149
Finn, D., 64, 65
Finney, A., 104
Flood-Page, C., 103
Folk Devils and Moral Panics (Cohen), 48, 105
France, A., 27, 60, 68, 69, 99, 107, 108, 109, 137, 146, 149
Freud, S., 32
Frith, S., 30, 38, 42, 127, 144
Frosh, S., 92
Frost, I., 128
Fuller, E., 137, 138
Furlong, A., 18, 70, 71, 79, 87, 88
Furnham, A., 118
Fyfe, A., 9

Garland, D., 27, 28, 29, 31, 32, 47, 153
generational theory, 42
Geraci, J., 118, 119
Gewirtz, S., 72, 93, 95

Giddens, Anthony, 1, 8, 9, 25, 62, 157
Gillies, V., 85, 90, 91, 92
Gillis, J.R., 6, 9
Gilroy, P., 20, 45, 126
Gintis, H., 46
Glueck, S., 29
Godfrey, J., 134, 135, 136
Goldson, B., 98, 104
Goldthorpe, J.H., 43, 87
Goodey, J., 110, 111
Goodnow, J., 108, 109
Gosling, V., 120
Gouldner, A.W., 39
Graham, K., 140
Gray, P., 101, 110
Green, E., 146
Greer, G., 128
Griffin, C., 2, 25, 26, 43, 45, 46, 48, 52, 53, 56, 74, 92, 93
Griffiths, P., 1, 6, 7, 8
The Guardian, 82
Guba, E., 158
Gunter, B., 118

Habermas, J., 164
Hall, G. S., 25, 26, 154
Hall, S., 6, 9, 20, 27, 29, 32, 43, 44, 48, 49, 50, 104, 105, 124, 126, 153
Halsey, A.H., 87
Hannigan, J., 148
Hansard, 139
Hargreaves, D.H., 47
Harris, A., 128
Hartnett, S., 102
Harvey, D., 116
Haywood, C., 77
Heath, S., 69
Hebdige, D., 43, 44, 117
Heidensohn, F., 54
Heim, M., 125
Henderson, S., 135
Hendrick, H., 13, 26, 27
Her Majesties Stationary Office (HMSO), 84
Hetherington, K., 133, 134
Higher Education Funding Council for England (HEFC), 67, 68
Hill, A., 134, 136
Hine, J., 99
HMSO *see* Her Majesties Stationary Office
Hobbs, D., 148
Hobsbawm, E.J., 9, 10, 11, 14
Hodkinson, P., 65, 145
Holdaway, S., 100
Holland, J., 70
Hollands, R., 130, 148
Hollin, C., 29
Holloway, L.S., 121, 123
Home Office, 51, 103, 139, 140, 162
Homel, R., 99, 108, 109
Hooton, E., 29
Horkheimer, M., 24
Huddleston, P., 89
Hudson, A., 12
Hudson, B., 55, 56
Humphery, S., 115
Hunt, G., 112, 113
Hurd, Douglas, 68
Hutson, S., 46

information and communication technology (ICT), 118, 119, 121
Institute of Alcohol Studies, 137
Internet, 118, 119, 120, 123, 125
introduction to the book, 1–5
  government and youth, 1
  history of worries about youth, 1
  modernity defined as the last twenty years, 1
  outline of the book, 3–5
  politics and youth, 1, 2
  social science and youth, 2
  youth research, 1, 2, 3
Irwin, S., 10

Jackie (magazine), 125
James, A., 98, 99
James, A.L., 98, 99
Jamieson, R., 75
Jefferson, T., 43
Jeffery, C., 90
Jenkins, R., 46, 47
Jephcott, P., 16
Jewkes, Y., 105, 106
Johnson, R., 22
Jones, G., 69, 70
Jones, S., 60, 125

Kelling, G., 40, 101
Kemshall, H., 146
Kenway, J., 116, 117, 118, 119, 128
Kidd-Hewitt, D., 105

Klein, R., 161
Kline, S., 117
Krotoski, A., 120
Kumar, K., 116

Laidler, K., 112, 113
Lanuza, G., 60
Lather, P., 163
Laub, J., 109
Lauder, H., 164, 165
Lawson, N., 86
Learning to Labour (McRobbie), 53
Lee, L., 41, 119, 121
Lee, M, 117
Lees, S., 53, 54
Leiss, W., 117
Liazos, A., 50
Licensing Act (2004), 140
Lincoln, Y., 158
Lingard, B., 93, 94
Lister, R., 69
Little, A., 17
Livingstone, S., 118, 119, 120, 121, 122, 130
Loader, I., 100, 101, 163, 164
Local Government Act, 22
Lombroso, C., 28, 29, 30, 32
Lucey, H., 92
Lupton, D., 146, 149
Lydon, N., 93
Lyng, S., 149
Lyon, J., 10

Mac an Ghaill, M., 45, 77, 92
MacDonald, R., 65, 69, 72, 80, 90, 91, 140, 147, 149, 159
MacKay, H.D., 34, 40
Maczewski, M., 125
Maffesoli, M., 144
making of modern youth, 6–23
  arrival of the 'teenager,' 16–17
    existence of new sub-cultures, 16
    seen by some as threat to existing social order, 17
    but counterculture based in middle-classes, 17
  early modernity, 8–12
    child labour, 11
    domestic service, 10
    effects of industrialism, 9–10
    employment of women, 9–10
    juvenile deliquency, 11
    scope and impact of modernity, 8–9
    young women and society, 12
    youth as 'social barometer,' 11
  girl question, 21–23
    changes in culture, 21
    feminist movement, 21
    'natural' family, 22
    problem of single mothers, 22
    sex education, 22–23
    sexual behaviour, 22
  growth of interventionist state, 12–14
    anxiety about the 'condition of youth,' 12–14
    boy labour problem, 13
    education for girls, 14
    legislation for reformitories, 13–14
    youth as 'national asset,' 13
    youth problems attributed to poor family culture, 14
  pre-modernity, 6–8
    adults anxiety about youthful behaviour, 6–8
    apprenticeships and class, 7
    custom of charivari, 8
    differences between genders, 7
    regulation of youth, 8
    rites of passage to adulthood, 7
    role of youth culture, 6
  welfare capitalism (1945-80), 14–16
    Albermarle Commission, 16
    Children and Young People's Act (1969), 15
    educational reform, 16
    Government intervention in youth regulation, 15
    Labour Government and major social reforms, 15
    Youth Service, 15–16
  youth and unemployment, 17–19
    decline in jobs for youths, 18
    extended schooling, 18
    Goverment training and the Youth Opportunities Programme (YOP), 18
    youth training successful in creating the work ethic, 18–19
  youth disorder and race, 19–20
    problems with the Children's Act, 19
    racial element in disturbances, 20
    urban rioting in 1980's, 20

Malbon, B., 135
Malone, K., 101
Mamon, S., 80
Mannheim, Karl, 42
Manpower Services Commission (MSC), 18, 19
Mansell, R., 129
marketisation and commodification of youth, 115–132
consumption in late modernity, 115–123
consumer culture, 115–116
effects of globalisation and new technologies, 116–117
emergence of the young consumer, 117–118
growth of teenage market, 117–118
market segmentation, 117
specialised market and 'medicalisation,' 117
inclusive consumption of new media, 120–121
digital media in schools, 121
ICT policy and employability, 121
New Labour and the digital age, 120
mass market and Fordist production, 116
moral panics, new media and technology, 122–123
little evidence of harm from new media, 122–123
possible dangers of new technology to the young, 122
responses to fear of the unknown, 123
net generation and digital divide, 119–120
middle classes have greater access to technology, 119
new uses of technology give power, 119
variations with age and gender, 119–120
niche marketing, 115–123
youth, new media technology and consumption, 118
information and communication technology (ICT), 118
inclusive consumption of new media, 120–121
youth consumption identities, 123–132
'girl power' and feminism, 127–130
commodification of girlhood, 129
marketing and 'being a girl,' 128, 129
popular culture and 'girl power,' 128–129
young girls as advertising targets, 130
importance of difference, 125–127
experimenting with identities, 126
'identity work' and commodities, 125
media studies and creativity of youth, 127
racial identities and 'difference,' 126–127
political economy of consumption, 127
consumption as part of capitalism, 127
emptiness of some youth activities, 127
post-structuralism and 'identity work,' 124–125
creative consumption, 124
importance of music, 124–125
Internet and creation of identities, 125
structural positions and locations, 130–131
creative consumption of youth, 131
framework of post-structuralism, 130–131
Marsh, J., 65, 69, 72, 90, 91, 140, 147, 149, 159
Marshall, G., 87
Martell, L., 62
Martin, G., 133
Massey, D., 17
Mawby, B.I., 111
May, T., 24
Mayhew, Henry, 31
McCahill, M., 101, 103
McClelland, K., 10
McDowell, L., 74, 75, 76, 90
McGuigan, J., 43, 44, 45, 53
McRobbie, Angela, 53, 54, 56, 105, 125
Merton, Robert, 36
Messerschmidt, J., 112

Miles, S., 92, 93, 94, 117, 118, 143
Miller, J., 113
Millie, A., 101, 102
Ministry of Education, 16
Mintel, 118, 129, 135
Mitchell, W., 137, 149
Mitteraurer, M., 7
Mizen, P., 15, 18, 19, 57, 63, 64, 65, 66, 67, 80, 104
Mobilization of Youth Project, 39
Moffitt, T., 108
Muggleton, D., 143
Muncie, J., 11, 29, 36, 37, 52, 97, 98, 103, 105, 106
Musgrove, F., 17

Nagy, J., 118
National Academy for Gifted and Talented Youth, 89
National Deviance Conference, 48
National Grid for Learning, 120
National Vocational Qualifications (NVQ's), 19
Naughton, M., 160, 161
Nava, M., 125
Nava, O., 125
Nayak, A., 75
Neill, J., 90, 91
Nelson, M., 119
Nesbet, R.A., 24
Neustatter, A., 105
New Age travellers, 133–134
New Deal employment programme, 63, 64
New Labour:
  and anti-social behaviour, 101
  and citizenship, 68
  crime prevention, 99
  and digital age, 120
  and education, 4
  inclusive education, 80–83
  managing youth transitions, 63–66
  meritocracy, 86
  new times, 62
  penal sentences for youth, 99
  problem of race in education, 95
  respect agenda, 139, 140
  and responsible citizenship, 153
  and Social Science, 160
  youth justice policy, 98
New Opportunities Fund, 120
New Right, 18, 22, 41, 45, 46, 51, 57
Newburn, T., 19, 20, 51, 52, 97, 98, 99, 103, 104, 110, 112, 138, 139, 148
Newby, H., 41
Nichols, G., 148
Noble, M., 79
Noden, P., 95
Norris, C., 103
Novak, T., 19
Nuffield College, Oxford, 87
Nutley, S., 161
NVQ *see* National Vocational Qualifications

Oakley, A., 52
Office for National Statistics, 137
Office for Standards in Education (Ofsted), 79
Oh, S., 89
Ohlin, L., 36, 39
Ong, A., 88
Osborne, R., 105
Osgerby, B., 15, 16, 17, 21, 133, 134
Osler, A., 68, 85, 94

Park, A., 162
Park, Robert, 33
Parker, H., 51, 55, 138, 147, 149
Parsons, C., 35, 38, 84
Parsons, Talcott, 34
Paterson, M., 115
Payne, G., 36, 158
Pearson, G., 1, 10, 11, 14, 31, 39, 49, 97, 100, 105
Percy-Smith, B., 163, 164
Pevalin, D., 87
Phillips, C., 20, 101
Phipps, L., 120
Pilcher, J., 42
Pilkington, H., 144
Pitts, J., 104, 106
Plant, M., 137
Plummer, G., 94
Pratt, J., 55
Prime, D., 69
Projansky, S., 129
Putman, R.D., 40

Raby, R., 145
Raffe, D., 59, 60
Randall, J., 163

Rattansi, A., 94
Reay, D., 90
Redhead, S., 142
Reed, Raphael, 94
Reeve, A., 101
Release, 135
Richardson, A., 137, 138, 139
Riley, R., 65
Roberts, K., 18, 19, 46, 60, 70, 71
Robins, D., 18, 51
Rock, P., 33, 38, 39, 40, 52, 106, 110
Rose, N., 87, 152
Rugg, J., 60
Russell, R., 129, 130
Rutherford, A., 51
Rutter, M., 10, 86

Sabrina, the Teenage Witch (TV), 128, 129
Sampson, R.J., 108, 109
Sanderson, I., 3, 160, 161, 162, 163
Saunders, N., 135
Savage, M., 71, 73, 87, 88, 90, 131
Savage, S., 18
Scarman Report, 20
science and the age of reason, 24–40
  adolescence, 25–27
    basis of Victorian philosophy, 26
    ideas based on theory, science and 'common sense,' 27
    influence of psychology, 25–26
    role of G. Stanley Hall, 25–26
  American social science, 38–40
    assumptions based on 'Middle America,' 38
    British subculture related to class, 39
    tackling social disorganisation, 40
  anomie and delinquency, 36–37
    causes of delinquency lie within society, 36
    problems of subcultures, 36–37
    sociological positivism, 37
    strains caused by frustration, 36
  Chicago School and early sociology, 32–34
    causes of juvenile delinquency, 34
    focus on youth problem, 33
    social disorganisation and delinquency, 34
    study of social life in the city, 33
  criminology and positivist science, 27–28
    behaviour and biology, 28
    female delinquency, 28
    'science of the criminal,' 28
  functionalism and youth as a social institution, 34–36
    adaptive social systems, 35–36
    age differentiation, 34–35
    biologism and positivism, 35
    separation of youth culture, 35
    structural functionalism, 34
    teaching children about society, 35
  modernity, science and the age of reason, 24–25
    'instrumental rationality,' 24
    reflexivity of modern life, 24–25
  positive criminology, 29–32
    criminal characteristics, 31, 32
    criminology and social science, 32
    'developmental criminology,' 30
    girls and delinquency, 30
    influence of psychology and positivism, 29
    multiple causes of juvenile delinquency, 29–30
    'pathological family' and genetics, 29
    science and the youth problem, 31
Scott, J., 10, 71, 74, 87
Scraton, P., 105, 106
Seabrook, T., 146
Selwyn, N., 119, 120, 121
Servon, L., 119
SEU *see* Social Exclusion Unit
Sewell, T., 95
Shain, F., 95, 96
Sharpe, S., 52
Shaw, C.R., 34, 39
Shaw, I., 162
Shearing, C., 100
Sheldon, W., 29
Shildrick, T., 147
Shiner, M., 110, 138, 139, 140, 148
Sibley, D., 101
Skeggs, B., 73, 131
Skelton, C., 92, 161
Skogan, W, 102
Slee, R., 85
Smart, C., 28, 30, 31, 37
Smith, A., 8, 101
Smith, C., 79
Smith, D., 69, 76, 107
Social Exclusion Unit (SEU), 63, 64, 81, 83, 94, 120

social science and politics, 41–58
class, culture and youth, 43–45
Centre for Contemporary Culture Studies (CCCS), 43, 44, 45
as political party, 45
and racial resistance subcultures, 44
youth and subcultures, 43
concept of bricolage, 43
embourgeoisement seen as myth, 43
importance of consumption in youth activity, 45
neo-Marxist Gramscian hegemony theory, 43
punk as subculture absorbed by society, 44
race and resistance, 44
subcultures and class experience, 43
developments in criminology, 47–52
moral panics and labelling theory, 48–49
'black mugger' label, 49
development of labelling theory, 48
'hooligans' in history, 49
moral panics and deviance amplification, 48
new deviancy theory, 48, 50–52
and authoritarian populism, 51
ethnographic youth studies, 51
influence on education in criminology, 52
little impact on policy, 51
radical criminology, 49–50
as class issue, 50
and New Left Realism, 50
victimisation studies, 50
feminism, 52–58
avoiding gender subordination, 53
concerns about conformity, 54, 56
contribution to social theory, 52–53
feminist youth research, 56–57
mainly limited to social life, 56
research restricted despite political impact of feminism, 56–57
girls defined by their sexuality, 54–55
'sexual problems' of girls, 55–56
social control of 'problem girls,' 55
studies by McRobbie, 53
working-class kids and working-class jobs, 46–47
counter-school culture, 47
educational differentiation examined, 46
youth training programmes and existing structures, 47
youth as 'a generation for itself,' 41–42
biological rhythm of life, 42
generation and class, 42
generational theory, 42
youth unemployment, 45–46
mainly considered due to individual failings, 46
social contract between young people and society considered broken, 45–46
Social Science Research Council, 160
Solomos, J., 20
Special Educational Needs and Disability Act (2001), 83
Spice Girls, 128, 129
Springhall, J., 7, 8, 13, 16, 25, 42, 108
Squires, P., 110
Stanko, E., 112
Starkey, H., 68, 85
Stephen, D., 110
Stewart, F., 117
Sutherland, E., 34
Sweeting, H., 137

Taft, J., 129
'*Talk to Frank*' (website), 140
Tapscott, D., 119
Taylor, D., 147
Taylor, I., 34, 49, 50
Taylor, R., 66, 68, 75
Technical and Vocational Education Initiative (TVEI), 19
Thatcherism, 41
Thompson, R., 22, 23
Thomson, R., 69, 70, 76
Thornton, D., 100, 142, 143
Thorpe, D., 22, 55
threatening youth and risky futures *see* crime and youth
Thrupp, M., 86
Tierney, J., 32, 33, 34, 37, 38, 48, 49, 50, 51, 106, 108, 110
Tilly, L., 10
Tomlinson, S., 21, 66, 67, 70, 79, 80, 81, 82, 83, 86, 87, 88, 89, 95
Toofail, J., 104
Training and Enterprise Council, 79

transitions of youth in the age of uncertainty, 59–77
changes in the transition from school to work, 59–62
expansion of education over age 16, 59–60
individualisation in transitions, 60–62
biographical project, 61
importance of choice, 61–62
labour market for youth remains stagnant, 59
markers of status, 60
similar changes world-wide, 60
training by Government in vocations and skills, 60
youth leaving homeand then returning, 60
inequality and transitions into adulthood, 70–76
inequality cause of youth problems, 70
masculinity studies, 74–76
effect of changes in work, 74–75
masculinity and service-sector employment, 75–76
structure agency and culture, 72–74
cultural context of transition and gender, 73
'cultural turn' in class analysis, 72
'fields' and 'habitus,' 73
structure versus agency debate, 74
'structured individualism' in youth transitions, 71–72
dichotomy between structure and agency, 72
fallacies about individualism, 71
reconciling social change and continuity, 71
structured pathways and individualism, 70–71
new times and New Labour, 62–70
core principles, 62–63
life-long learning, 66–68
belief in education, 66–67
blaming young individuals for problems, 67
University education mainly middle-class, 66–68
New Labour and managing youth transitions, 63–66
'blame culture,' 65
continuing problems, 66
New Deal employment programme, 63, 64
Social Exclusion Unit (SEU), 63, 64
work-to-welfare progammes, 64
politics of citizenship, 68–69
active citizenship as 'deficit model,' 69
citizenship training, 68–69
New Labour and work ethic, 68
research and transitions into adulthood, 69–70
New Labour and citizenship, 69
pathways for transition to adulthood, 69–70
'third-way' politics, 62
Tyler, M., 129, 130

United Nations Convention on the Rights of the Child, 98, 100
Utting, D., 99, 107

Valentine, G., 121, 123
Vande Berg, L., 129
Vincent, K., 94

Walford, G., 10
Walker, R., 161
Walkerdine, V., 73, 77, 90, 91, 92, 94
Walklate, S., 40
Wallace, C., 46, 60
Warwick University, 89
Webb, J., 161
websites:
Talk to Frank, 140
Webster, C., 71, 111
Weil, S., 163, 164
Wells, S., 140
West, D.J., 107, 137
Whitty, G., 85
Wikström, P.O-.H., 108, 109
Wilber, S, 125
Wiles, P., 161
Williams, M., 24
Williams, S., 146, 158
Williamson, H., 109
Willis, P., 46, 47, 74, 124
Wilson, D., 110
Wilson, J.Q., 40, 101
Woods, P., 47

Wright Mills, C., 2, 164
Wyn, J., 59, 61

Xena: Warrior Princess (TV), 128

Yamashita, H., 88
Young, A., 65, 97
youth culture *see* culture of youth and risk-taking
youth education *see* education and politics
Youth Justice Board, 102
Youth Lifestyles Survey, 103
Youth Opportunities Programme (YOP), 18
youth transitions *see* transitions of youth in the age of uncertainty

Open up your options
Education
Health & Social Welfare
Management
Media, Film & Culture
Psychology & Counselling
Sociology
Study Skills
for more information on our publications visit www.openup.co.uk
OPEN UNIVERSITY PRESS
McGraw - Hill Education